Teaching Primary Programming with Scratch

Pupil Book – Year 5

PHIL BAGGE

A research informed scheme of work by Phil Bagge HIAS Computing Inspector/Advisor
Part of the HIAS Teaching Primary Programming from Scratch Series

Published in 2023 by University of Buckingham Press,
an imprint of Legend Times Group
51 Gower Street
London WC1E 6HJ
info@unibuckinghampress.com
www.unibuckinghampress.com

Published by arrangement with Hampshire Inspection and Advisory Service (part of Hampshire County Council)

ISBN 978-1-91505-4-265

CONTENTS

If you can only pick two modules due to time constraints, I would choose either **Making Choices** or **Wizards Choice Two** and either **Butterfly Fun** or **Ocean Pollution**.

INTRODUCTION & PROGRESSION

INTRODUCTION

Scheme

This book is a complete scheme of work for teaching primary programming using Scratch in Year 5 for 9–10 year olds.

Part of a Series

It is part of a five-book series. Three other books include projects for other year groups.

Teaching Primary Programming with Scratch, Year 3

Teaching Primary Programming with Scratch, Year 4

Teaching Primary Programming with Scratch, Year 4

If you are interested in the methodology and research-informed practice behind this series, as well as well as a wealth of other insights gained from teaching block-based programming for thousands of hours then

Teaching Primary Programming with Scratch – Research-Informed Approaches

will be an informative read.

Permissions

It includes permission to photocopy the pupil and teacher help sheets for your class and school.

It includes links to example code, project templates and slides to introduce new programming concepts.

Progression

There is a clear, research-informed progression through the series and the graphic on the right on a grey background shows which programming concepts are introduced in this book.

Pedagogy in a Few Paragraphs

Introduction to Programming Concepts Away from Code

Pupils are taught key programming concepts away from programming to lower cognitive load and make it easier to transfer these ideas from one programming language to another.

Paired Programming

Pupils are encouraged to work in same ability pairs for some parts of the projects, because this has shown to be particularly helpful for pupils working within or below the expected outcomes.

PRIMM

Pupils are encouraged to read and understand code before they create their own code. We use the PRIMM method in this book.

Predict

Run

Investigate

Modify (change)

Make

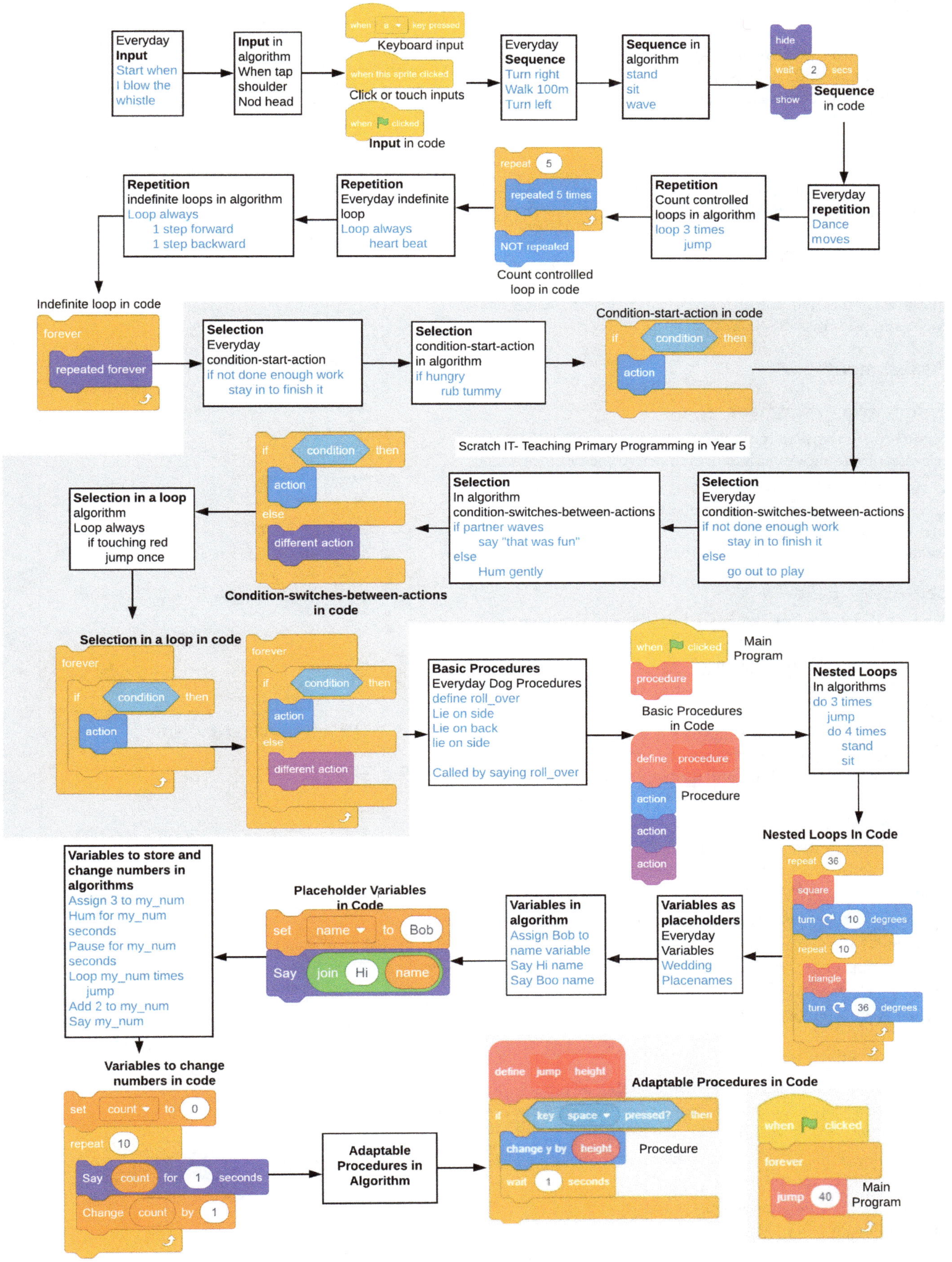
Everyday Input
Start when I blow the whistle
Input in algorithm
When tap shoulder
Nod head
Keyboard input
Click or touch inputs
when this sprite clicked
when clicked
Input in code
Everyday Sequence
Turn right
Walk 100m
Turn left
Sequence in algorithm
stand
sit
wave
hide
wait 2 secs
show
Sequence in code
Everyday repetition
Dance moves
Repetition
Count controlled loops in algorithm
loop 3 times
jump
repeat 5
repeated 5 times
NOT repeated
Count controllled loop in code
Repetition
Everyday indefinite loop
Loop always
heart beat
Repetition
indefinite loops in algorithm
Loop always
1 step forward
1 step backward
Indefinite loop in code
forever
repeated forever
Selection
Everyday
condition-start-action
if not done enough work
stay in to finish it
Selection
condition-start-action
in algorithm
if hungry
rub tummy
Condition-start-action in code
if condition then
action
Scratch IT- Teaching Primary Programming in Year 5
Selection
Everyday
condition-switches-between-actions
if not done enough work
stay in to finish it
else
go out to play
Selection
In algorithm
condition-switches-between-actions
if partner waves
say "that was fun"
else
Hum gently
if condition then
action
else
different action
Condition-switches-between-actions in code
Selection in a loop
algorithm
Loop always
if touching red
jump once
Selection in a loop in code
forever
if condition then
action
else
different action
Basic Procedures
Everyday Dog Procedures
define roll_over
Lie on side
Lie on back
lie on side
Called by saying roll_over
when clicked
procedure
Main Program
Basic Procedures in Code
define procedure
action
action
action
Procedure
Nested Loops
In algorithms
do 3 times
jump
do 4 times
stand
sit
Nested Loops In Code
repeat 36
square
turn 10 degrees
repeat 10
triangle
turn 36 degrees
Variables as placeholders
Everyday Variables
Wedding
Placenames
Variables in algorithm
Assign Bob to name variable
Say Hi name
Say Boo name
Placeholder Variables in Code
set name to Bob
Say join Hi name
Variables to store and change numbers in algorithms
Assign 3 to my_num
Hum for my_num seconds
Pause for my_num seconds
Loop my_num times
jump
Add 2 to my_num
Say my_num
Variables to change numbers in code
set count to 0
repeat 10
Say count for 1 seconds
Change count by 1
Adaptable Procedures in Algorithm
define jump height
if key space pressed? then
change y by height
wait 1 seconds
Procedure
Adaptable Procedures in Code
when clicked
forever
jump 40
Main Program

Creative

Each project provides time and stimulus to be creative in code within the zone of proximal development provided by the taught concepts and explored projects. In other words, it has reasonable projects that can be created independently or with minimum teacher support.

Knowledge

Key knowledge is introduced in the concept introductions and reinforced in each of the activities.

Revisiting Learning

It is important to revisit prior learning so each module has questions and activities which revise learning from Year 4 on loops and prior modules in Year 5.

Assessment

Summative Assessment

Summative assessment is baked into every stage of the PRIMM process, providing a wealth of data to determine progress.

If you have used earlier versions of these resources on the code-it website, then you will enjoy the new project assessment grid that combines pupil's self-assessment and quick teacher assessment ideally within the lesson.

Self-Assessment

Pupils self-mark to help them see how they have progressed, reducing teachers' workload and enabling teachers to concentrate on the pupils that might need more support.

Hints & Tips

Every pupil's resource also includes a copy of the resource annotated with extra information to further teachers programming knowledge, hints and formative assessment opportunities in case pupils are stuck and tips to adapt or support whole class teaching.

Many of these extra hints and tips will not be needed, but the more informed the teacher is the better quality learning opportunity pupils will have.

Yellow highlighted hints and tips are whole class suggestions

Lilac highlighted hints and tips are information to help teachers support SEN pupils.

Green highlighted hints and tips are suggestions to help the teacher support individual pupils stuck on a specific question.

Can We Start Here?

If pupils have never programmed with Scratch before a basic introduction project such as that provided in *Teaching Primary Programming with Scratch, Year 3* is a must.

I would also recommend a single module of count-controlled loops and one on indefinite loops found in

Teaching Primary Programming with Scratch, Year 4

Many of the projects in the book build on prior learing.

Committed to Improvements

HIAS, Hampshire's Inspection & Advisory Service, is committed to developing and improving these resources. We recognize that primary programming is still its infancy in comparison with other subjects, and that new research and primary practice will refine and improve teaching and learning in this area. All royalties earned from this series will be used to write more computing books and revise these resources as needed.

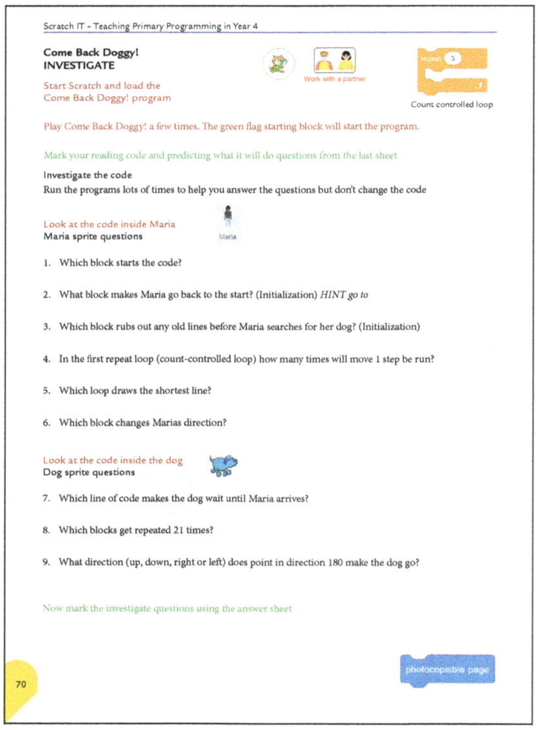

Scratch IT - Teaching Primary Programming in Year 4

Come Back Doggy!
INVESTIGATE

Work with a partner

Start Scratch and load the Come Back Doggy! program

Count controlled loop

Play Come Back Doggy! a few times. The green flag starting block will start the program.

Mark your reading code and predicting what it will do questions from the last sheet

Investigate the code
Run the programs lots of times to help you answer the questions but don't change the code

Look at the code inside Maria
Maria sprite questions

Maria

1. Which block starts the code?
2. What block makes Maria go back to the start? (Initialization) *HINT go to*
3. Which block rubs out any old lines before Maria searches for her dog? (Initialization)
4. In the first repeat loop (count-controlled loop) how many times will move 1 step be run?
5. Which loop draws the shortest line?
6. Which block changes Marias direction?

Look at the code inside the dog
Dog sprite questions

7. Which line of code makes the dog wait until Maria arrives?
8. Which blocks get repeated 21 times?
9. What direction (up, down, right or left) does point in direction 180 make the dog go?

Now mark the investigate questions using the answer sheet

70

photocopiable page

Photocopiable resource for pupils

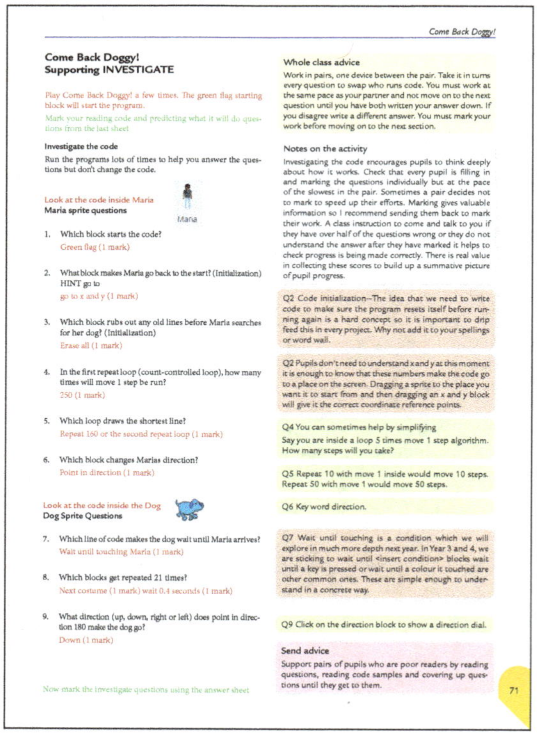

Come Back Doggy!

Come Back Doggy!
Supporting INVESTIGATE

Play Come Back Doggy! a few times. The green flag starting block will start the program.

Mark your reading code and predicting what it will do questions from the last sheet

Investigate the code

Run the programs lots of times to help you answer the questions but don't change the code.

Look at the code inside Maria
Maria sprite questions

Maria

1. Which block starts the code?
   Green flag (1 mark)
2. What block makes Maria go back to the start? (Initialization) HINT go to
   go to x and y (1 mark)
3. Which block rubs out any old lines before Maria searches for her dog? (Initialization)
   Erase all (1 mark)
4. In the first repeat loop (count-controlled loop), how many times will move 1 step be run?
   250 (1 mark)
5. Which loop draws the shortest line?
   Repeat 160 or the second repeat loop (1 mark)
6. Which block changes Marias direction?
   Point in direction (1 mark)

Look at the code inside the Dog
Dog Sprite Questions

7. Which line of code makes the dog wait until Maria arrives?
   Wait until touching Maria (1 mark)
8. Which blocks get repeated 21 times?
   Next costume (1 mark) wait 0.4 seconds (1 mark)
9. What direction (up, down, right or left) does point in direction 180 make the dog go?
   Down (1 mark)

Now mark the investigate questions using the answer sheet

Whole class advice

Work in pairs, one device between the pair. Take it in turns every question to swap who runs code. You must work at the same pace as your partner and not move on to the next question until you have both written your answer down. If you disagree write a different answer. You must mark your work before moving on to the next section.

Notes on the activity

Investigating the code encourages pupils to think deeply about how it works. Check that every pupil is filling in and marking the questions individually but at the pace of the slowest in the pair. Sometimes a pair decides not to mark to speed up their efforts. Marking gives valuable information so I recommend sending them back to mark their work. A class instruction to come and talk to you if they have over half of the questions wrong or they do not understand the answer after they have marked it helps to check progress is being made correctly. There is real value in collecting these scores to build up a summative picture of pupil progress.

Q2 Code initialization--The idea that we need to write code to make sure the program resets itself before running again is a hard concept so it is important to drip feed this in every project. Why not add it to your spellings or word wall.

Q2 Pupils don't need to understand x and y at this moment it is enough to know that these numbers make the code go to a place on the screen. Dragging a sprite to the place you want it to start from and then dragging an x and y block will give it the correct coordinate reference points.

Q4 You can sometimes help by simplifying

Say you are inside a loop 5 times move 1 step algorithm. How many steps will you take?

Q5 Repeat 10 with move 1 inside would move 10 steps. Repeat 50 with move 1 would move 50 steps.

Q6 Key word direction.

Q7 Wait until touching is a condition which we will explore in much more depth next year. In Year 3 and 4, we are sticking to wait until <insert condition> blocks wait until a key is pressed or wait until a colour it touched are other common ones. These are simple enough to understand in a concrete way.

Q9 Click on the direction block to show a direction dial.

Send advice

Support pairs of pupils who are poor readers by reading questions, reading code samples and covering up questions until they get to them.

71

Teacher Hints & Tips on the same photocopiable resource

WE ARE LEARNING ABOUT CONDITIONAL SELECTION IN ALGORITHMS AND PROGRAMMING

Condition-starts-action algorithm

A condition is a state we can check to see if it is true or false

Conditional Selection Vocabulary
condition, true false, selection, choice, pathways, equal

Conditions

Start with an if

Only checked once unless they are in a loop

Two possible pathways: True and False

Are only checked when reached in flow of control

Extension Conditions can be combined with AND & OR
Reversed with NOT

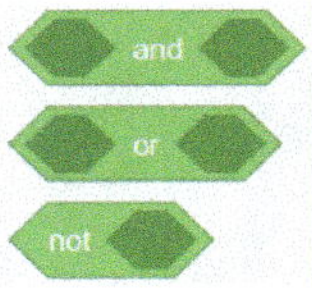

and
or
not

Making friends Algorithm

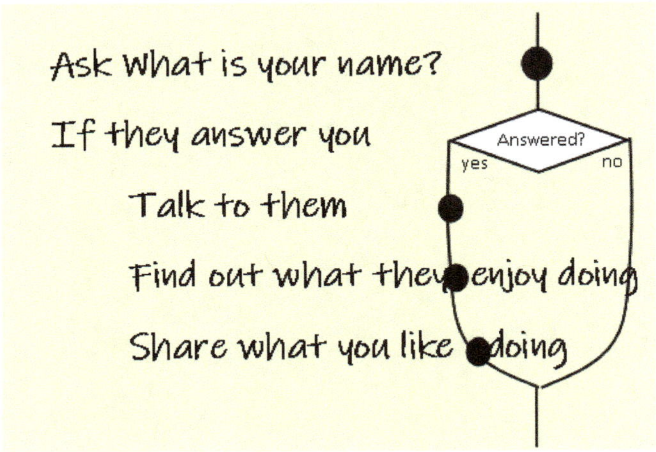

Ask What is your name?
If they answer you
Talk to them
Find out what they enjoy doing
Share what you like doing
Answered?
yes
no

Condition-within-infinite-loop

Decomposition

Breaking up a project into parts to solve separately.

Algorithms

A set of instructions or rules to do something.

We are indenting to show what actions are started if a condition is true

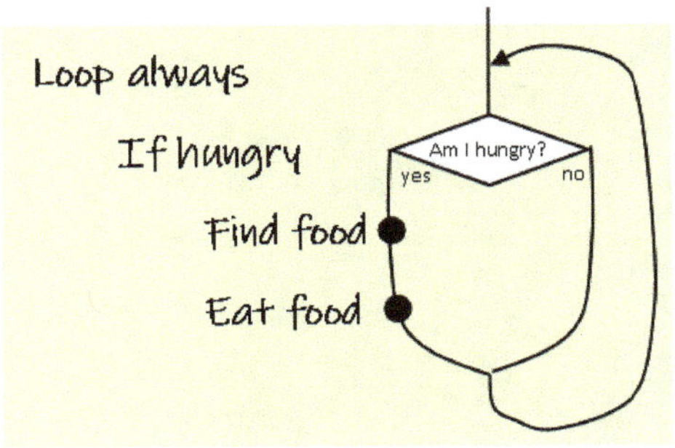

Loop always
If hungry
Find food
Eat food
Am I hungry?
yes
no

INTRODUCING NEW CONCEPTS

CHAPTER 1 Condition-Starts-Actions

Introducing Condition-Starts-Actions

These slides can be downloaded from https://computing.hias.hants.gov.uk/course/view.php?id=51.

Delivery

They are designed to be delivered to the whole class before pupils move on to using a condition-starts-action module such as

Making Choices

They can also be delivered to a small group or pairs of pupils if they are working independently through resources.

Format

Slides are provided in PDF and PowerPoint formats, and teachers who purchased the book are authorised to adapt the resources within their school or on closed learning platforms such as Seesaw, Google Classroom or Teams, as long as they are not shared outside the school community.

Hints

Extra hints and tips on usage are provided alongside each slide on the following pages.

Resources

Pupils will need whiteboards and pens or paper and pencils.

Summary Sheet

There is a summary sheet on page 11 that pupils can use to write their algorithms on and be reminded about key knowledge.

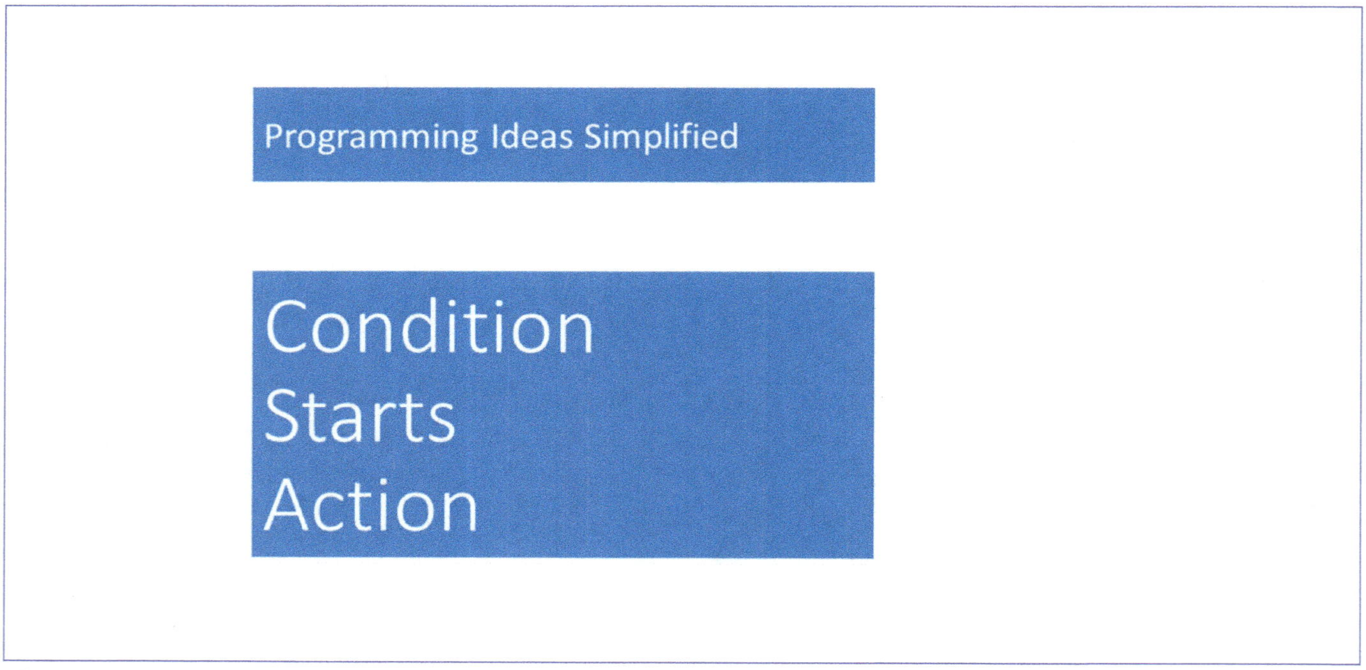

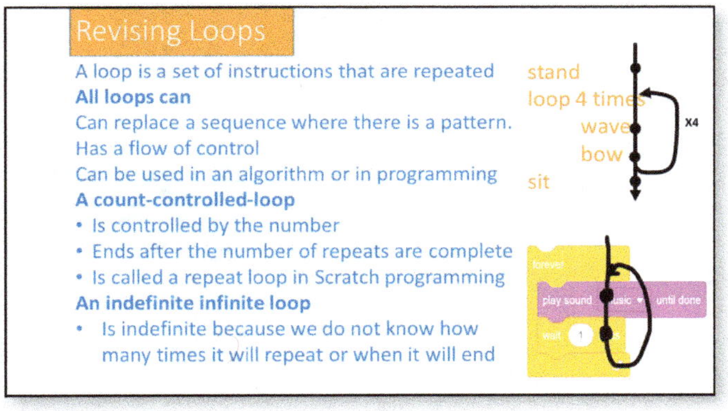

Go through loop essential knowledge that pupils learnt last year. They can use loops this year while learning new knowledge about conditions. Ask them what projects they did.

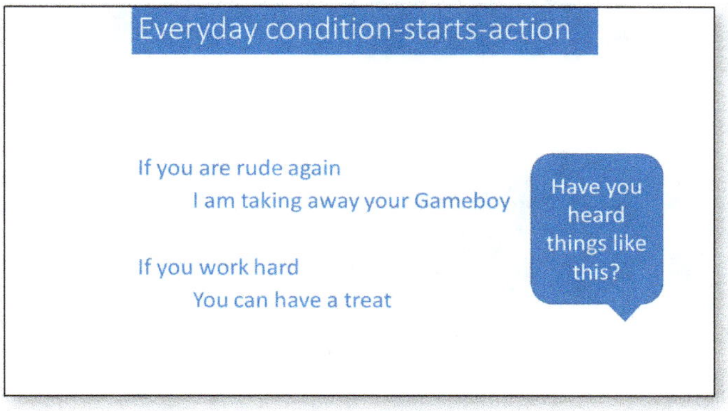

If you have any common class examples, now is a good time to mention these.

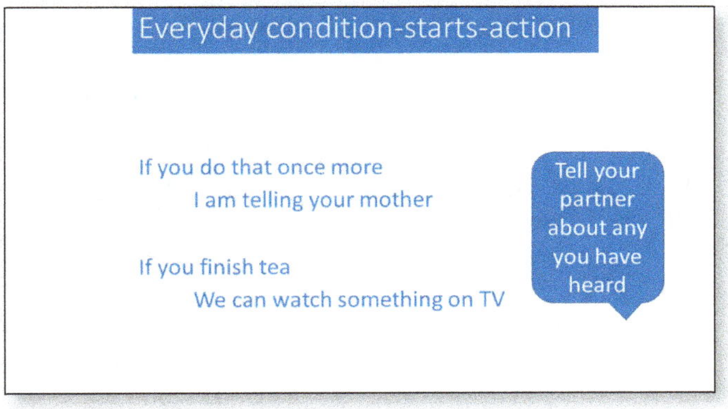

Give pupils a minute to share examples they have heard or used.

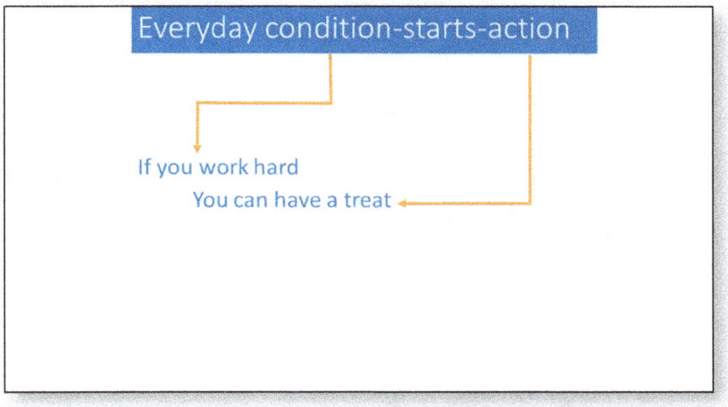

Point out that top part is the condition and the bottom part is the action or actions.

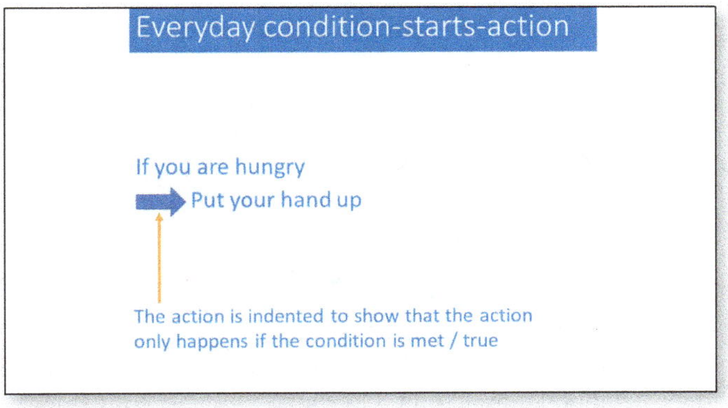

Text is indented to show that actions only happens when the condition is true. So here you only put your hand up if you are hungry. If it is NOT indented, it is not part of the condition and everyone would act it out.

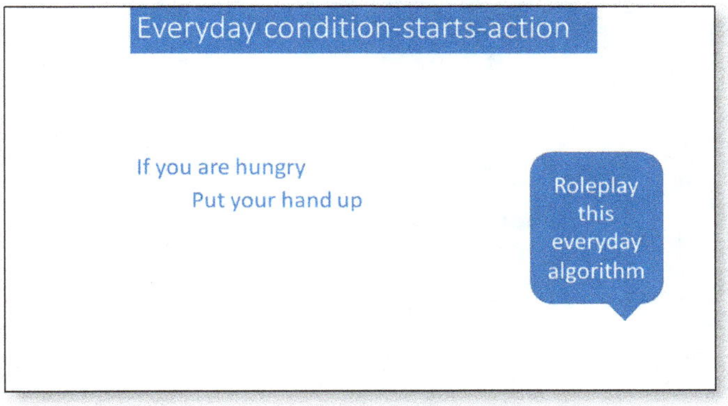

If you see any pupils putting their hand up multiple times, challenge this as the condition is only checked once.

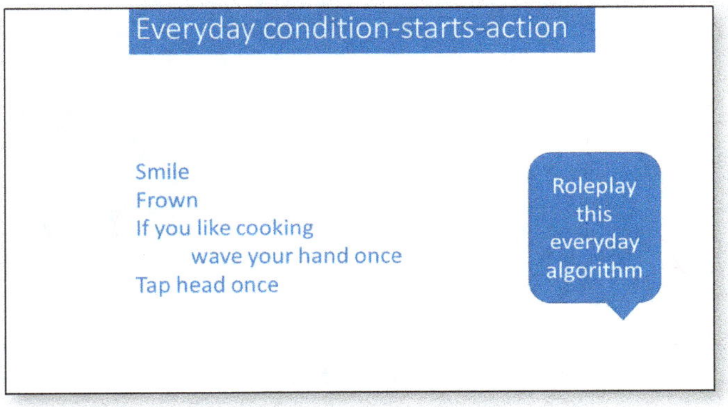

Watch to see if anyone is copying other pupils rather than reading themselves. When they write their own algorithms, check the understanding of those pupils.

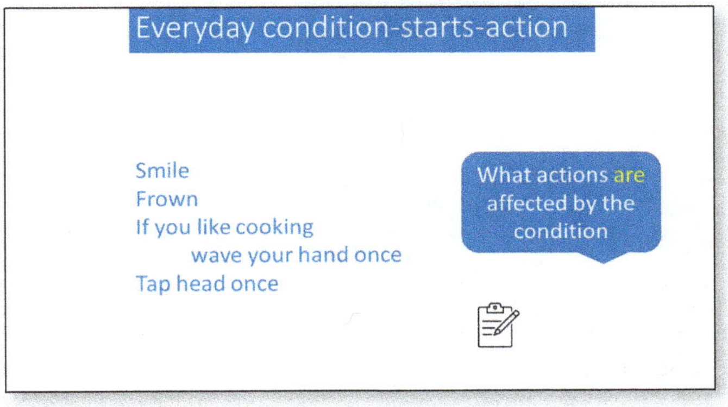

Ask them to write answers on their whiteboards.

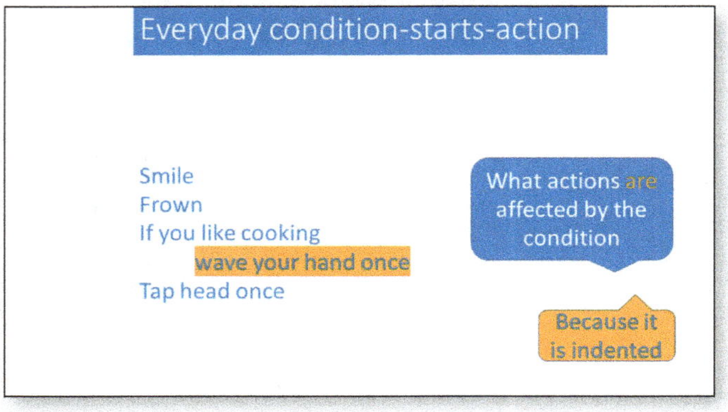

Check answers on whiteboards.

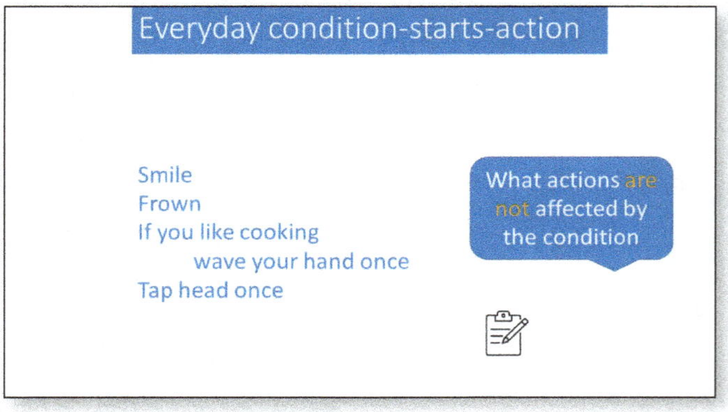

Answers on a whiteboard.

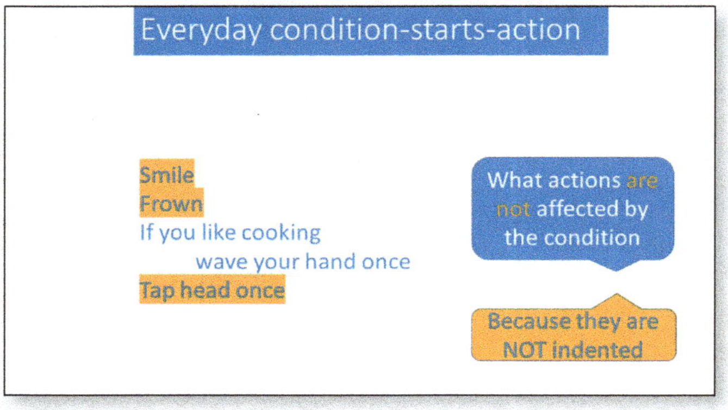

Check answers on whiteboards.

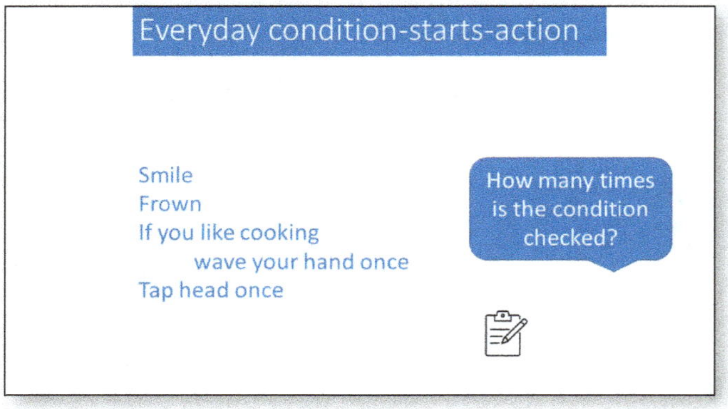

This is a very common misconception that conditions are checked over and over without being within a loop.

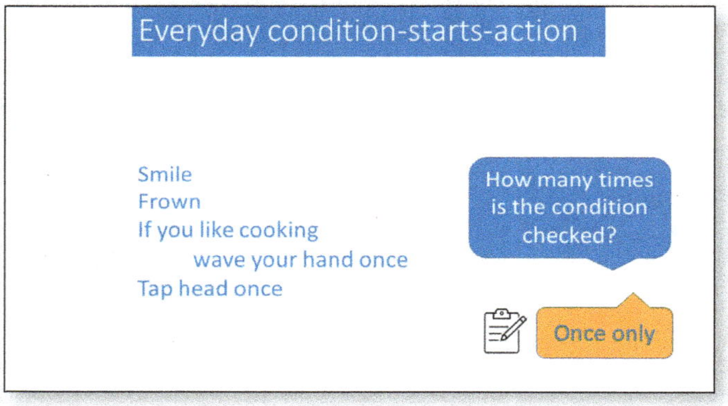

Once only

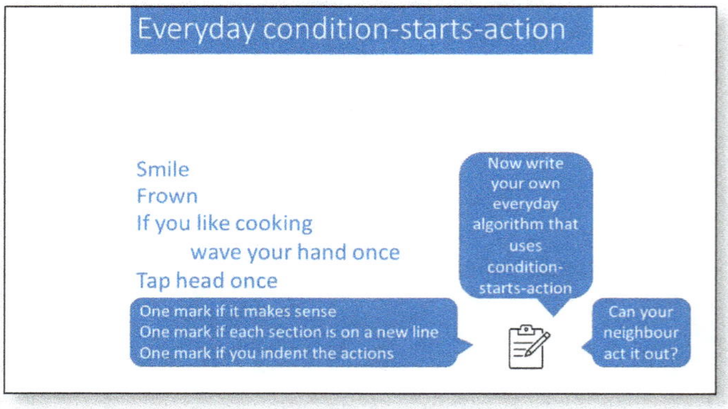

Give pupils time to write their own versions and give them to their neighbours to act out. Go round and check on work of any pupil who was slow or incorrectly acting out algorithms from earlier.

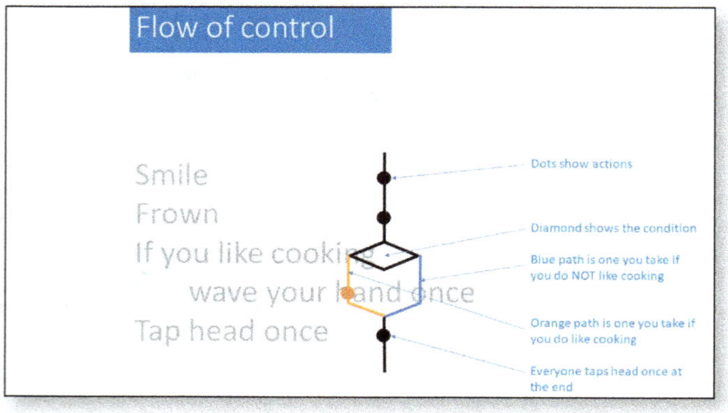

Read out the key on the left whilst pointing to the parts of the algorithms and flow of control. Do not call these diagrams flow charts as they are not. Go through the algorithm twice, once as true and once as false. Point out that you can only travel one path depending on your response to the condition.

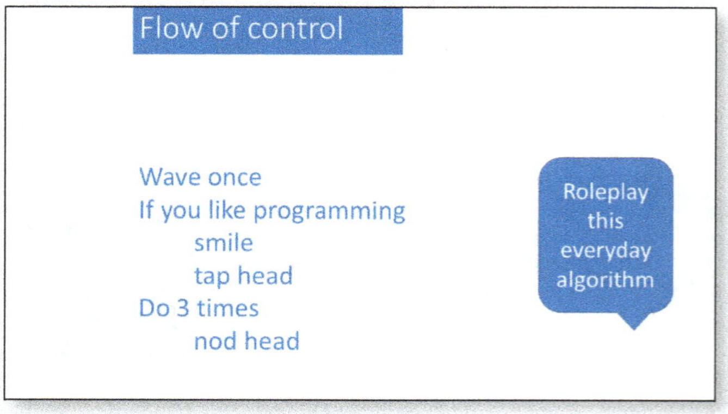

Ask pupils to roleplay this algorithm.

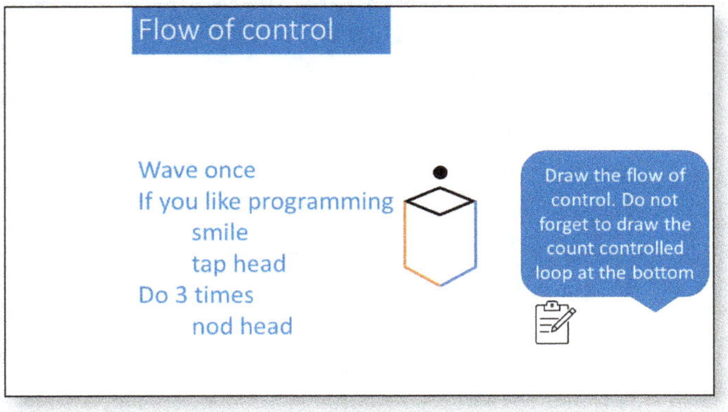

Now ask pupils to complete the flow of control. You might want to flick back to slide 15 to show pupils a previous example. Explain that they do not need to draw the paths in different colours.

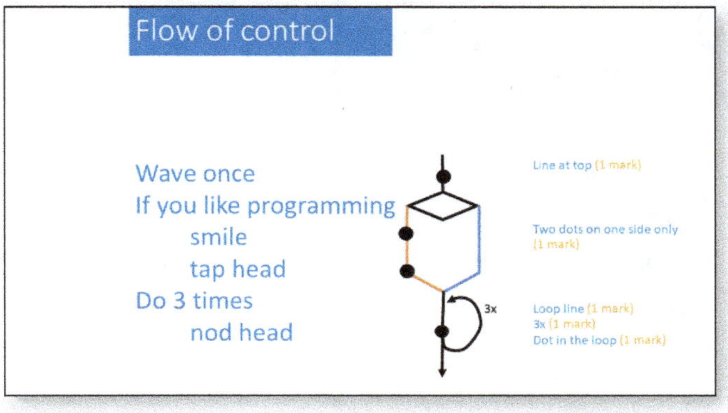

Go through the marking on the right so pupils can get some marks for partial success.

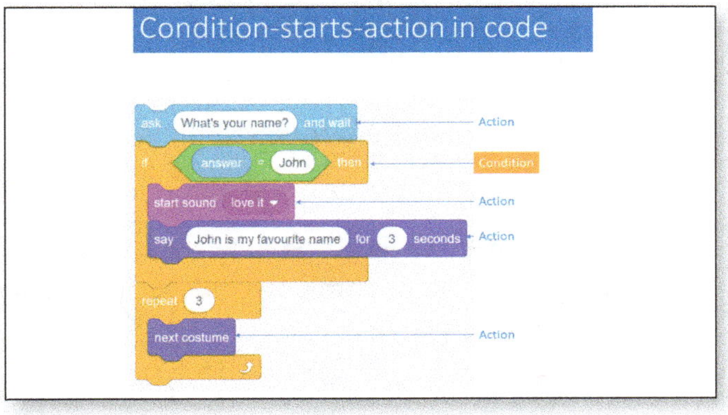

Point out the if block, which is the condition-starts-action code block. Point out the condition shape as well.

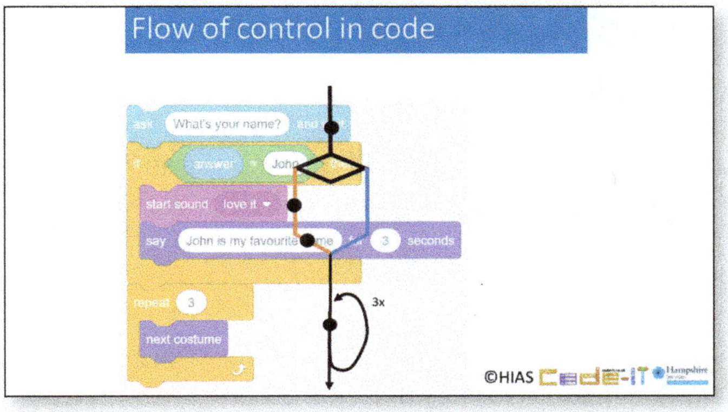

Show how flow of control works just as well for code as for algorithms.

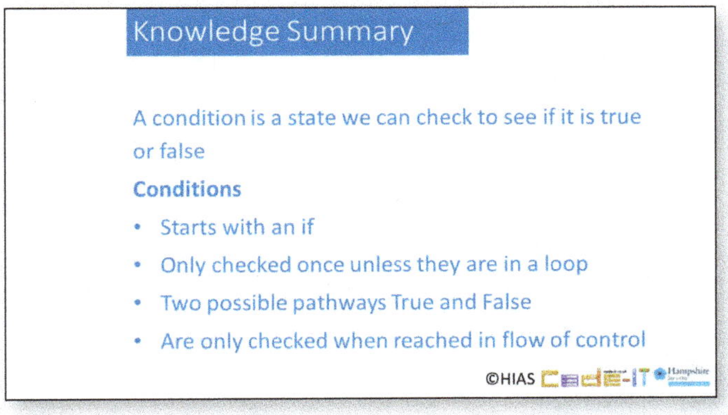

Finish with a revision of key knowledge gained through this introduction to the concept.

CHAPTER 2 Condition-Starts-Action-in-a-Loop

Introducing Condition-starts-action-in-a-loop

These slides can be downloaded from https://computing.hias.hants.gov.uk/course/view.php?id=51.

Delivery

They are designed to be delivered to the whole class before pupils move on to using a condition-starts-action in a loop module such as.

Butterfly fun

Diving Beetle

They can also be delivered to a small group or pairs of pupils if they are working independently through resources.

Format

Slides are provided in PDF and PowerPoint formats, and teachers who purchased the book are authorized to adapt the resources within their school or on closed learning platforms such as Seesaw, Google Classroom or Teams, as long as they are not shared outside the school community.

Hints

Extra hints and tips on usage are provided alongside each slide on the following pages.

Resources

Pupils will need whiteboards and pens or paper and pencils.

Slides

Slides 1–17 go with both modules.

Summary Sheet

These is a summary sheet on page 11 that pupils can use to write their algorithms on and be reminded about key knowledge.

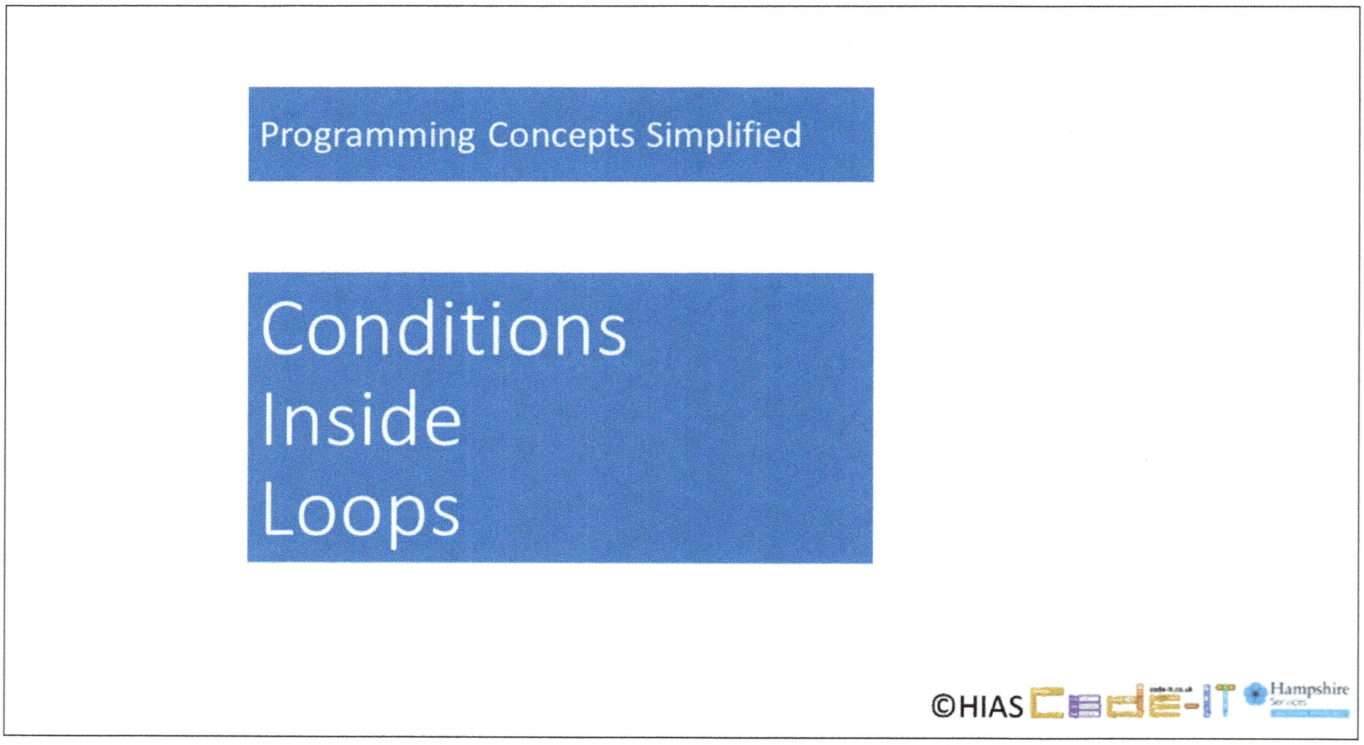

Example Slide

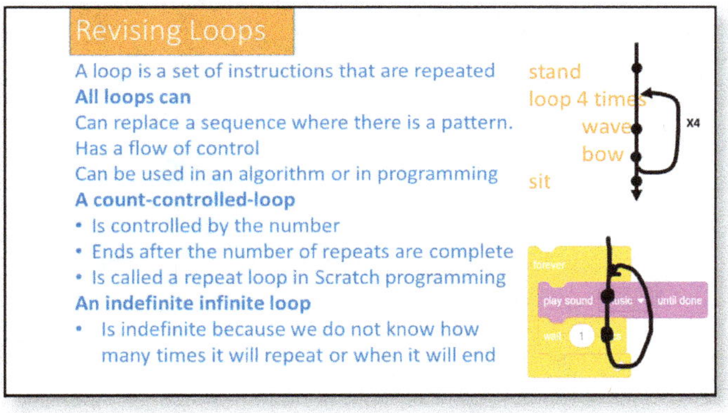

Briefly remind pupils of what they learnt in Year 4 when studying loops. They will be using indefinite loops in this module.

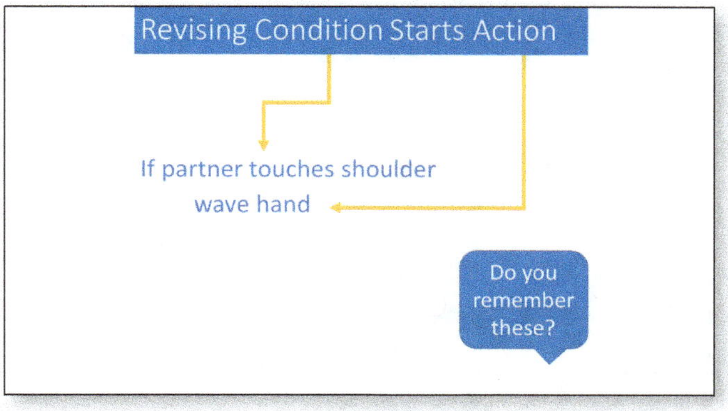

Can pupils remember any they wrote or the if and indents structure?

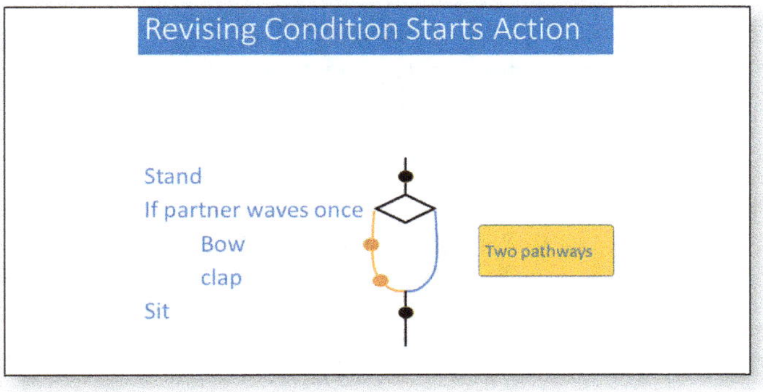

Do you remember that the condition forced you to go down a pathway? You either met the condition and went down the orange path or did not met the condition and went down the blue path.

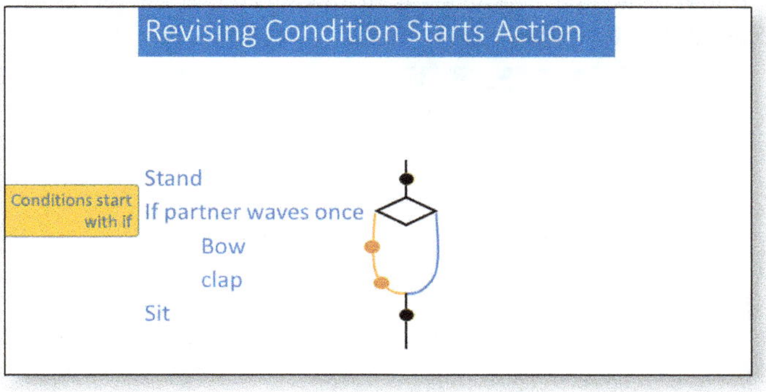

Remind pupils that they can spot conditions by looking for if.

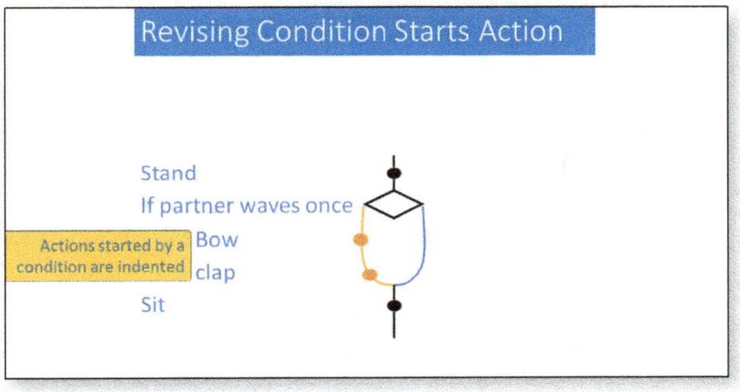

Do they remember that actions started by a condition are indented?

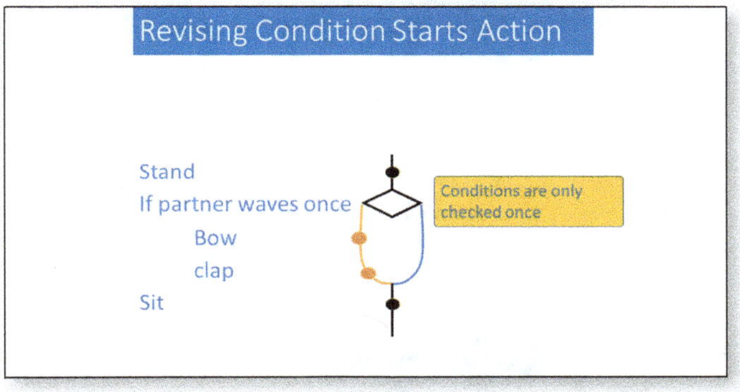

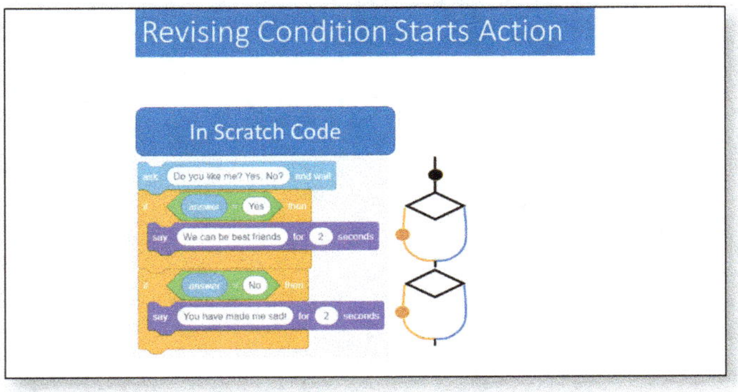

These conditions work well in Scratch code. Ask them what they built in code using conditions.

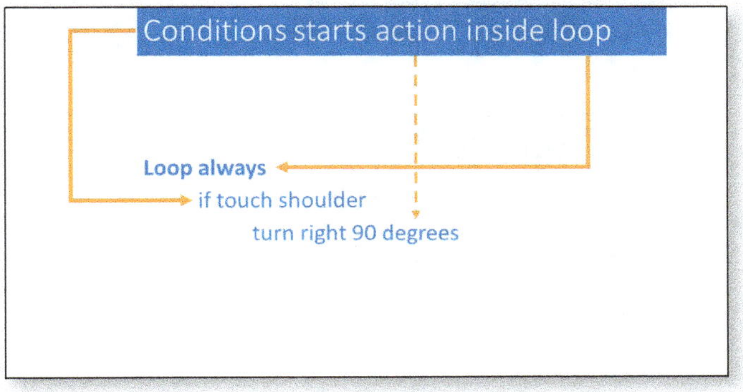

What will happen if we put these conditions that start action within a forever loop? Can they tell their partner what they think will happen?

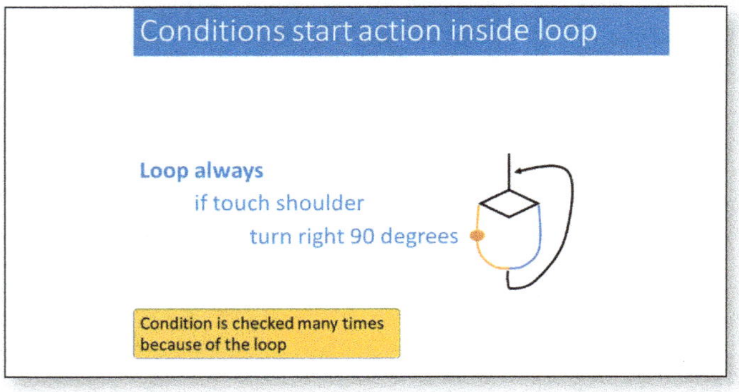

Ask two sensible pupils to come and help you. One can slowly go through the stages of the algorithm, pointing to it. The other pupil can touch your shoulder when they want but not all the time. When you get to if, ask the question, are they touching my shoulder? If they are, go down orange pathway and turn 90 degrees. Do this lots of times, as it helps pupils to understand what is going on in the algorithm to see it acted out.

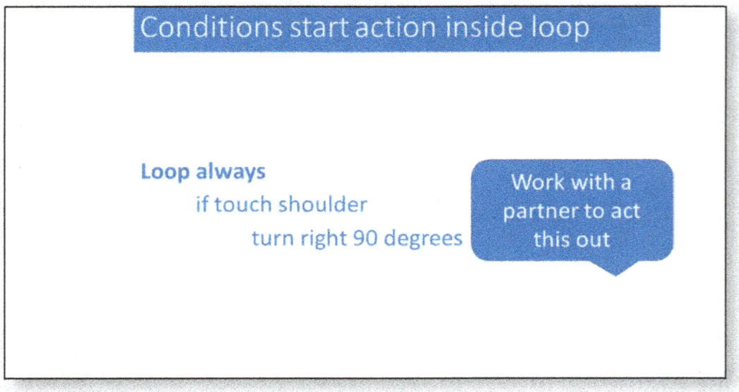

Ask pupils to say the question like you did. Only check if they have touched your shoulder when you get to that part of the algorithm. Pointing this out can help them to see how their algorithms and code works. Give pupils time to play both roles.

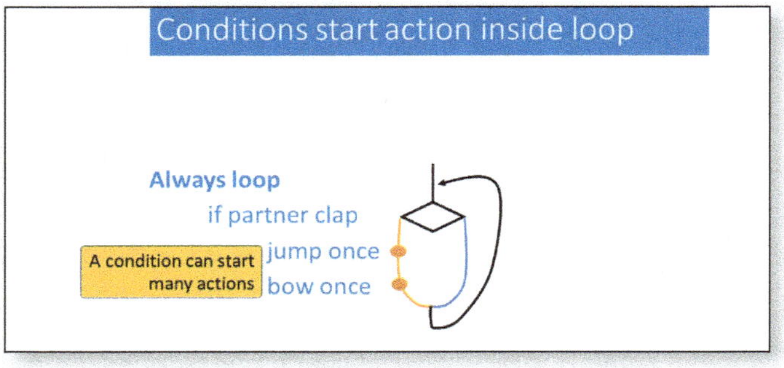

Point out that a condition can trigger multiple actions.

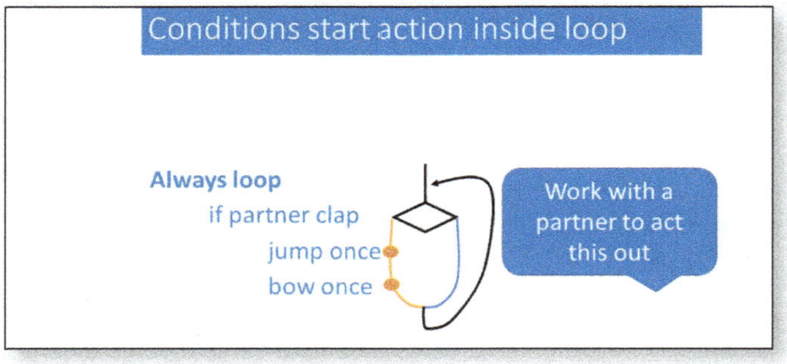

Ask pupils to say the question like you did. Only check if they have touched your shoulder when you get to that part of the algorithm. Pointing this out can help them to see how their algorithms and code works. Give pupils time to play both roles.

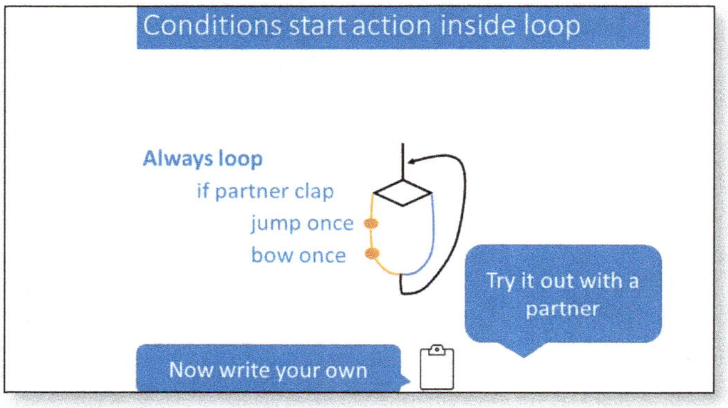

Ask pupils to write their own algorithms inside loops and to test them with their partners.

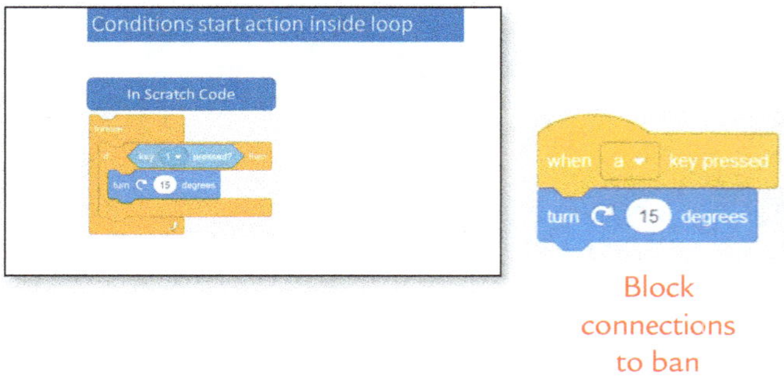

Show pupils how this works in code. It can be useful to ban the simple key pressed so do something blocks. Explain that in all other programming languages, this would not work.

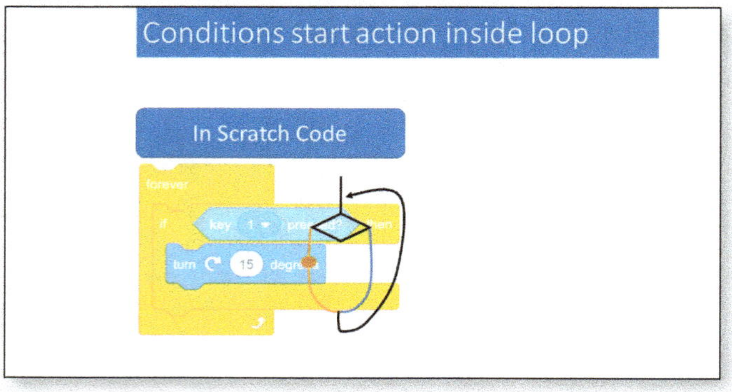

THIS IS THE LAST SLIDE. The next two slides are a role play activity to help make what is happening inside a loop more concrete.

Point out that flow of control works in code as it does in algorithms.

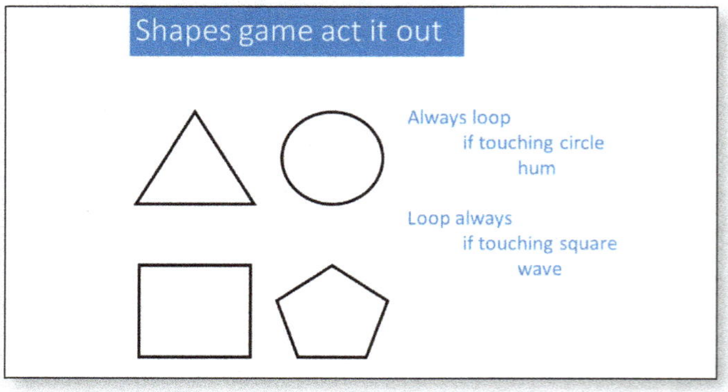

Make sure you have masking-taped or chalked some circles, squares, triangles and pentagons in an area. Say that pupils can walk normally using a hidden algorithm. Can they act out these instructions?

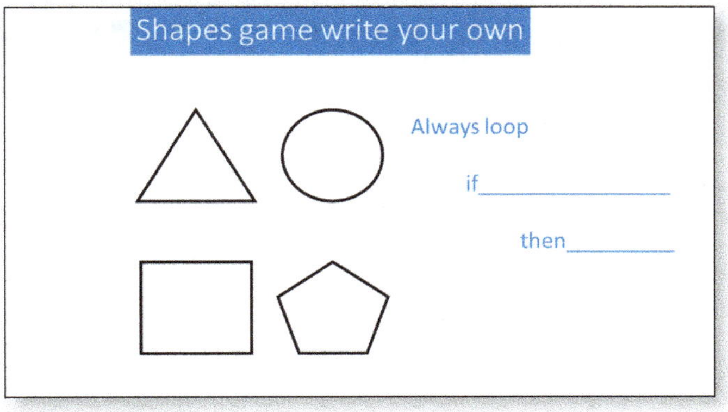

Now ask pupils to use the template to write and act out their own algorithms inside an indefinite loop.

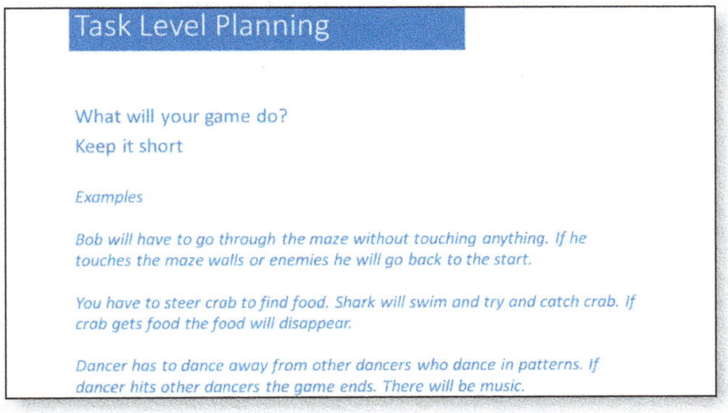

Talk through the examples and show pupils where on the planner they can fill in their game idea. Give them time to write their own idea.

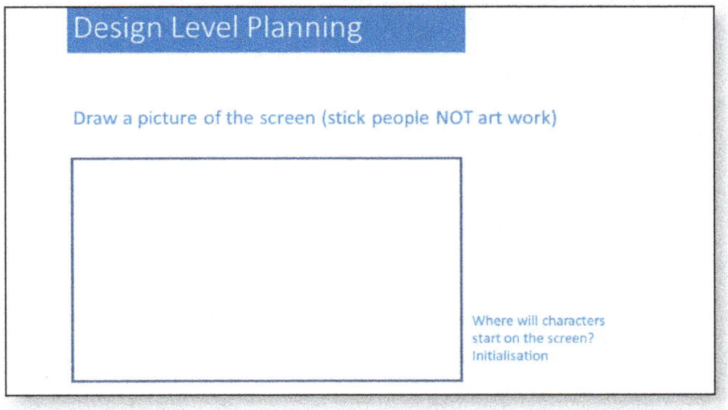

Ask them to draw their characters on the planner and indicate where they will start. Give them time to do this.

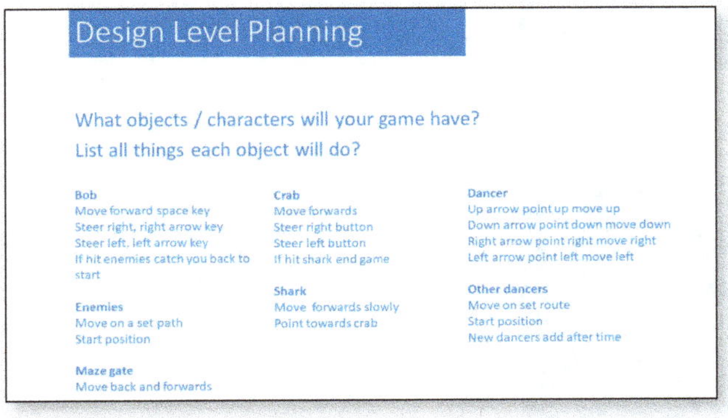

Give them plenty of time to list all the actions their characters will need to do. Point out that every action has been decomposed into separate actions. They cannot put steer; it must be steer right and steer left. Check to see if they are doing this.

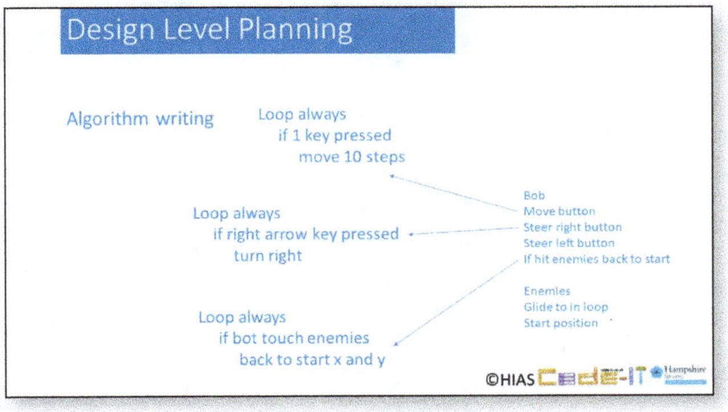

Finally, get every pupil to write at least three algorithms for actions they decomposed in the last section. Check them for forever loops and ifs. Point out the blocks sheet on the back of their planner to use to help them design algorithms to plan code.

Supporting the planning process

The slides can help you work with either the whole class or a small section of pupils to help them plan their own game.

CHAPTER 3 Condition-Switches-Between-Actions

Introducing Condition-Switches-Between-Actions

These slides can be downloaded from https://computing.hias.hants.gov.uk/course/view.php?id=51.

Delivery

They are designed to be delivered to the whole class before pupils move on to using a condition-switches-between-actions module such as

Wizards Choice Two.

They can also be delivered to a small group or pairs of pupils if they are working independently through resources.

Format

Slides are provided in PDF and PowerPoint formats, and teachers who purchased the book are authorized to adapt the resources within their school or on closed learning platforms such as Seesaw, Google Classroom or Teams, as long as they are not shared outside the school community.

Hints

Extra hints and tips on usage are provided alongside each slide on the following pages.

Resources

Pupils will need whiteboards and pens or paper and pencils.

Summary Sheet

These is a summary sheet that pupils can use to write their algorithms on and be reminded about key knowledge on page 11.

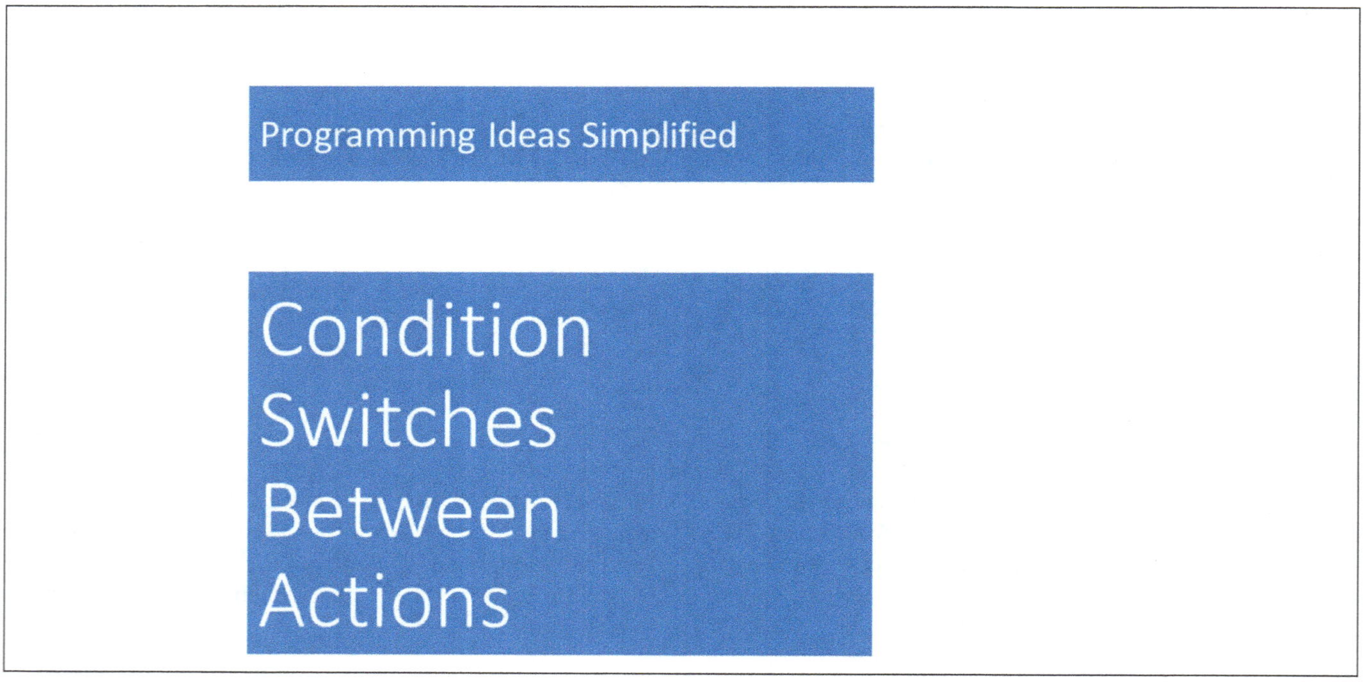

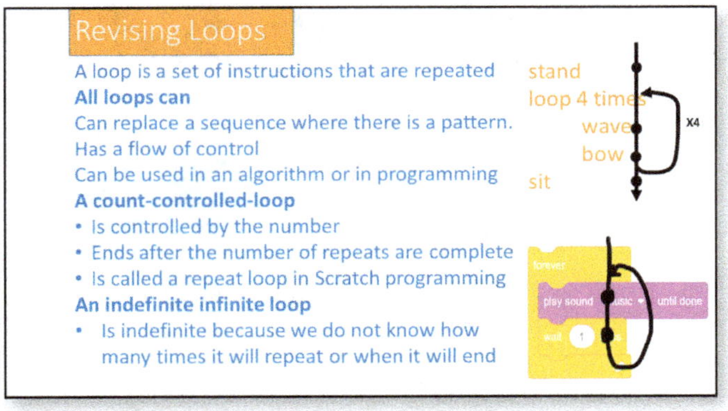

Revise loops from Year 4 and tell pupils that they will have opportunity to use loops this year while also learning new knowledge about conditions.

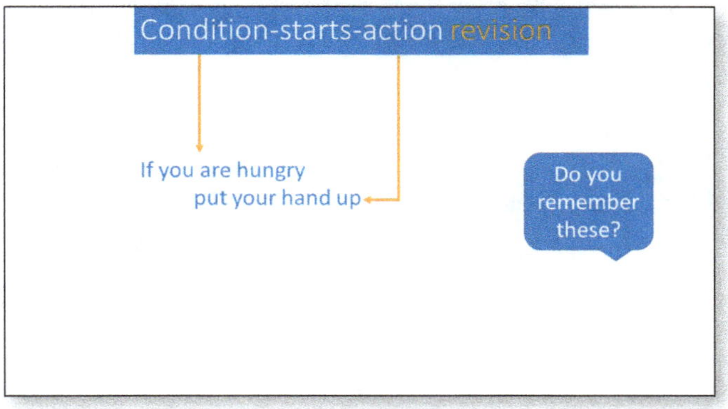

If you have not covered condition starts actions (if else), then skip this slide.

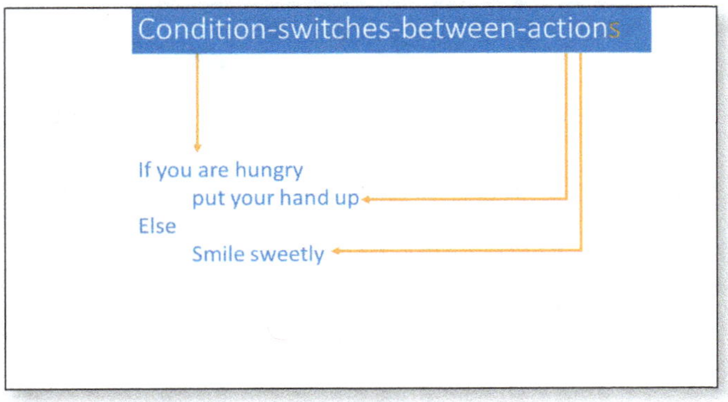

Point out which parts are conditions and which are actions.

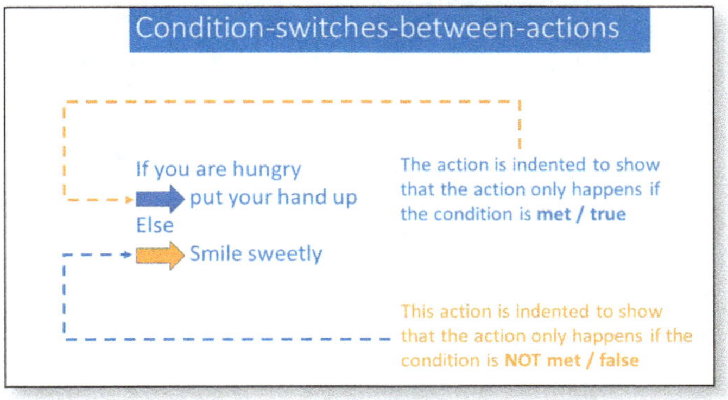

Ask pupils to explain to their neighbours how the two indented sections work.

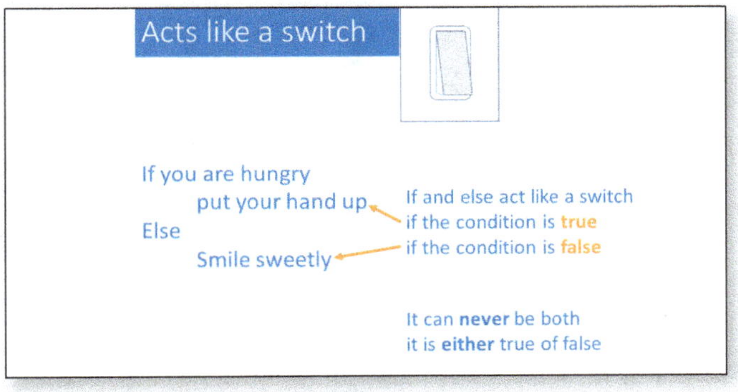

Use the switch analogy to enforce that a condition can either be true or false but never both at same time or neither at same time. Humans have room for ambiguity, but algorithms and code do not.

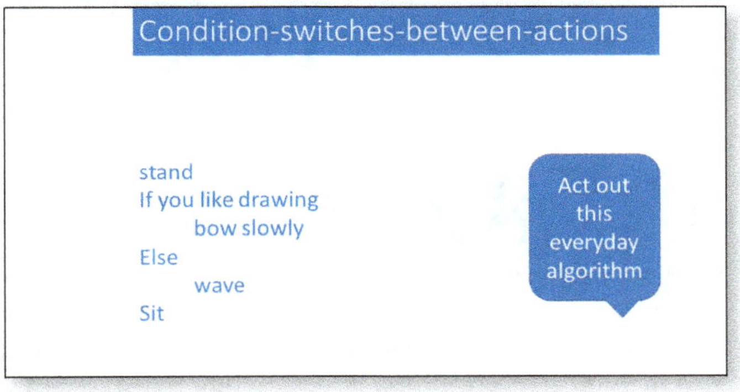

Watch to see if anyone is copying other pupils rather than reading themselves. When they write their own algorithms, check the understanding of those pupils.

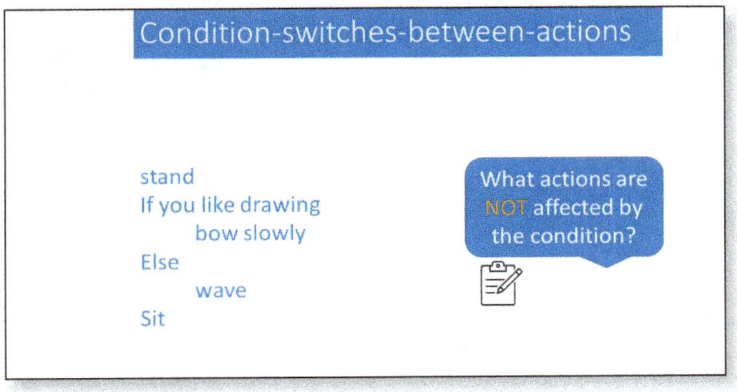

Answers on a whiteboard.

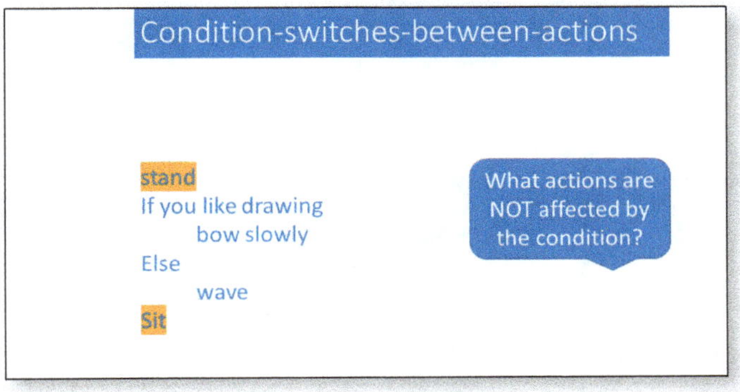

Point out that these are not indented.

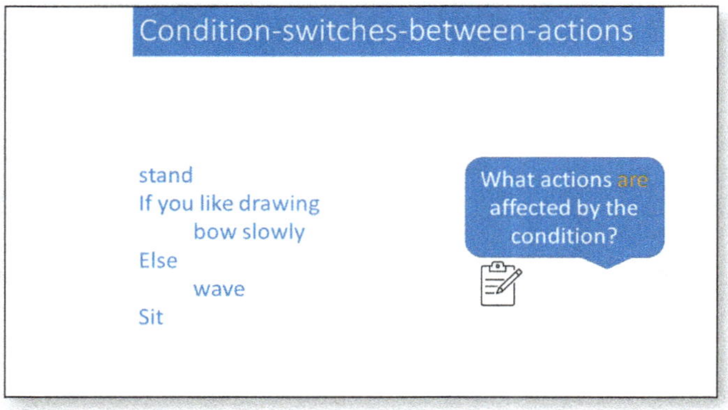

Answers on a whiteboard.

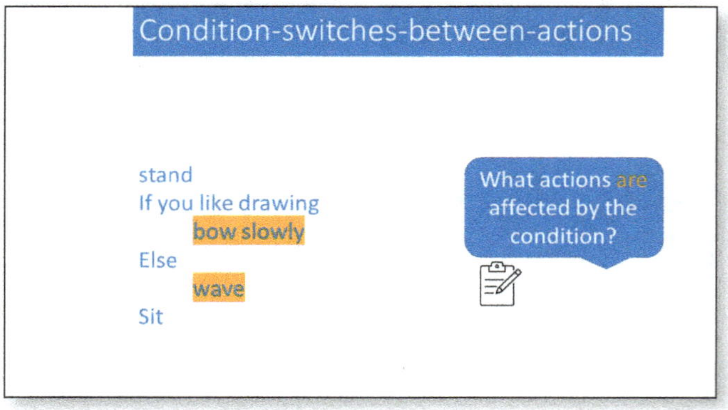

Point out that these are indented.

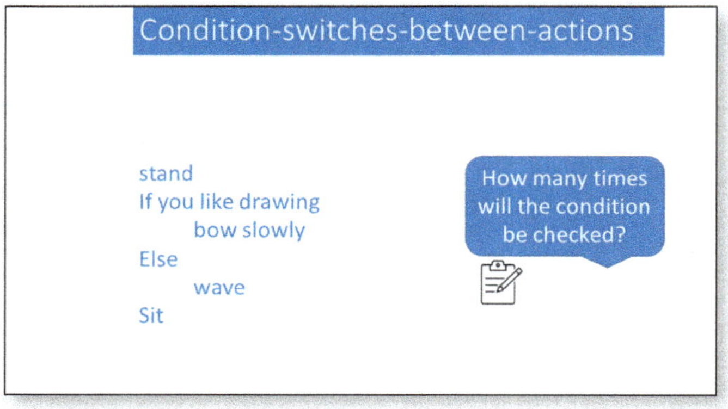

Answers on a whiteboard.

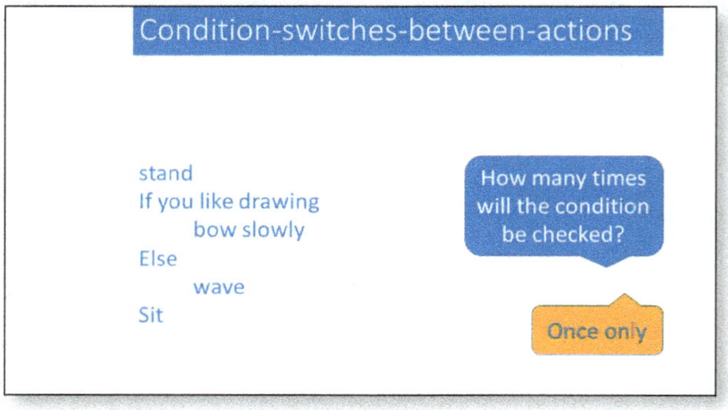

This is a very common misconception that conditions are checked over and over without being within a loop.

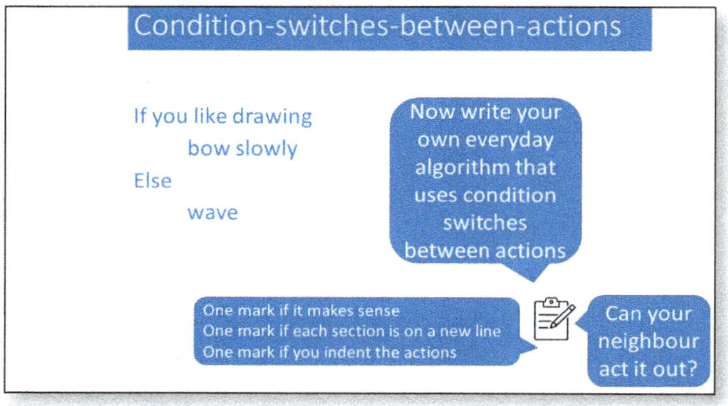

Give pupils time to write their own versions and give them to their neighbours to act out. Go round and check on work of any pupil who was slow or incorrectly acting out algorithms from earlier.

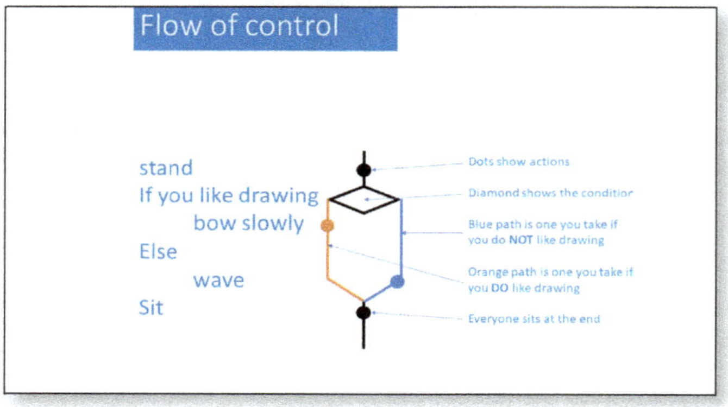

Read out the key on the left while pointing to the parts of the algorithms and flow of control. Do not call these diagrams flow charts, as they are not. Go through the algorithm twice once as true and once as false. Point out that you can only travel one path depending on your response to the condition.

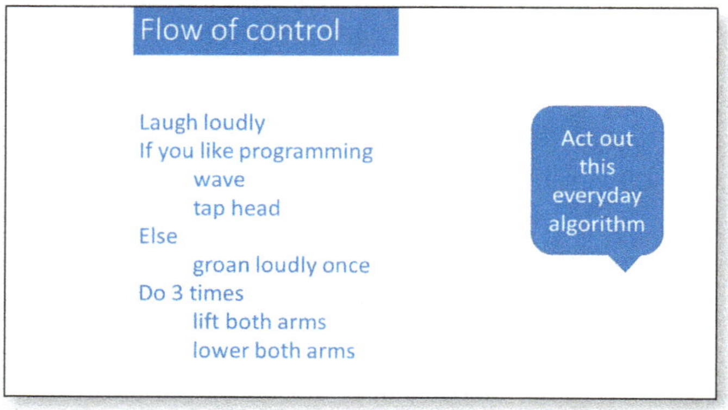

Ask pupils to roleplay this algorithm.

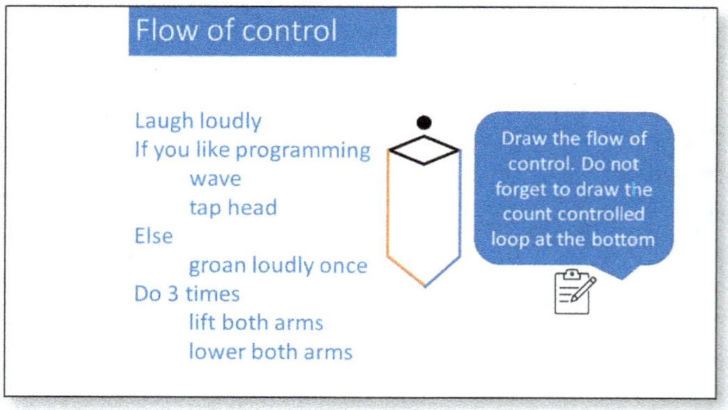

Now ask pupils to complete the flow of control. You might want to flick back to an earlier slide to show pupils a previous example. Explain that they do not need to draw the paths in different colours.

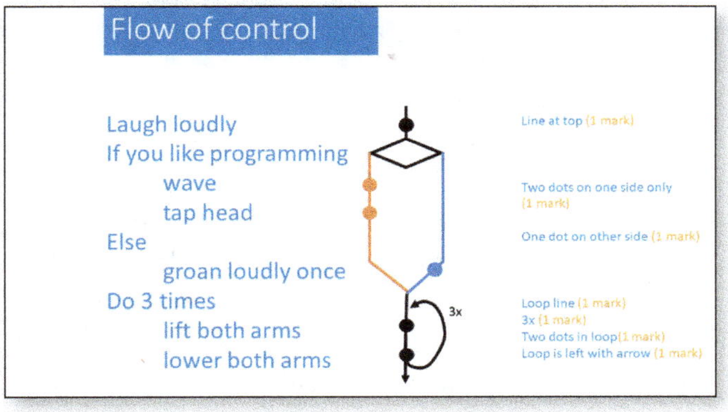

Go through the marking on the right so pupils can get some marks for partial success.

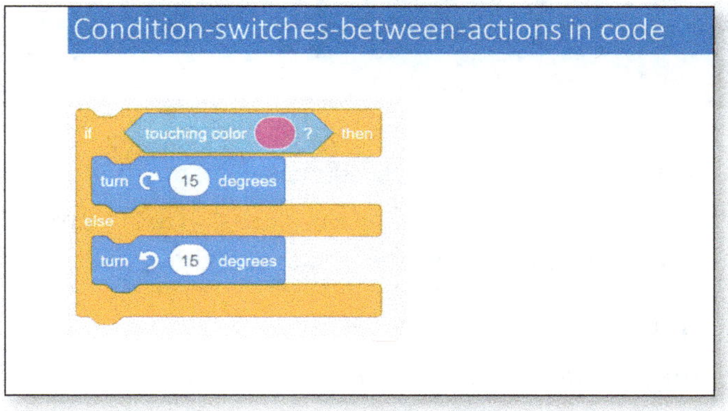

Point out the if else block, which is the condition switches between actions code block. Point out the condition shape as well.

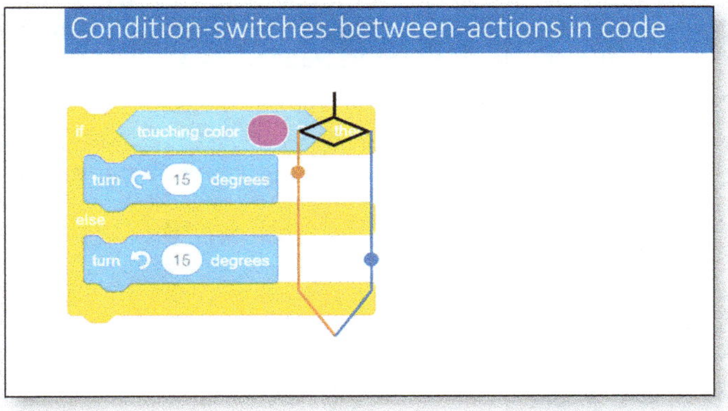

Show how flow of control works just as well for code as for algorithms.

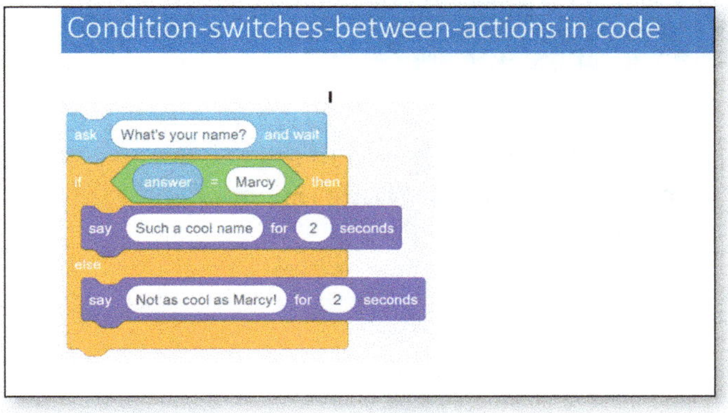

If you are not using Parsons you could also build and demonstrate how this code can be built.

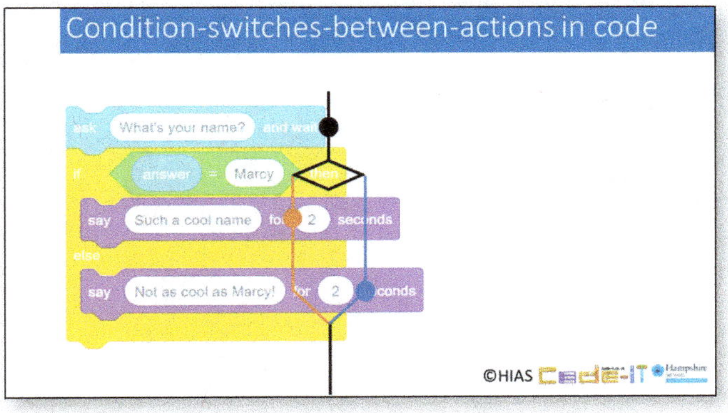

Go though the flow of control choices for both pathways. Make sure you point out that the code would need to be restarted to test it for the second path.

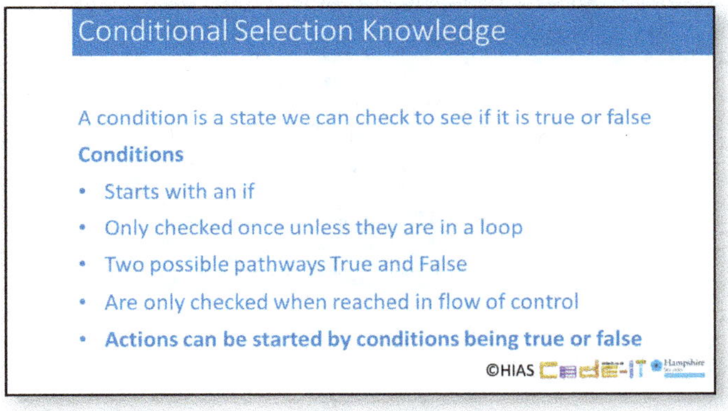

Finally go through key knowledge learned in these slides.

CHAPTER 4 Condition-Ends-Loop

Introducing Condition-Ends-Loop

These slides can be downloaded from https://computing.hias.hants.gov.uk/course/view.php?id=51.

Delivery

They are designed to be delivered to the whole class before pupils move on to using a condition-ends loop module such as

Catch the Ball (which you can find on the resource website at the link above)

They can also be delivered to a small group or pairs of pupils if they are working independently through resources.

Format

Slides are provided in PDF and PowerPoint formats, and teachers who purchased the book are authorised to adapt the resources within their school or on closed learning platforms such as Seesaw, Google Classroom or Teams as long, as they are not shared outside the school community.

Hints

Extra hints and tips on usage are provided alongside each slide on the following pages.

Resources

Pupils will need whiteboards and pens or paper and pencils.

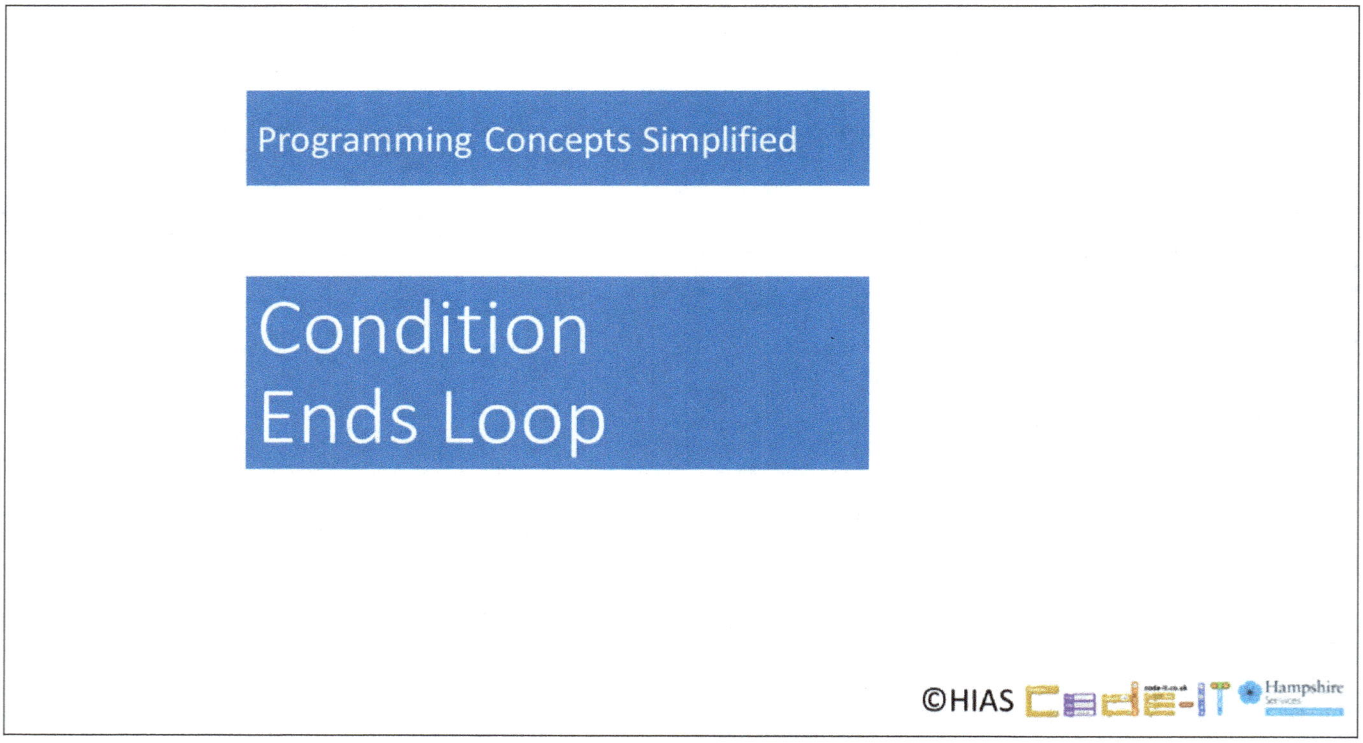

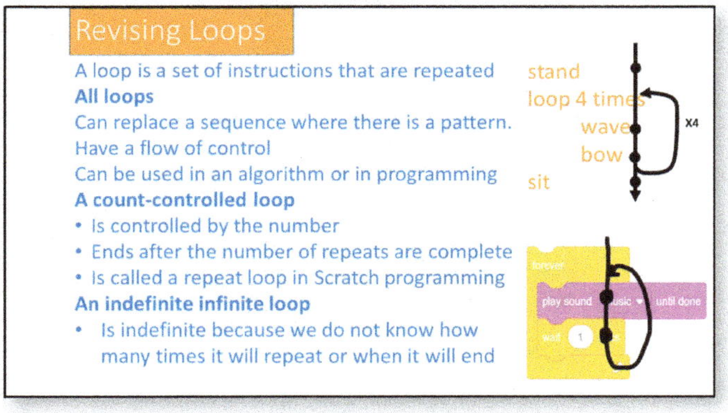

Go through loop essential knowledge that pupils learnt last year. They can use loops this year while learning new knowledge about conditions.

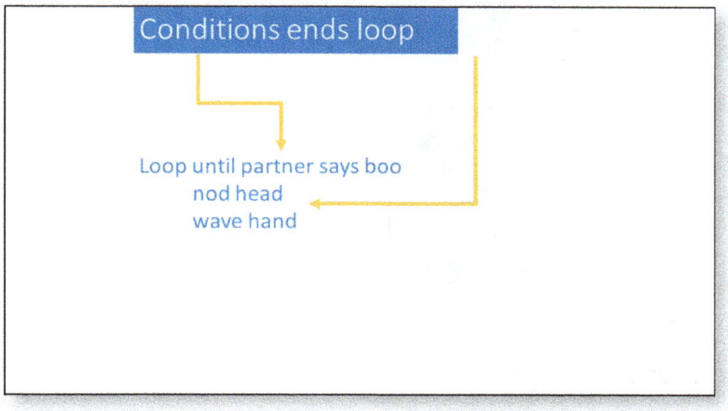

Nod and wave are inside a new type of indefinite loop that can only be ended when a condition is true. Remember an indefinite loop is called this because we don't know when it will end. We don't know when the partner will say boo, or even if they will say it.

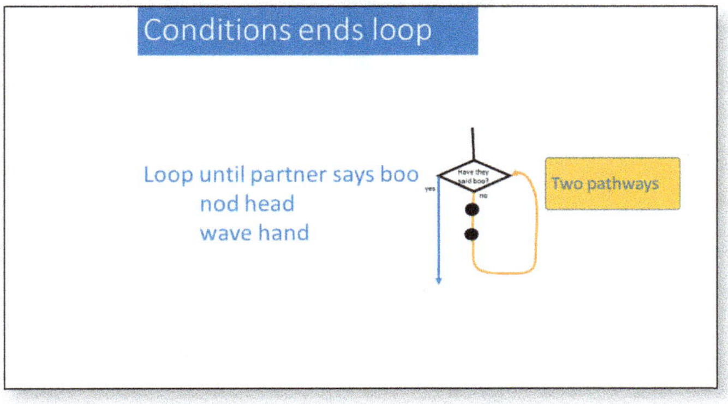

There are two pathways? If partner does not say boo, we follow the orange loop pathway. Once we get back to the condition, we check it, and if our partner says boo we go down the blue pathway.

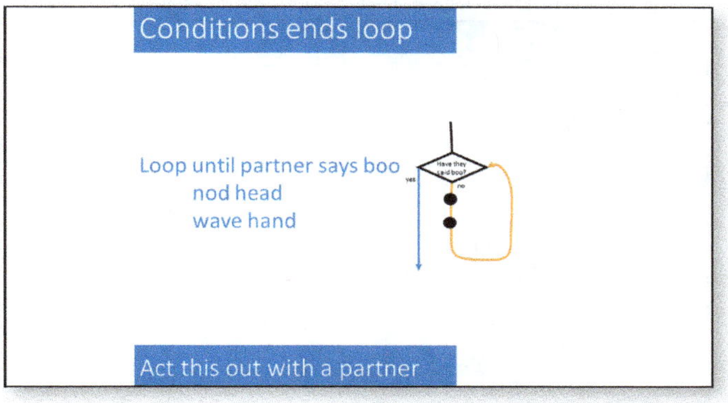

Now take it in turns to act this out. Ask the question out loud every time you get to the condition, but not before.

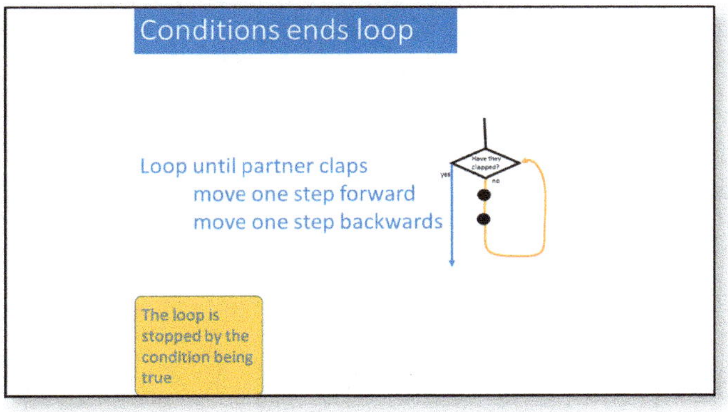

Can you see how the loop is only stopped by the condition being true?

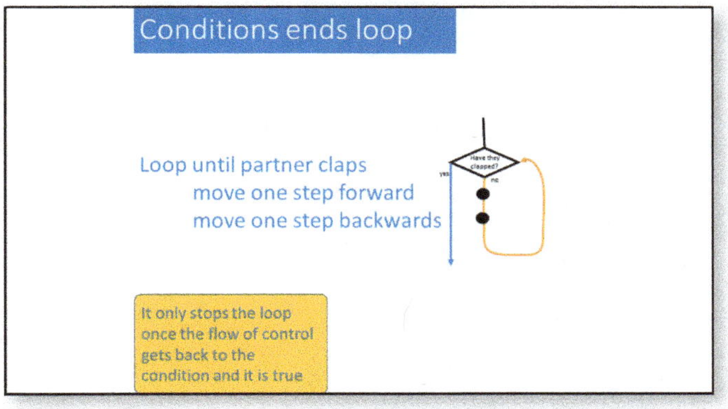

Only when we reach the condition and it is true, at that exact moment will we leave the loop.

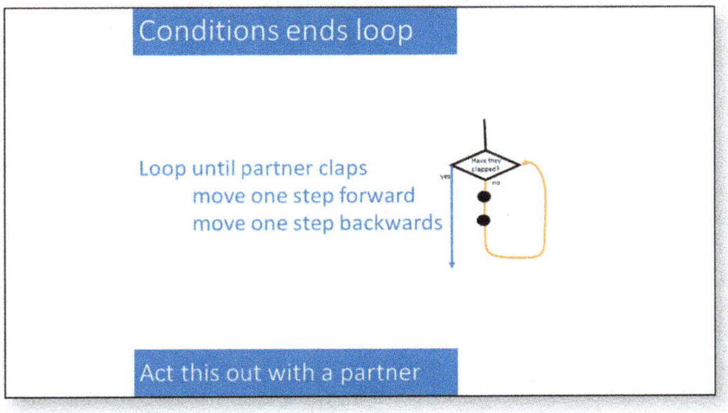

Now take it in turns to act this out. Ask the question out loud every time you get to the condition but not before.

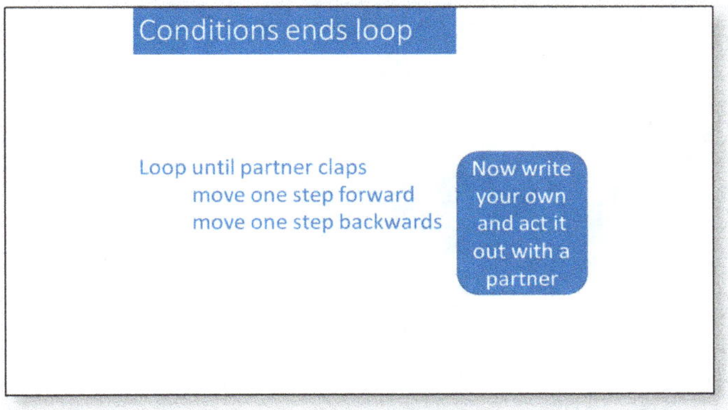

Now write your own condition that ends a loop. You can include any other algorithmic concepts you have used before.

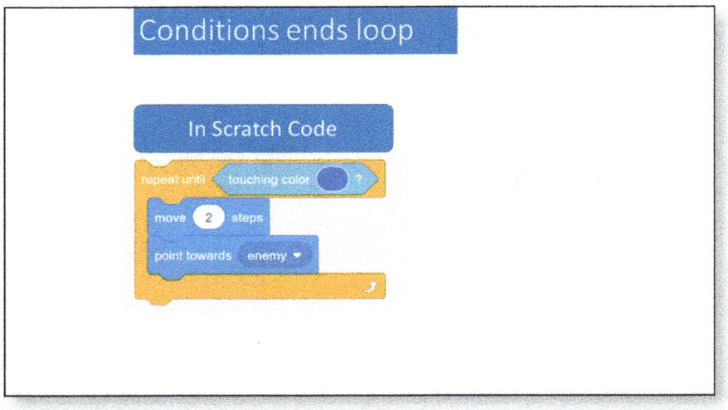

Point out that in Scratch condition ends loop are repeat until blocks. Point out that repeat until blocks can have other code after them.

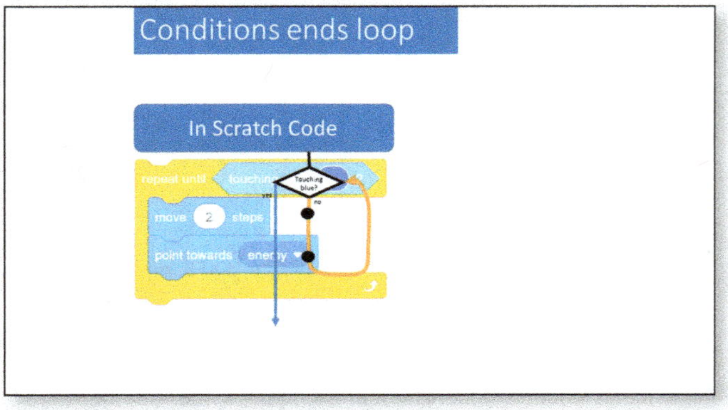

In Scratch code, they follow the same flow of control as our algorithmic examples.

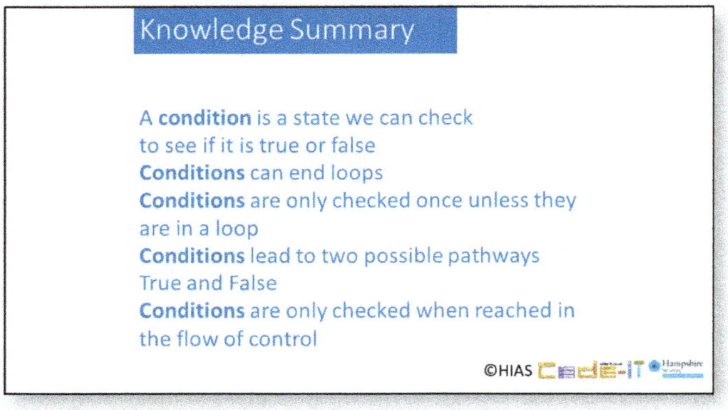

Go over the knowledge summary – are there any parts that pupils do not understand?

PROGRAMMING MODULES THAT USE CONDITION-STARTS-ACTION

CHAPTER 5 Making choices

Overview

Pupils identify where conditional selection can be found in their everyday lives before roleplaying and writing everyday conditions. They then examine code that uses conditions that start actions before building their own programming that uses conditions.

To do before the session

1. Look at the grid below and decide which optional and SEN activities you are going to include and exclude.
2. Print pupil worksheets for each activity chosen and staple into a booklet, one for each pupil.
3. Print marksheets for activities chosen to be placed where pupils can access them.
4. Download the code needed and place in a templates folder on your school network or add to a Scratch Studio or link on your learning platform.
5. Download the slides that go with the concept introduction.
6. Study the notes that go with the slides.
7. Examine the teacher help notes that are provided alongside every activity.
8. Photocopy some support cards for OR, AND & NOT for more ABLE.

To do at the start of the session

If you have not introduced condition-starts-action with this class before, do this first as a whole class activity.

To do after the concept has been introduced

Each activity has whole class notes to help you explain what is needed if it is the first time pupils have carried out this type of activity. There are also core instructions underneath in case you are sticking to the core activities only.

How this module fits into a programming progression

Sequence and Input
↓
Count-controlled loops
↓
Indefinite loops
↓
Conditional selection
↓
Conditional selection in a loop
↓
Procedures
↓
Variables
↓

Vocabulary

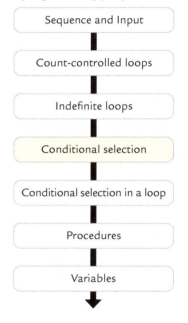

Condition, selection, true, false, condition met, pathway, decomposition, , input ask block, answer block, equals means same as, choice

Resource Name	Core Optional SEN	Teacher	Pupil Grouping	How Assessed	SCRATCH ACCESS
CONCEPT condition-starts-action	**CORE**	Leads Session	Solo Whole Class Activity	Formative	NO
PARSONS	OPTIONAL SEN OPTIONAL ALL **(predict or parsons not both)**	Support Poor Readers	Solo or Paired (Teacher choice)	Pupil Marked Marksheet Provided	YES Making Choices Parsons
PREDICT	OPTIONAL ALL **(predict or parsons not both)**	Support Poor Readers	Paired	Pupil Marked Marksheet Provided	NO
FLOW	OPTIONAL ALL	Support Poor Readers	Solo or Paired (Teacher Choice)	Pupil Marked Marksheet Provided	NO
INVESTIGATE	**CORE**	Support Poor Readers	Paired	Pupil Marked Marksheet Provided	YES Making Choices
CHANGE	**CORE**	Support Poor Readers	Paired	Pupil Marked Marksheet Provided	YES Making Choices
CREATE	**CORE**	Assesses Pupil Work and Checks Pupil Self-Assessment	Solo	Pupil Assessed & Teacher Assessed	YES Making Choices

Core activities general instructions

1. Group pupils in roughly same ability pairs. For **investigate** and **change** worksheets, pupils will work in pairs, for **create** they will work separately.
2. Give out the pupil booklets and explain that pupils need to follow the instructions on the sheets to explore how **count-controlled loops** work.
3. Explain that each pupil will record separately whilst working alongside their partner and keeping to the same pace as their partner.
4. Demonstrate where they can find the template code and explain that pupils will share one device for investigate and change.
5. Explain that during each question, only one person should touch the shared device and they should swap who that person is when there is a new question.
6. Encourage them to discuss their answers with their partner. If they disagree with their partner, they can record a different answer in their own booklet.
7. Show pupils where it says they should mark their work on the sheet where the answer sheets are in the classroom.
8. Remind pupils to return marksheets after marking, because there are not enough for every pair to have their own.

Key programming knowledge

A condition is a state we can check to see if it is true or false

Conditions starts with an if

Conditions are only checked once unless they are in a loop

Conditions lead to two possible pathways True and False

Conditions are only checked when reached in the flow of control

An algorithm is any set of instructions to carry out a task that can be understood by another human

Decomposition is breaking up a project into parts to solve separately

Resources

Making Choices	https://scratch.mit.edu/projects/343948560/editor/
Making choices PARSONS	https://scratch.mit.edu/projects/329426702/editor/

	On the sheet, if it says no Scratch, they must work only on the sheet.
	If it says Scratch with a green tick, they can use one device between the pair.
	If it says work with a partner, they must work at the same speed as their partner.
	If it says work on their own, they must do this using a separate device each working alone.

Scottish Curriculum for Excellence Technologies

I understand the instructions of a visual programming language and can predict the outcome of a program written using the language. TCH 1-14a

I can explain core programming language concepts in appropriate technical language TCH 2-14a

I can demonstrate a range of basic problem solving skills by building simple programs to carry out a given task, using an appropriate language. TCH 1-15a

I can create, develop and evaluate computing solutions in response to a design challenge. TCH 2-15a

English Computing National Curriculum Programs of Study

Pupils should be taught to:

- **design, write and debug programs that accomplish specific goals**, including controlling or simulating physical systems; **solve problems by decomposing them into smaller parts.**
- **use sequence, selection** and **repetition in programs;** work with variables **and various forms of input and output.**
- **use logical reasoning to explain how some simple algorithms work and to detect and correct errors in algorithms and programs.**

Welsh National Curriculum Relevant Strands

Progression Step 3.

- I can use conditional statements to add control and decision-making to algorithms.
- I can explain and debug algorithms.

MAKING CHOICES PARSONS

Start Scratch and Load
Making Choices PARSONS

Work with a partner

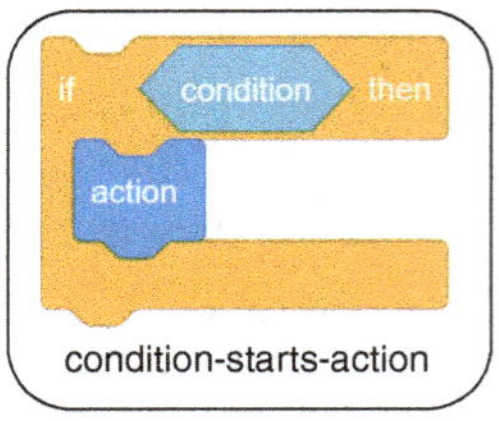

Use the algorithm below to help you connect the Scratch blocks in the correct places in Sprite A.

Start the quiz when the a key is pressed
Show the sprite on the screen
Say a welcome
Ask the question 20+10=?
If the answer is the same as 30 then
    Say correct
Ask the question 13–7=?
If the answer is the same as 6 then
    Say well done etc
Ask the question 50×3=?
If the answer is the same as 150 then
    Say Great answer
Pause for 3 seconds
Hide the sprite

Run the code and check your answer using the PARSONS ANSWERS sheet

photocopiable page

PARSONS teacher help notes
Making Choices

Notes on the activity

Parsons problems were originally designed for university students to make sense of text-based programming by ordering chunks of code rather than writing all the code out. It was designed as a scaffold to reduce the time spent in the minute detail of code and concentrate on the logical order needed to solve a problem.

This example makes pupils think about how an algorithm can be written differently than the code, as it uses similar language to the code but not always the same. An algorithm is designed for another human to understand and can be created with a wide variety of commands and symbols. A machine can only follow the precise code language that the blocks are written in.

If pupils still need time to develop their code-connecting skills, it can be a good activity to start with. It is popular with pupils as it is a hands-on activity. If this is the case, you might ask pupils to complete this in pairs, but both having a device to do this individually.

Alternatively, it could be an option you only give to pupils who have struggled in other modules to help them familiarize themselves with the code first before moving on to investigating and modifying code.

Whole class advice

Remember an algorithm plan does not have to be written in code so the algorithm will not be the same as the code in every line.

Start the quiz when the a key is pressed
Show the sprite on the screen
Say a welcome
Ask the question 20+10=?
If the answer is the same as 30 then
    Say correct
Ask the question 13–7=?
If the answer is the same as 6 then
    Say well done etc
Ask the question 50×3=?
If the answer is the same as 150 then
    Say Great answer
Pause for 3 seconds
Hide the sprite

Run the code and check your answer using the answers sheet

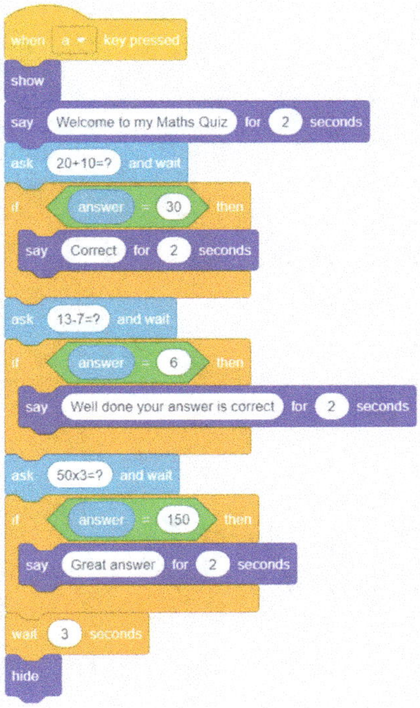

Send able advice

Use something to block all of the algorithm but the line pupils are working on, thus revealing one line of the algorithm at a time.

This makes it easier to concentrate on the immediate task rather than be overwhelmed by all of the algorithm.

If supporting pupils one to one, you could also get them to work with just three bits of code, one of which must be the code they need.

You could also part-build some of the code, so there are even fewer sections, as shown below.

You can use this version https://scratch.mit.edu/projects/578541554/editor/

Individual advice

The first word in every line is the most important and will often give you a good clue as to which block you need.

Don't forget to run your code to check that it works before moving on.

Understanding programming

The downside of Parsons problems is that if they are the only activity that pupils use in coding, they can encourage pupils to believe that there is only one right way to program a quiz question, whereas there are many ways to ask and check a quiz question. A couple of these have been coded on the right.

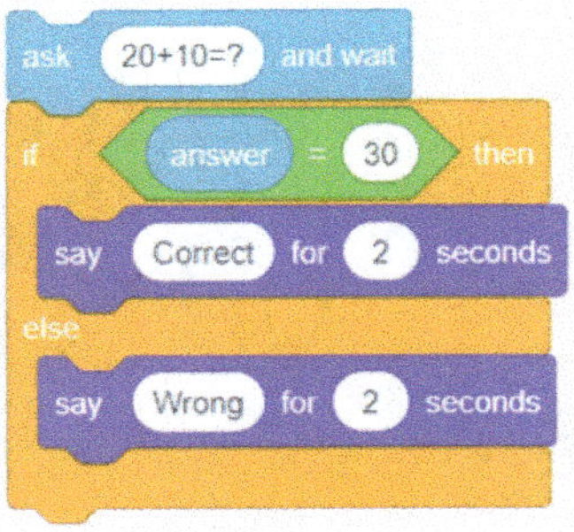

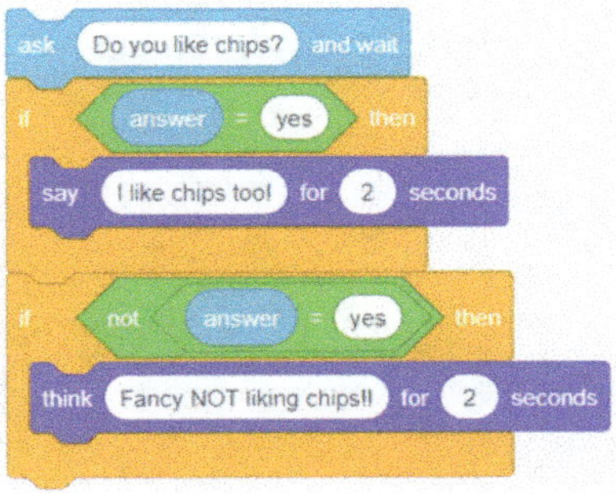

Making choices
PREDICT

Work with a partner

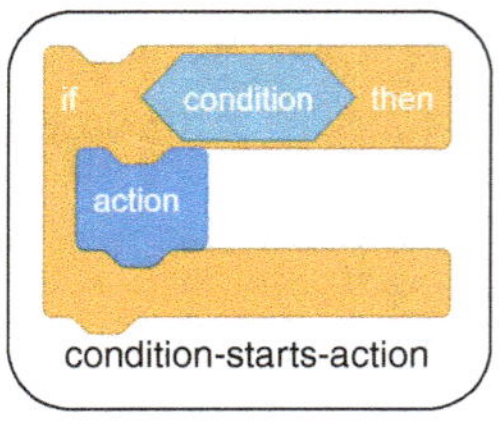

Draw a line to connect the code description to the correct code

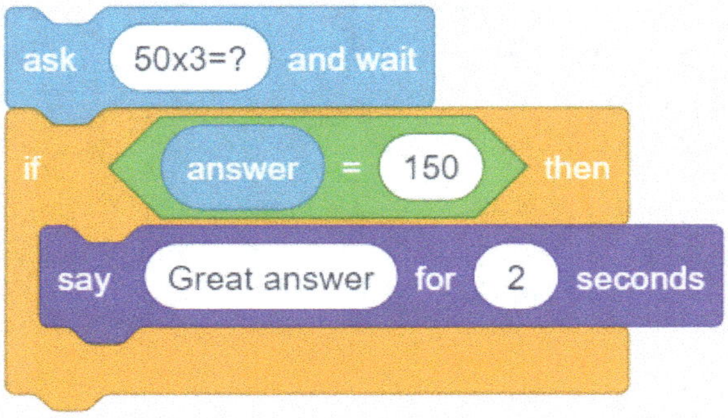

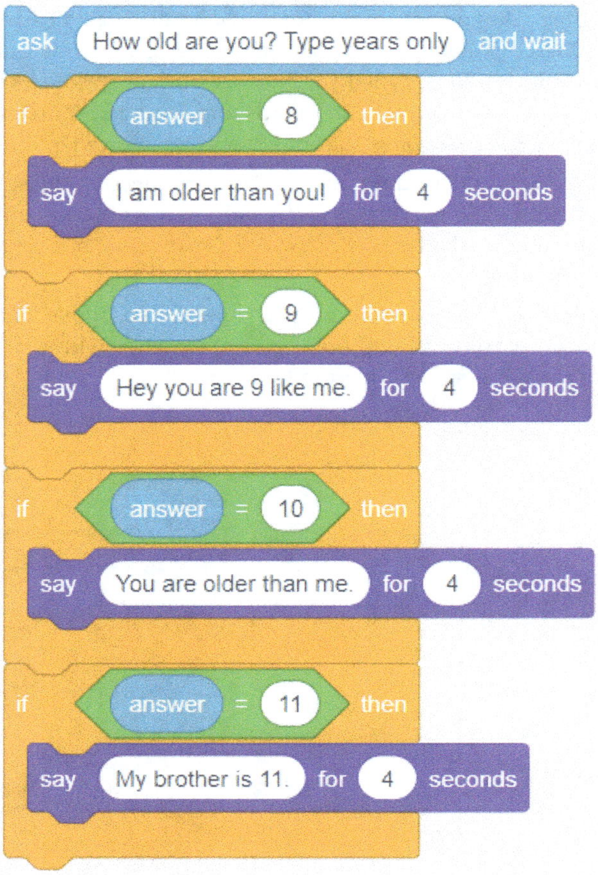

The user is asked a question, and if their answer is a yes or a no the sprite changes costumes as well as taking to them.
The user is asked a question and if their answer is the same as 150, they are told, great answer.
The user types a number in and that number is checked four times to see if it is the same as an 8, 9, 10 or 11. The program talks to the user if you type in one of these numbers only.

Code Description

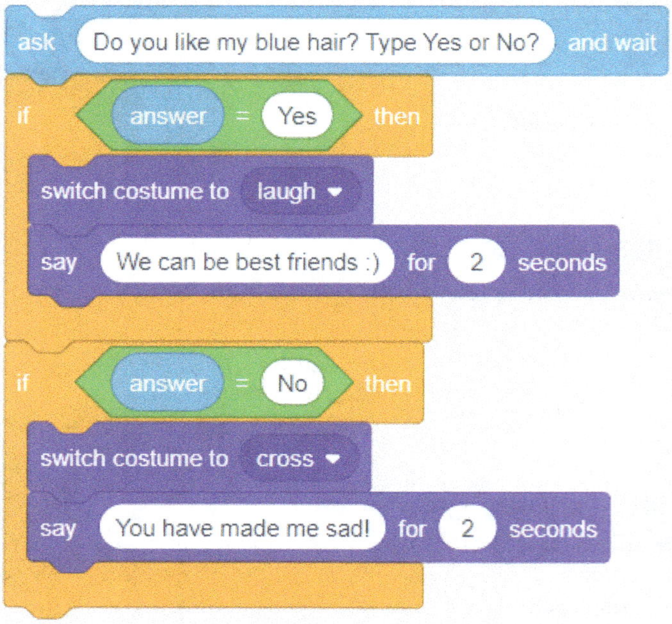

photocopiable page

PREDICT TEACHER HELP NOTES MAKING CHOICES

Whole class advice

Make sure you work with your partner on this sheet. Take it in turns to read the code and definitions out loud to each other.

Notes on the activity

Prediction helps pupils to think about the bigger purpose of the code before they run the code and experience what it actually does. It is carried out away from their digital devices.

Individual advice

Instead of reading equals read the same as.

Instead of reading answer read the answer the user gave.

Demonstrate this by reading one with the pupil

For example,

Ask 50×3=?

If the answer the user typed in is the same as 150,

Say, great answer.

Send able advice

Cover up the two longer bits of code with an exercise book or paper. Read the shortest code and circle the key facts. Now ask your pupil if they can spot those facts in the definitions as you read them one by one. Now cover up two more sections of code and repeat the process. In doing so, you are reducing the amount of visual information the pupil has to process.

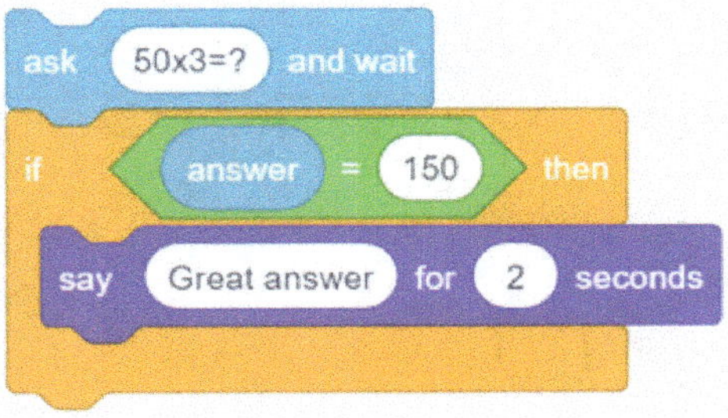

The user is asked a question, and if their answer is a yes or a no the sprite changes costumes as well as taking to them.

The user is asked a question, and if their answer is the same as 150 they are told, great answer

The user types a number in and that number is checked four times to see if it is the same as an 8, 9, 10 or 11. The program talks to the user if you type in one of these numbers only.

Individual advice

Read the definitions one by one slowly.

Underline any key words.

Are those same key words in the code?

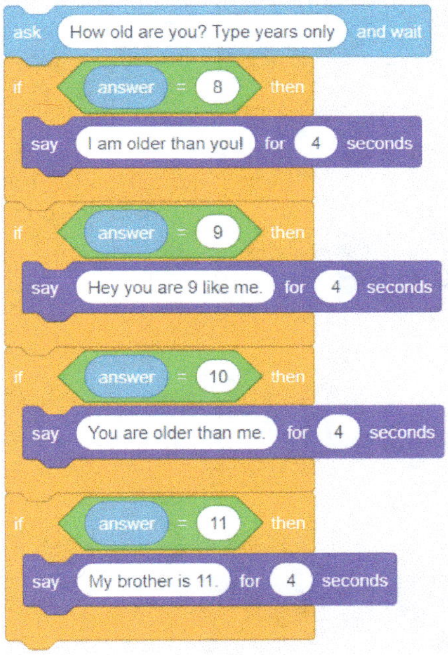

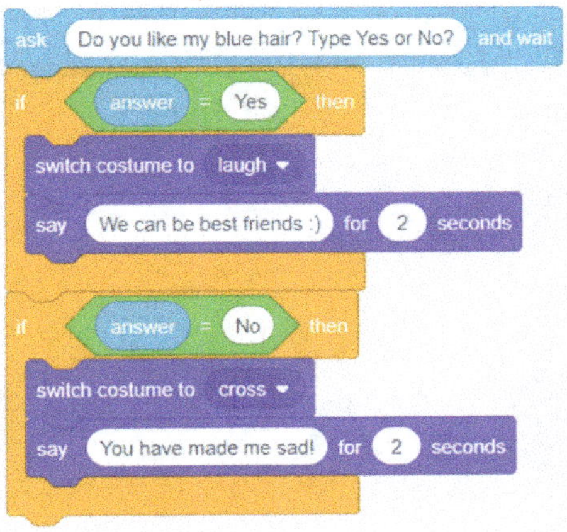

Understanding programming

While these examples are appropriate for our upper KS2 pupil, they are all incomplete, as they don't have any method of catching answers that are outside the conditions.

One simple way to do this would be with a condition-switches-between-actions block. Any code within the second else section would be run if the condition is NOT true.

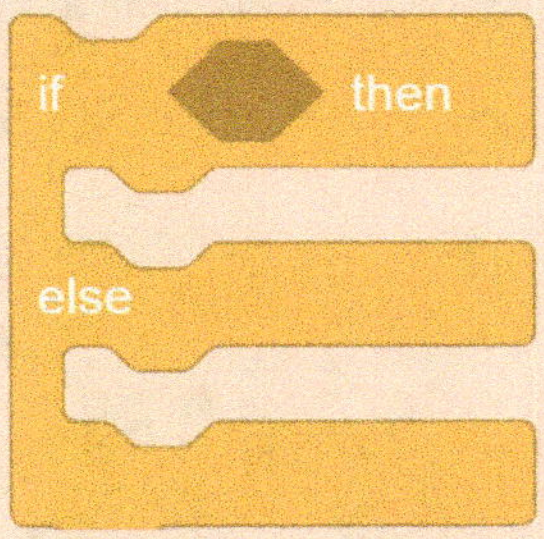

Another way would be the use of the NOT block as shown below.

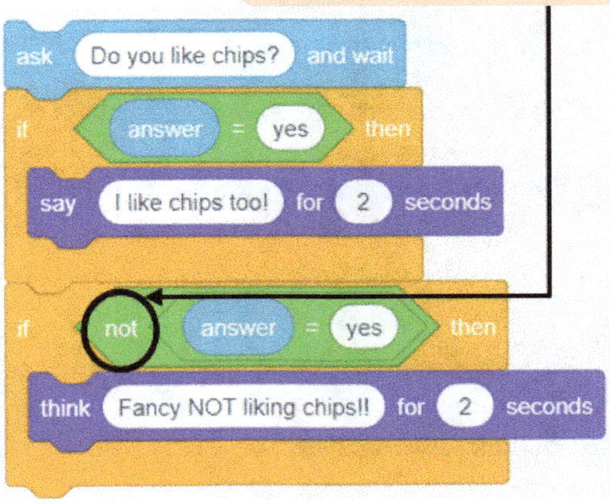

MAKING CHOICES FLOW

Work with a partner

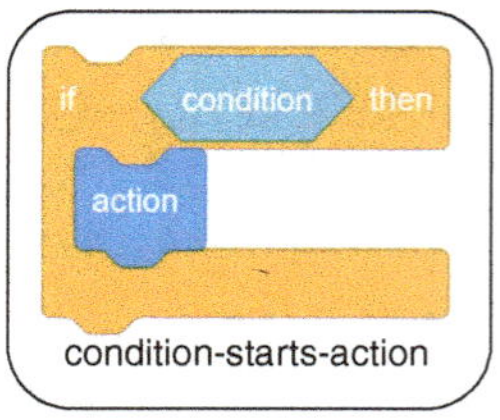

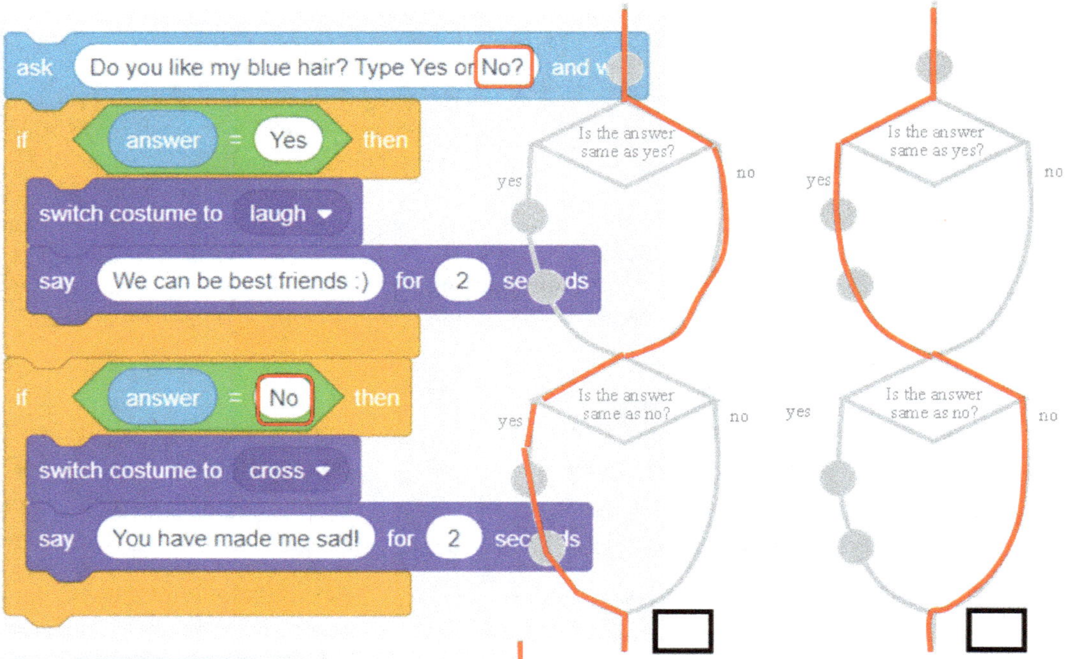

Tick the red pathway the code took when **No** was the answer.

Which costume was run

- ☐ laugh
- ☐ cross

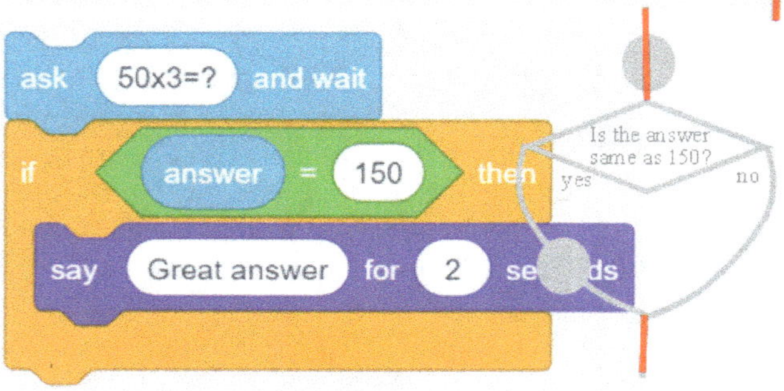

Draw the route the code took if 200 was typed in by the user.

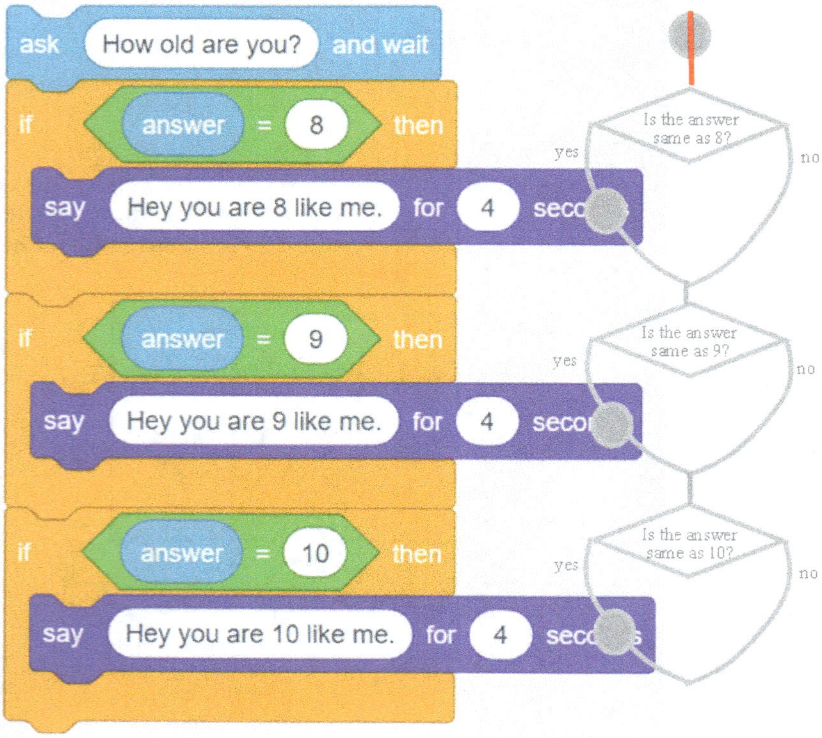

Draw the route the code took when 9 was typed in by the user.

photocopiable page

FLOW TEACHER HELP NOTES MAKING CHOICES

Whole class advice

Make sure you work with your partner on this sheet. Work together on one code section and flow of control. Read the code out loud and trace the flow of control with your finger.

Notes on the activity

Thinking about the order the code runs in can help pupils make sense of the code as well as checking that they understand key information about conditional selection.

This activity can also be kept by the teacher and used as a tool to discuss selection formatively with any pupil or pair of pupils to check they understand the order the code will be run in.

Send able advice

Cover up the code and flow of control sections that pupils are not working on. You could always chop the page up into three sections to reduce cognitive load.

Read the code aloud pointing to each line of code as you do this. If a pupils fine motor control is a particular issue, you could also draw in the line as long as they point to or describe where it should go.

Individual advice

One person reads the code on the left while the other person points to the part of the flow of control it links to. The person who is reading the code needs to choose what the user types in that is collected by the answer blocks (point to answer blocks). In this case, we know it is NO as there is a red rectangle round it (point to this).

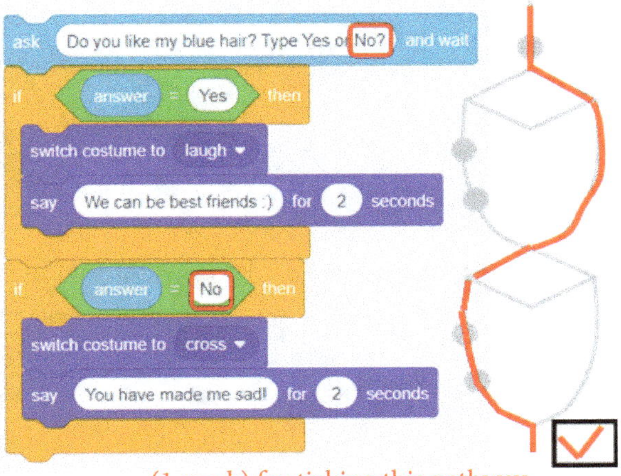

(1 mark) for ticking this pathway

Tick the red pathway the code took when No was the answer.

Which costume was run

☐ laugh

☐ cross (1 mark) if ticked

Individual advice

Read the code out loud like this, pointing to each part as you read it.

Ask 50x3 and wait until the user has typed in an answer. The users answer will then be inside the answer block. We know that they typed in 200. Is 200 the same as 150? Pause for them to tell you it is or is not the same.

No, it is not the same, so the condition is NOT met, it is FALSE. So say great answer is NOT run.

Now let us do this again and this time you point to the pathway it goes down on the flow of control.

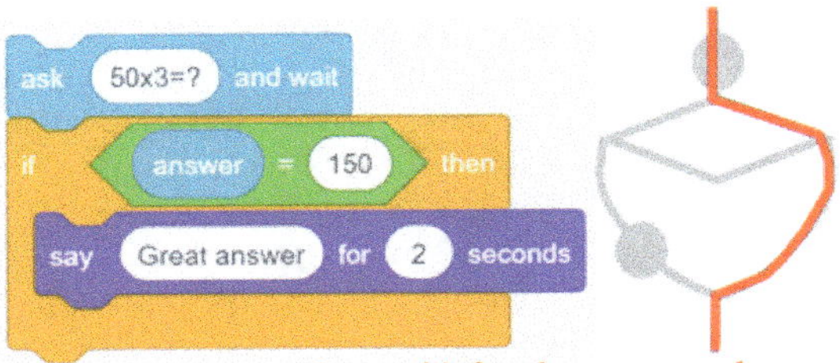

(1 mark) for the same pathway

Draw the route the code took if 200 was typed in by the user.

Individual advice

Point out that the answer typed in by the user (9 in this case) is checked by all three condition blocks starting with the one at the top.

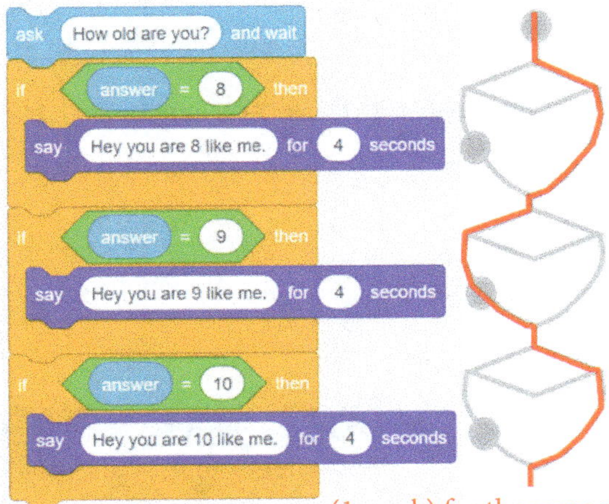

(1 mark) for the same pathway

Draw the route the code took when 9 was typed in by the user.

Understanding programming

When asked, typically a half to two-thirds of classes indicate that understanding the order that the code is executed/run in helps them understand how conditional selection works. However, there is no research into this aspect for primary pupils at the time of writing this, although Sue Sentence, the author of the PRIMM methodology, talks about flow of control as a good activity to use with PRIMM, as we are doing here.

MAKING CHOICES
INVESTIGATE

Work with a partner

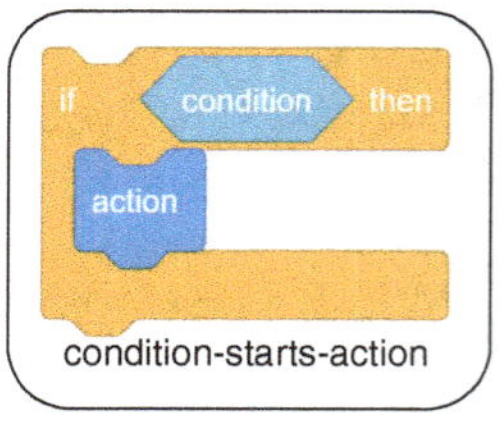

Start Scratch and Load
Making choices

A

INVESTIGATE (Run the programs lots of times but don't change the code)

Run the code inside spite **A** and answer these questions.

1. How many ***if-then*** **condition-starts-action** blocks are there? *HINT You can include the loose one*

HINT

2. What does = mean in these conditions? *HINT Read comments*

3. In the second question 13–7 what will the program say if the user types the answer 6?

4. What will the program do if the user gets the answer wrong?

Run the code inside sprite **B** and answer these questions.

B

5. In the question ***What is your favourite colour?*** what does the program do with the answer you type in? *HINT Look in say block with joins*

6. In the question **How old are you?** what happens if you are less than 8 or more than 12 years old? *HINT Try inputting an age less than 8 or more than 11*

7. In the question **Do you like me? Yes or No?** can you get the program to give both responses by typing in yes and no at the same time? *HINT Type yes no*

8. In the question **Are you happy or sad?** what happens to the B sprite when you are sad?

Run the code inside sprite **C** and answer these question

C

9. What happens if you get any of the first three questions wrong?

10. What happens if you get any of the first three questions right?

11. Look at the **condition-starts-action** blocks connected on their own (scroll right). Which one best shows how the code blocks are connected on the left? AA, BB or CC?

Now mark these questions using the INVESTIGATE ANSWER sheet

photocopiable page

INVESTIGATE TEACHER'S NOTES

MAKING CHOICES

Whole class advice

Work in pairs, one device between the pair. Take it in turns every question to swap who runs code. You must work at the same pace as your partner and not move on to the next question until you have both written your answer down. If you disagree, write a different answer. You must mark your work before moving on to the next section.

Send able advice

Support pairs of pupils who are poor readers by reading questions, reading code samples and covering up questions until they get to them.

Notes on the activity

Investigating code is a core activity in these modules, so I do NOT recommend that you skip this activity. Questions and code in sprites A and B are less complex than that in sprite C. If some pairs of pupils are taking much longer than their peers, you can always cross out the questions in the last section or use the flow of control at the end of the chapter. Sometimes one pupil in a pair decides to work faster than their partner; check that this is not happening and that every pupil is filling in and marking the questions individually but at the pace of the slowest in the pair. Sometimes a pair decides not to mark to speed up their efforts. Marking gives valuable information, so I recommend sending them back to mark their work if this is the case. A class instruction to come and talk to you if they have over half of the questions wrong or they do not understand the answer after they have marked it helps to check progress is being made correctly. There is real value in collecting these scores to build up a summative picture of pupil progress.

Individual advice

Point to the condition-starts-action example at top of page or say if block.

Sprite A

1. How many **condition-starts-action** blocks are there?

   3 plus an empty example block (one mark for 3 or 4)

2. What does = mean in these conditions?

   Same as (1 mark)

3. In the second question 13–7, what will the program say if the user types the answer 6?

   Well done your answer is correct (1 mark)

4. What will the program do if the user gets the answer wrong?

   Nothing or move onto the next question or won't say anything or hide (1 mark for any of these)

Sprite B

5. In the question ***What is your favourite colour?*** what does the program do with the answer you type in?

   Uses it in the next sentence or say, no way (any colour) is my favourite (1 mark)

6. In the question **How old are you?** what happens if you are less than 8 or more than 12 years old?

   Nothing happens or moves to next question or says, do you like me? (1 mark)

7. In the question **Do you like me? Yes or No?** can you get the program to give both responses by typing in yes and no at the same time?

   No (1 mark) typing more means it is not the same (=) as yes or no

8. In the question **Are you happy or sad?** what happens to the B sprite when you are sad?

   Costume changes or sprite looks sad or switch costume to tera-d (1 mark)

Sprite C

9. What happens if you get any of the first three questions wrong?

   You don't get any more questions asked or end of the quiz (1 mark)

10. What happens if you get any of the first three questions right?

    You get to answer next question (1 mark)

11. Look at the **condition-starts-action** blocks connected on their own. Which one best shows how the blocks are connected on the left? AA, BB or CC?

    AA (1 mark)

Q2 There is a comment next to the code that tells them what = does.

Q3 Have they run the code and tried typing in 6 as the answer?

Q4 Have you run the code and deliberately got the answer wrong?

Q5 Look at how the answer block is used in the next line.

Q6 Try it with 13 and 7 on two **separate** occasions.

Q8 Have you looked at what the character looks like when the code is run in that way?

Understanding programming

The ability to control very complex pathways like the one programmed in C where the path changes depending on conditions is a feature of more advanced programming logic. Drawing out the flow of control can help us understand how it works.

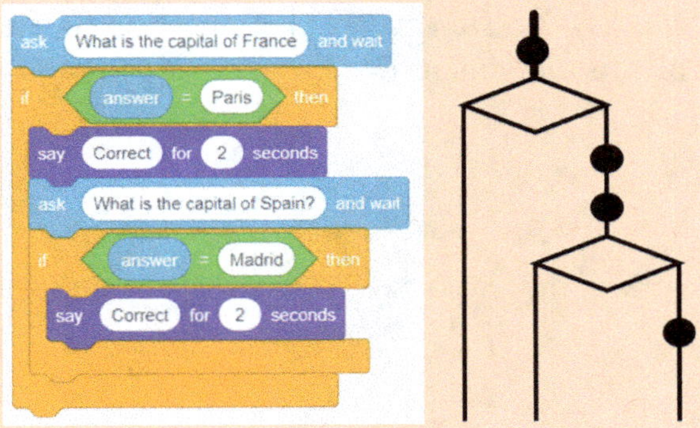
ask What is the capital of France and wait
if answer = Paris then
say Correct for 2 seconds
ask What is the capital of Spain? and wait
if answer = Madrid then
say Correct for 2 seconds

Sprite C Individual advice

The last page of this module is a flow of control for sprite c. Use this to help pupils understand how the code works.

MAKING CHOICES
CHANGE

Work with a partner

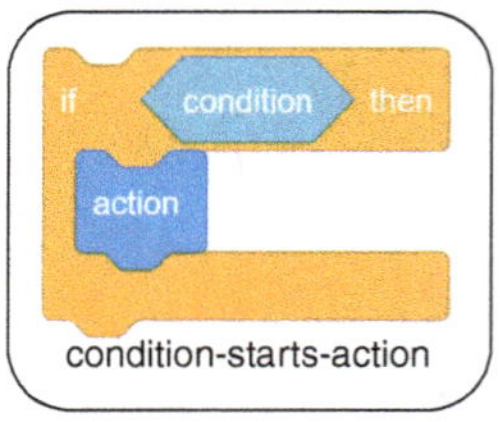

Change Code in Sprite A (Make small changes or small additions to the code)

1. Change the code to make the first question say something else rather than correct when the answer is the same as 30. What did you change it to?

2. Change the second question and correct answer. What did you change the question and correct answer to?

3. Add a short sound or simple graphic effect to question 3 if someone gets the answer right. What did you add? Where did you add it?

Change Code in Sprite B (Make small changes or small additions to the code)

4. Change the *'How old are you?'* question so it also gives an answer if someone is 7. What new blocks did you add?

5. Modify the *'Do you like me?'* question so it also gives an answer if the user types in sometimes. What new blocks did you add?

Now mark the these questions using the CHANGE ANSWER sheet

photocopiable page

CHANGE TEACHER NOTES MAKING CHOICES

Whole class advice

Work in pairs, one device between the pair. Take it in turns every question to swap who runs code. You must work at the same pace as your partner and not move on to the next question until you have both written your answer down. If you disagree, write a different answer. You must mark your work before moving on to the next section.

Notes on the activity

Changing or modifying the code is a core part of this module, so I suggest you do not leave it out. It is an important step towards creation of their own code.

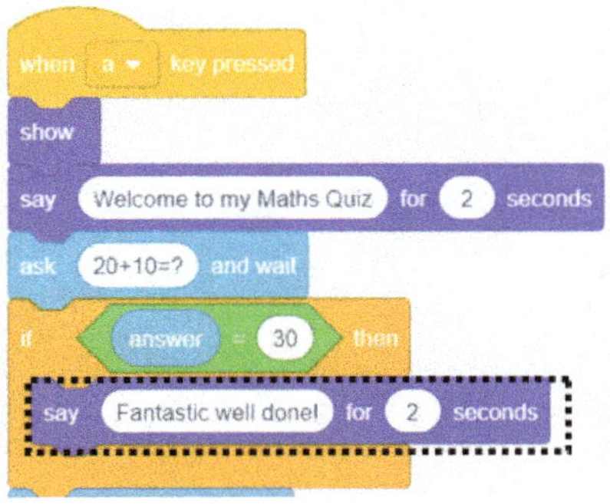

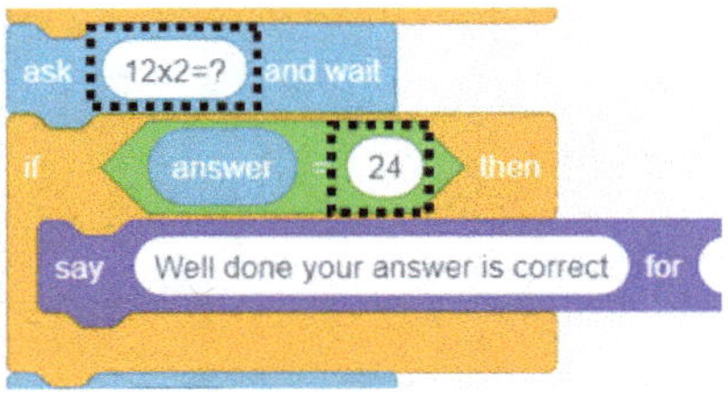

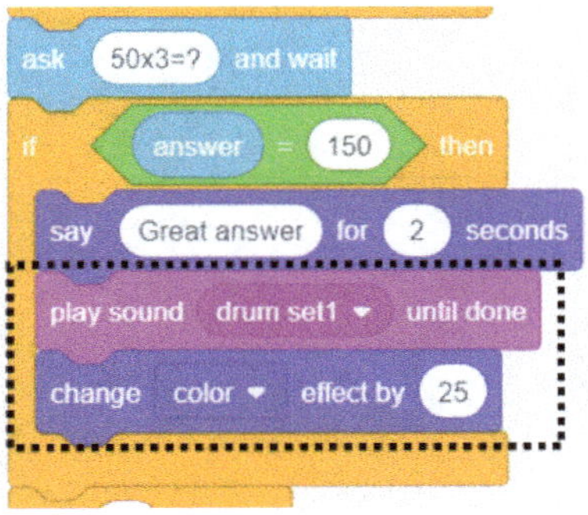

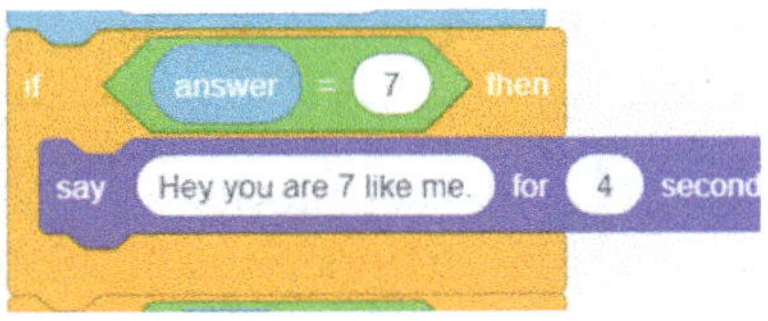

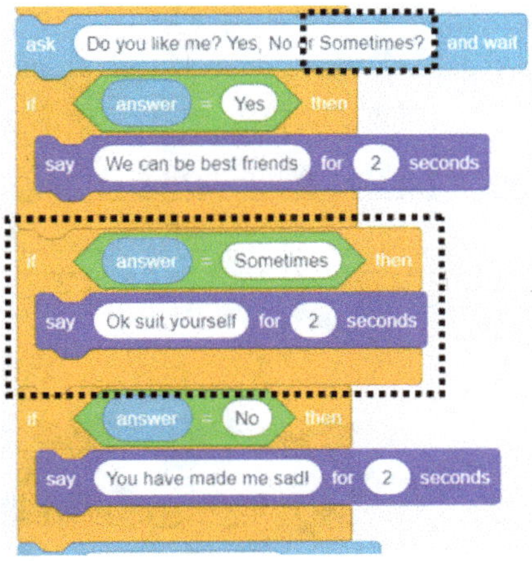

Modify Code in Sprite A ANSWERS

1. Adapt the code to make the first question say something other than correct when the answer is the same as 30. What did you change it to?

   Change word correct to something else that means right answer (1 mark)

2. Change the second question and answer. What did you change the question and answer to?

   New question in the ask block and new answer in the answer = block (1 mark)

3. Add a short sound or simple graphic effect to question 3 if someone gets the answer right. What did you add? Where did you add it?

   Any block inside the if block in the same place as the say Great answer for 2 secs block (1 mark)

Modify Code in Sprite B ANSWERS

4. Modify the *'How old are you?'* question so it also gives an answer if someone is 7. What new blocks did you add?

   Add a new section

   If answer = 7 then

   Say Hey you are 7 like me for 4 secs (1 mark)

5. Modify the *'Do you like me?'* question so it also gives an answer if the user types in sometimes. What new blocks did you add?

   Change the question to include sometimes as well as yes and no (1 mark)

   Add a new condition-starts-action section

   If answer = sometimes

   Say something linked to sometimes (1 mark)

Individual advice

Ask pupils to point out in the code where the question is and then where the right answer is.

Individual advice

The emphasis should be on the new code only being activated IF the condition is TRUE.

Individual advice

Most modify questions to this point have not involved much new code, so stating that they will need to add new code can help.

Also, stating that the new code will look very similar to existing code helps.

Individual advice

Explain that currently the user will only get a response from either yes or no but that now we need a response from sometimes. It can help to say that they will need to modify the ask block and add a new if block.

Send able advice

Support pairs of pupils who are poor readers by reading questions, reading code samples and covering up questions until they get to them.

MAKING CHOICES

CREATE

Work on your own

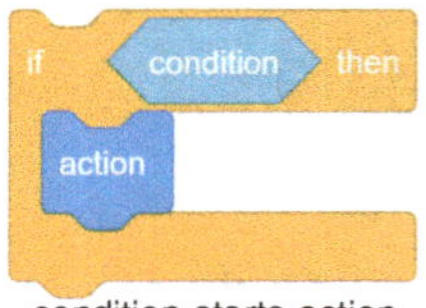

condition-starts-action

Plan your create second questions here

Create First (Choose one or more of these ideas first)

1. Add another question to the maths quiz in sprite A.
2. Add the question *'Do you like chips?'* to the bottom of the code in Sprite B. Give a funny answer if they do or don't like chips.
3. Add another capital city question to sprite C if the user gets the capital of the UK correct.

Create Second (Choose one or more of these ideas second)

1. Create your own fun quiz about any topic in a new sprite inside Making Choices. You can hide the A,B,C sprites now and delete them when you are finished.
2. Ask lots of questions about the user and give funny answers to each one inside a new sprite inside Making Choices. You can hide the A,B,C sprites now and delete them when you are finished.
3. Create a fun quiz on any topic, where you can only attempt the next question if you get the question before correct, inside a new sprite inside Making Choices. You can hide the old sprites now and delete them when you are finished.
4. Come up with your own idea that uses **condition-starts-actions** blocks. Tell your teachers about it before making it.

Teacher and Pupil Assessment

Circle one column on each row to show what you think you have achieved

	Not used **condition-starts-action** blocks	Used a single **condition-start-action** block in a question	Used more than one **condition-starts-action** blocks in a question	2 marks and Used either <, >, OR, AND or NOT in a condition
Condition-starts-action	0 marks	1 mark	2 marks	3 marks

	Not used previous programming concepts for real purpose	Used previous programming concepts for real purpose
Used previous programming concept such as count controlled or indefinite loops correctly	0 marks	1 mark

	No theme in planning or code	Has a theme in planning or code
Has a project theme in create second	0 marks	1 mark

photocopiable page

CREATE TEACHER NOTES MAKING CHOICES

Whole class advice

It helps if pupils work on their own for this while still supporting each other.

Individual advice

If you are providing hints at this point, then it should be reflected in your summative assessment.

Send able advice

Some pupils can really benefit from the teacher building a simple question as a demo at this point, just so they can see how the blocks snap together.

Send able advice

There are AND, OR & NOT extension support cards available for those who would benefit.

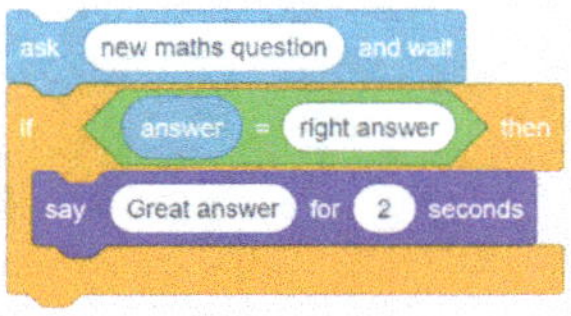

(1 mark)

(1 mark)

Create First (Choose one or more of these ideas first)

1. Add another question to the maths quiz in spite A.
2. Add the question *'Do you like chips?'* to the bottom of the code in Sprite B. Give a funny answer if they do or don't like chips.
3. Add another capital city question to sprite C if the user gets the capital of the UK correct.

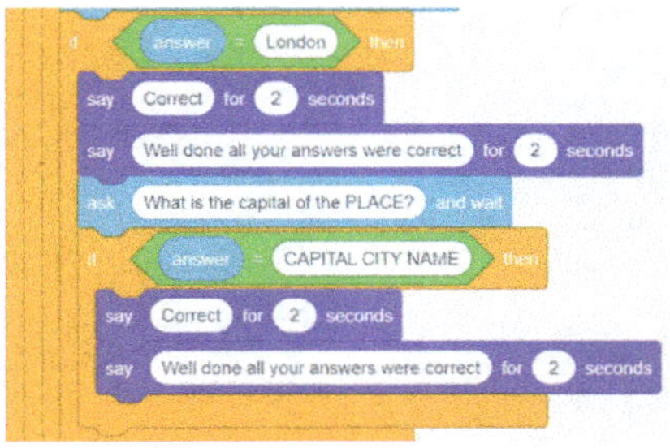

Must include new ask and if block within the last if block for London (1 mark)

Create Second (Choose one or more of these ideas second)

1. Create your own fun quiz about any topic in a new sprite inside Making Choices. You can hide the A,B,C sprites now and delete them when you are finished.
2. Ask lots of questions about the user and give funny answers to each one inside a new sprite inside Making Choices. You can hide the A,B,C sprites now and delete them when you are finished.
3. Create a fun quiz on any topic, where you can only attempt the next question if you get the question before correct, inside a new sprite inside Making Choices. You can hide the old sprites now and delete them when you are finished.
4. Come up with your own idea that uses **condition-starts-actions** blocks. Tell your teachers about it before making it.

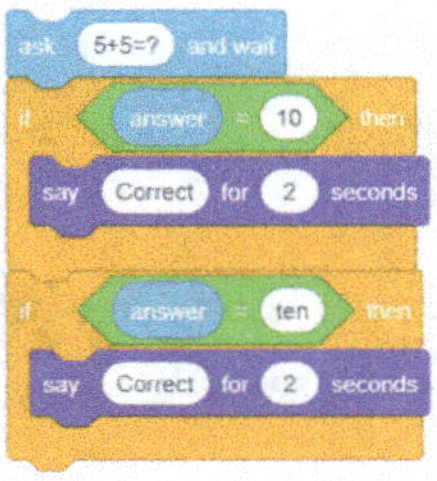

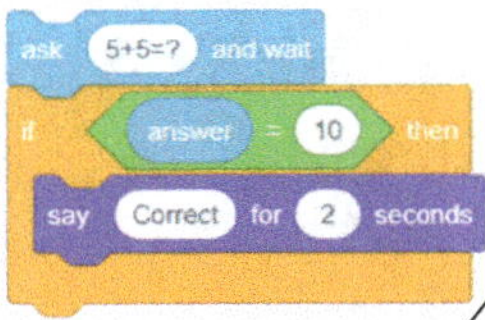

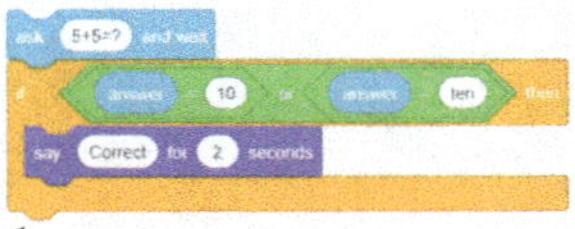

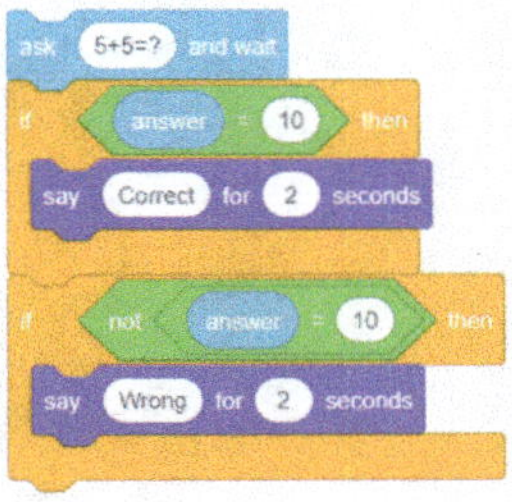

Teacher and Pupil Assessment

Circle one column on each row to show what you think you have achieved

	Not used **condition-starts-action** blocks	Used a single **condition-starts-action** block in a question or questions	Used more than one **condition-starts-action** blocks in a question	2 marks and used either <, >, OR, AND or NOT in a condition
Condition-starts-action	0 marks	1 mark	2 marks	3 marks

	Not used previous programming concepts for real purpose	Used previous programming concepts for real purpose
Used previous programming concept such as count controlled or indefinite loops correctly	0 marks	1 mark

Have pupils written any questions in the planning column?	No theme in planning or code	Has a theme in planning or code
Has a project theme in create second	0 marks	1 mark

These examples are not exhaustive, but help to give some guidance

PARSONS ANSWERS
MAKING CHOICES

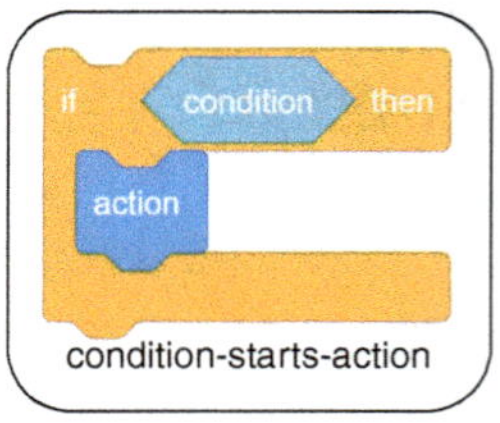

Start the quiz when the a key is pressed
Show the sprite on the screen
Say a welcome
Ask the question 20+10=?
If the answer is the same as 30 then
    Say correct
Ask the question 13–7=?
If the answer is the same as 6 then
    Say well done etc
Ask the question 50×3=?
If the answer is the same as 150 then
    Say Great answer
Pause for 3 seconds
Hide the sprite

Run the code and check your answer using the answers sheet

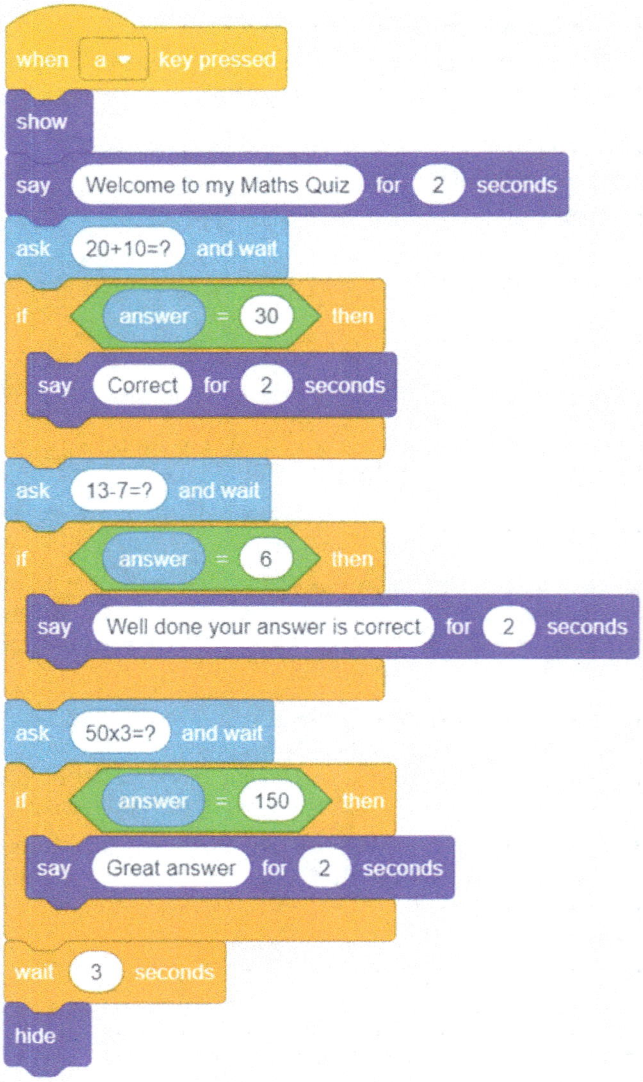

photocopiable page

PREDICT ANSWERS
MAKING CHOICES

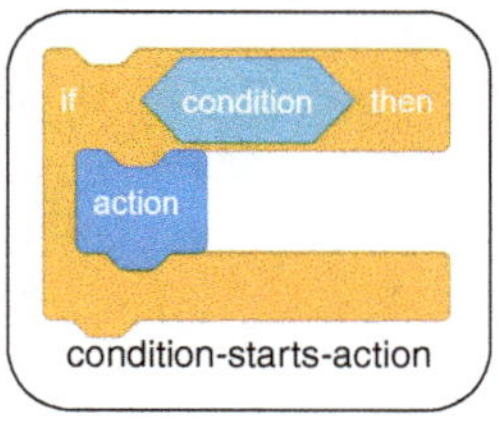

Draw a line to connect the code description to the correct code

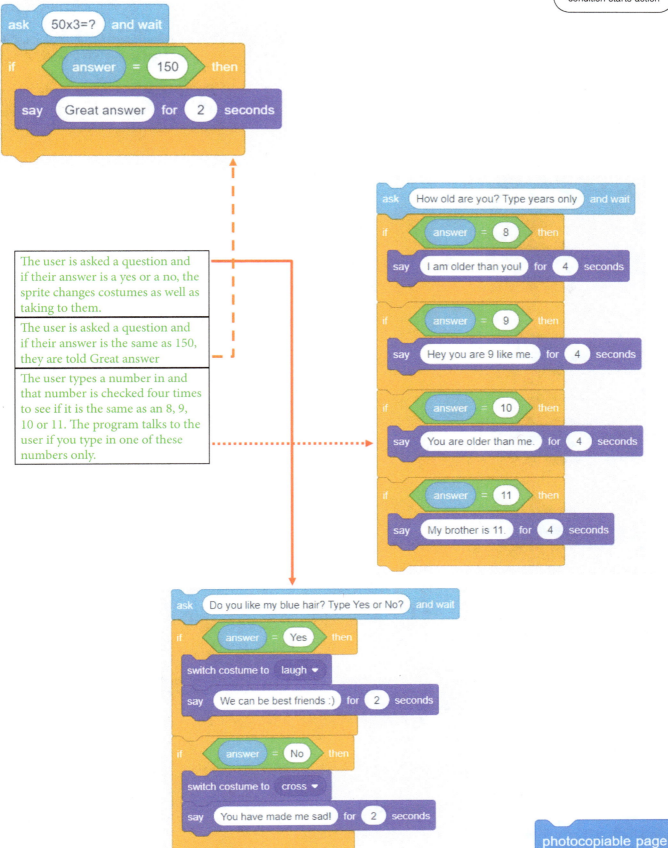

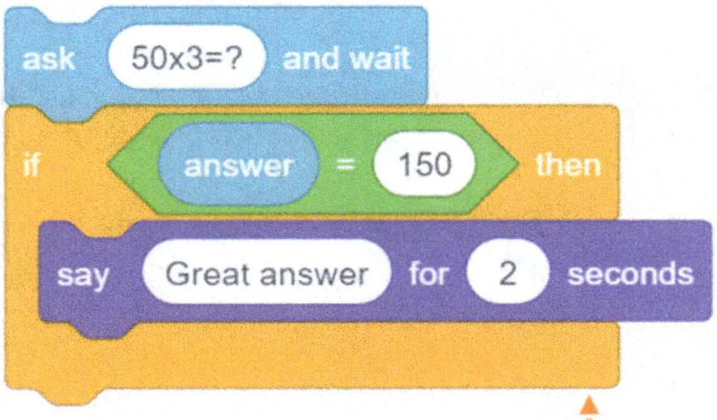

The user is asked a question and if their answer is a yes or a no, the sprite changes costumes as well as taking to them.
The user is asked a question and if their answer is the same as 150, they are told Great answer
The user types a number in and that number is checked four times to see if it is the same as an 8, 9, 10 or 11. The program talks to the user if you type in one of these numbers only.

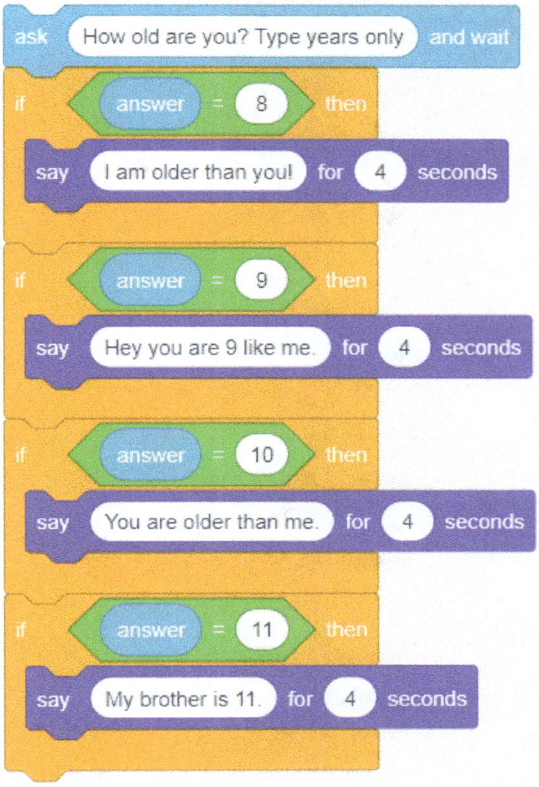

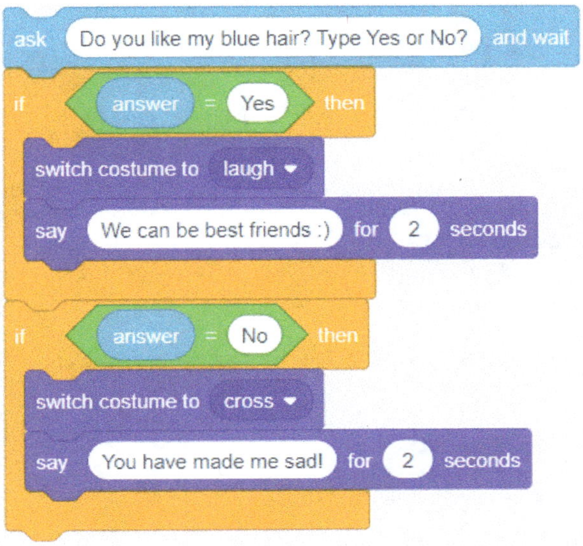

photocopiable page

FLOW ANSWERS
MAKING CHOICES

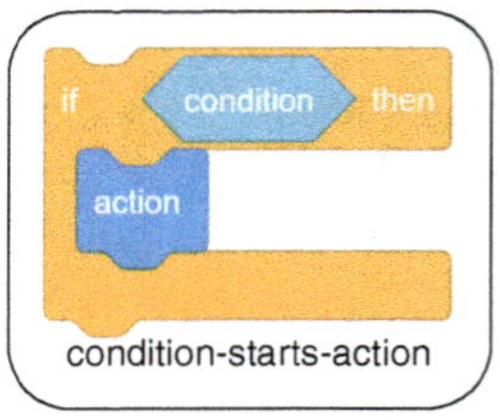

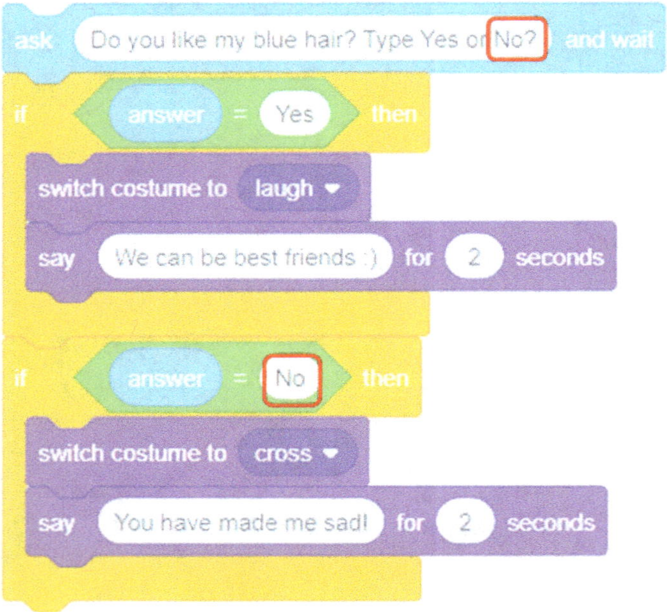

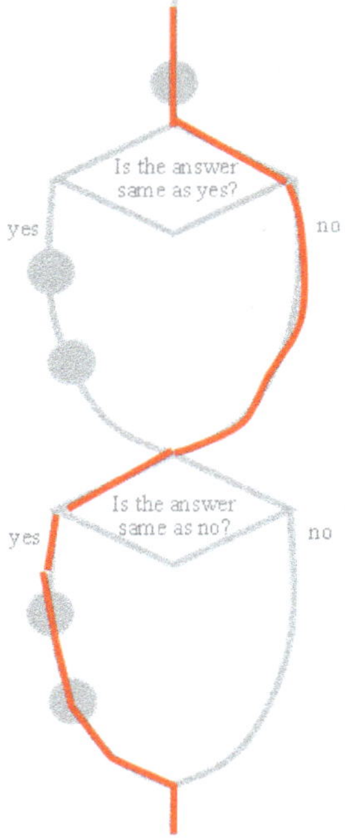

The red path shows the route the code took when **NO** was typed in by the user.

Which costume was run

Laugh ◯

Cross ✓ (1 mark for cross)

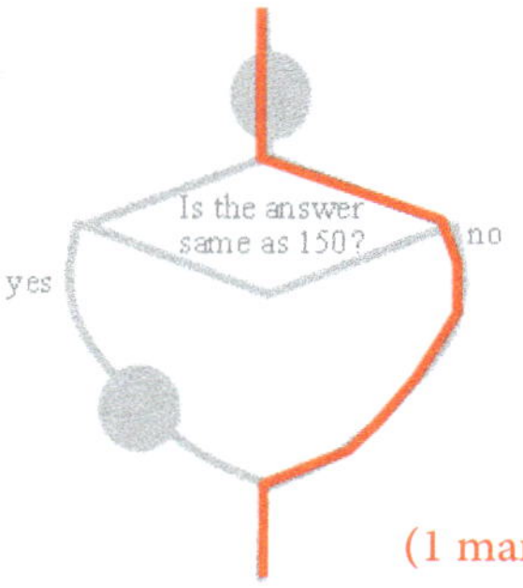

Draw the route the code took if 200 was typed in by the user.

(1 mark) for the same pathway

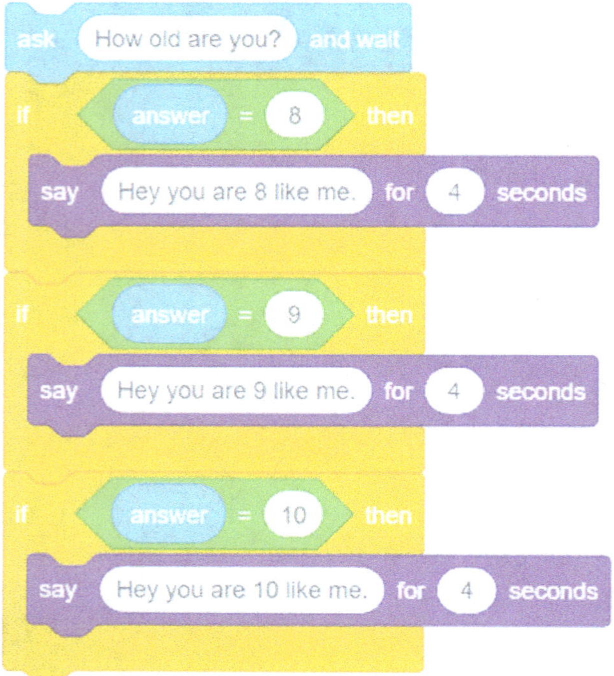

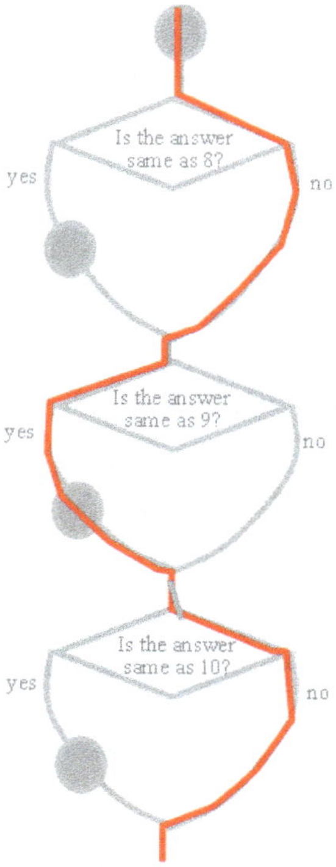

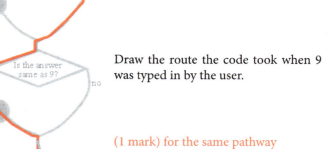

Draw the route the code took when 9 was typed in by the user.

(1 mark) for the same pathway

photocopiable page

INVESTIGATE ANSWERS
MAKING CHOICES

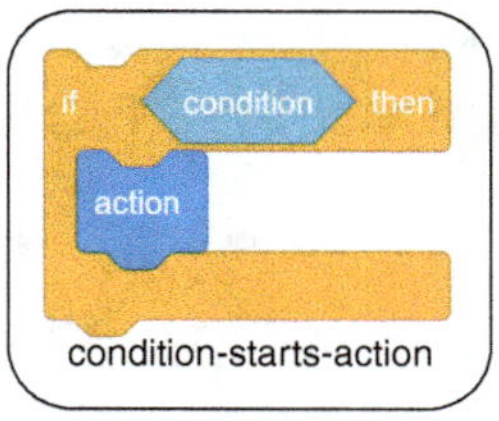

Sprite A

1. How many **condition-starts-action** blocks are there?

   3 plus an empty example block (one mark for 3 or 4)

2. What does = mean in these conditions?

   Same as (1 mark)

3. In the second question 13-7 what will the program say if the user types the answer 6?

   Well done, your answer is correct (1 mark)

4. What will the program do if the user gets the answer wrong?

   Nothing or move onto the next question or won't say anything or hide (1 mark for any of these)

Sprite B

5. In the question ***What is your favourite colour?*** what does the program do with the answer you type in?

   Uses it in the next sentence or says No way (any colour) is my favourite (1 mark)

6. In the question **How old are you**? what happens if you are less than 8 or more than 12 years old?

   Nothing happens or moves to next question or says do you like me (1 mark)

7. In the question **Do you like me? Yes or No?** can you get the program to give both responses by typing in yes and no at the same time?

   No (1 mark) typing more means it is not the same (=) as yes or no

8. In the question **Are you happy or sad?** what happens to the B sprite when you are sad?

   Costume changes or sprite looks sad or switches costume to tera-d (1 mark)

Sprite C

9. What happens if you get any of the first three questions wrong?

   You don't get any more questions asked or end of the quiz (1 mark)

10. What happens if you get any of the first three questions right?

    You get to answer next question (1 mark)

11. Look at the **condition-starts-action** blocks connected on their own. Which one best shows how the blocks are connected on the left? AA, BB or CC?

    AA (1 mark)

MODIFY ANSWERS
MAKING CHOICES

Modify Code in Sprite A ANSWERS

1. Adapt the code to make the first question say something other than correct when the answer is the same as 30. What did you change it to?

   Change word correct to something else that means right answer (1 mark)

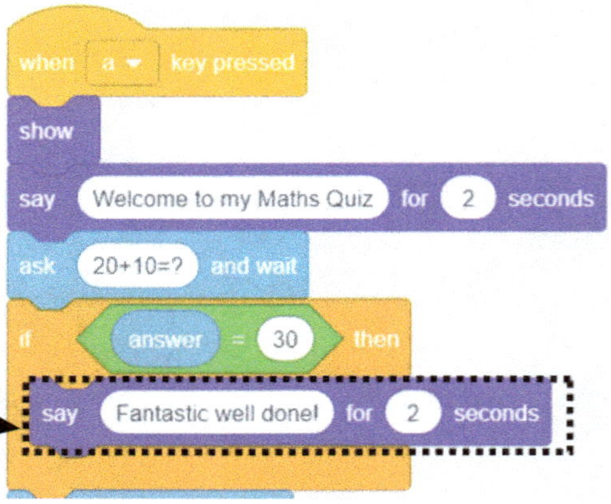

2. Change the second question and answer. What did you change the question and answer to?

   New question in the ask block and new answer in the answer = block (1 mark)

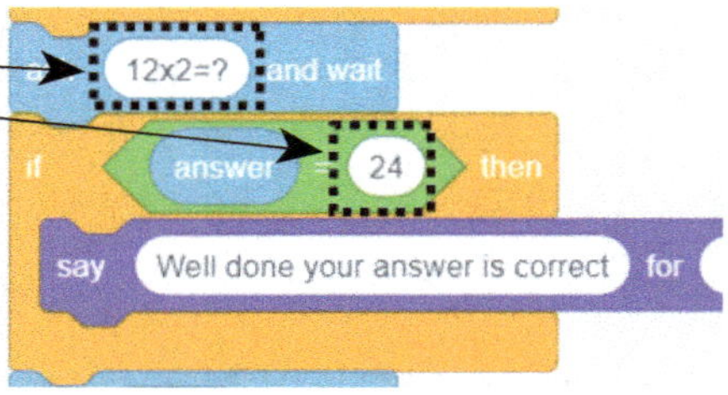

3. Add a short sound or simple graphic effect to question 3 if someone gets the answer right. What did you add?

   Any block inside the if block in the same place as the say Great answer for 2 secs block (1 mark)

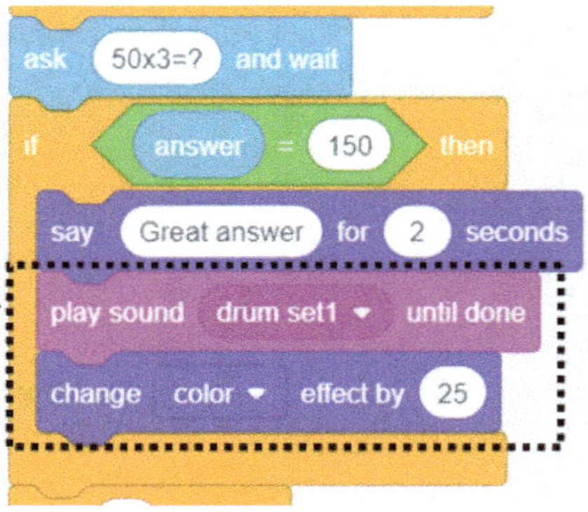

Modify Code in Sprite B ANSWERS

4. Modify the *'How old are you?'* question so it also gives an answer if someone is 7. What new blocks did you add?

   Add a new section

   If answer = 7 then

   Say Hey you are 7 like me for 4 secs (1 mark)

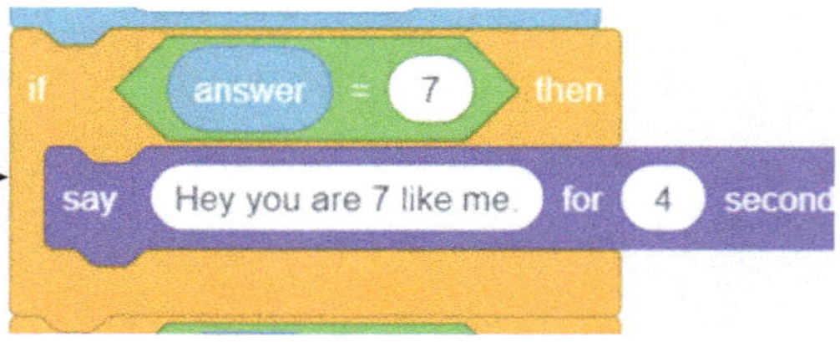

5. Modify the *'Do you like me?'* question so it also gives an answer if the user types in sometimes. What new blocks did you add?

   Change the question to include sometimes as well as yes and no (1 mark)

   Add a new condition-starts-action section

   If answer = sometimes

   Say something linked to sometimes (1 mark)

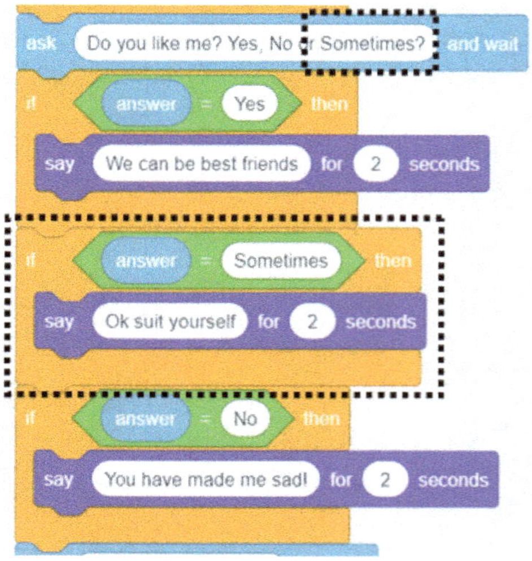

photocopiable page

MAKE ANSWERS
MAKING CHOICES

Create First (Choose one or more of these ideas first)

1. Add another question to the maths quiz in spite A.
2. Add the question *'Do you like chips?'* to the bottom of the code in Sprite B. Give a funny answer if they do or don't like chips.
3. Add another capital city question to sprite C if the user gets the capital of the UK correct.

Create Second (Choose one or more of these ideas second)

1. Create your own fun quiz about any topic in a new sprite inside Making Choices. You can hide the A,B,C sprites now and delete them when you are finished.
2. Ask lots of questions about the user and give funny answers to each one inside a new sprite inside Making Choices. You can hide the A,B,C sprites now and delete them when you are finished.
3. Create a fun quiz on any topic, where you can only attempt the next question if you get the question before correct, inside a new sprite inside Making Choices. You can hide the old sprites now and delete them when you are finished.
4. Come up with your own idea that uses **condition-starts-actions** blocks. Tell your teachers about it before making it.

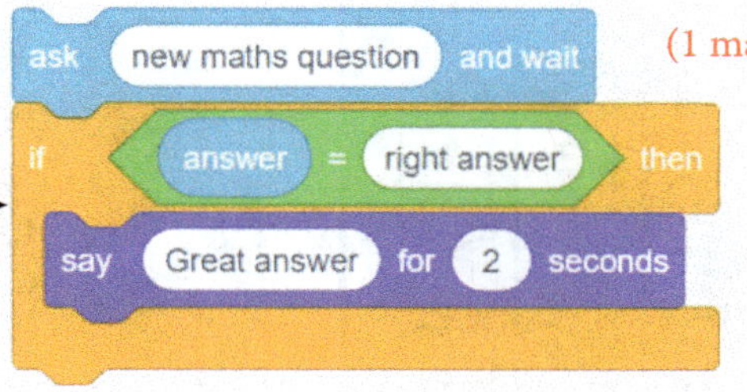

(1 mark)

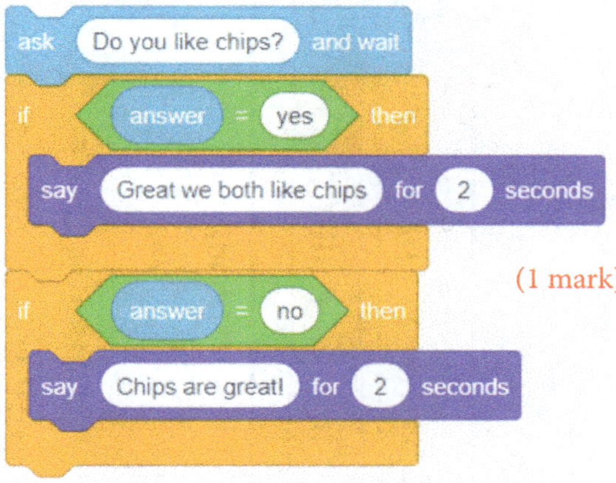

(1 mark)

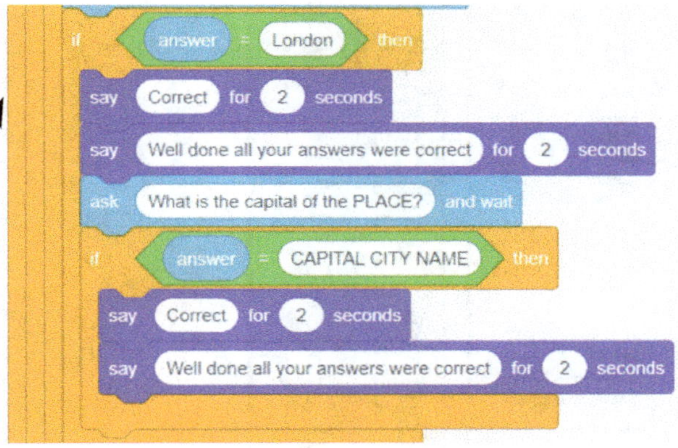

Must include new ask and if block within the last if block for London (1 mark)

Teacher and Pupil Assessment

Circle one column on each row to show what you think you have achieved

	Not used **condition-starts-action** blocks	Used a single **condition-starts-action** block in a question	Used more than one **condition-starts-action** blocks in a question	2 marks and Used either <, >, OR, AND or NOT in a condition
Condition-starts-action	0 marks	1 mark	2 marks	3 marks

	Not used previous programming concepts for real purpose	Used previous programming concepts for real purpose
Used previous programming concept such as count controlled or indefinite loops correctly	0 marks	1 mark

	No theme in planning or code	Has a theme in planning or code
Has a project theme in create second	0 marks	1 mark

Boolean AND

AND means that both conditions need to be met to start something.

Everyday Boolean AND

If you clean your bedroom and brush your hair, you can go swimming.

If you work hard in class and revise for tests you will do well in life.

Condition & Condition = Action

and

and - Both conditions need to be met to start something.

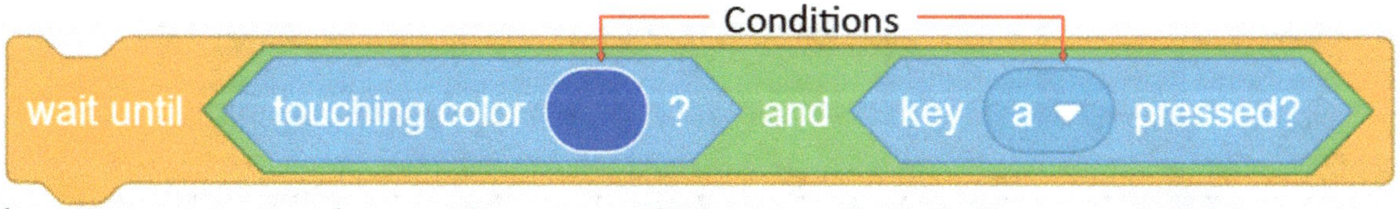
Conditions
wait until
touching color ?
and
key a pressed?

The program can't continue until the sprite touches the colour green **and** the a key is pressed. **Both** conditions need to be met.

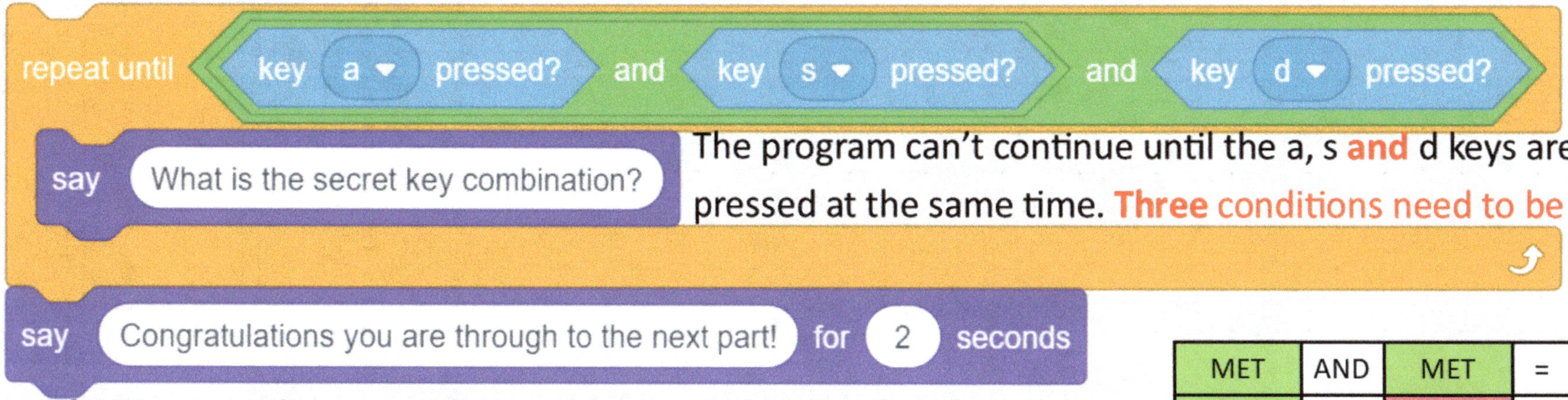
repeat until
key a pressed?
and
key s pressed?
and
key d pressed?
say
What is the secret key combination?
say
Congratulations you are through to the next part!
for
2
seconds

The program can't continue until the a, s **and** d keys are pressed at the same time. **Three** conditions need to be met.

and - Many conditions can be combined using AND. All of them would have to be met to start something.

and
and
and

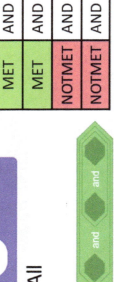

MET	AND	MET	=	TRUE
MET	AND	NOTMET	=	FALSE
NOTMET	AND	MET	=	FALSE
NOTMET	AND	NOTMET	=	FALSE

Boolean NOT

NOT reverses any condition.

It can be used with any condition

NOT works with simple conditions and combined with other more complex conditions

Everyday Boolean NOT If you are NOT hitting your brother you can play outside.

If NOT Condition then action. Action only happens if you are NOT meeting the condition.

Programming Examples

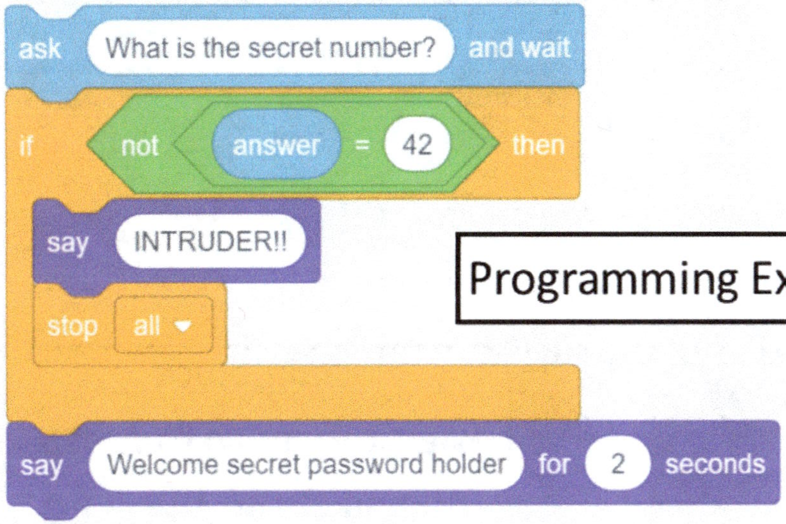
ask What is the secret number? and wait
if not answer = 42 then
say INTRUDER!!
stop all
say Welcome secret password holder for 2 seconds

What will this program do if 42 is typed in?

If answer typed in is NOT same as 42 then

say Intruder for 2 seconds

The condition is reversed by NOT

If NOT touching colour red then say

Not touching red

The condition is reversed by NOT

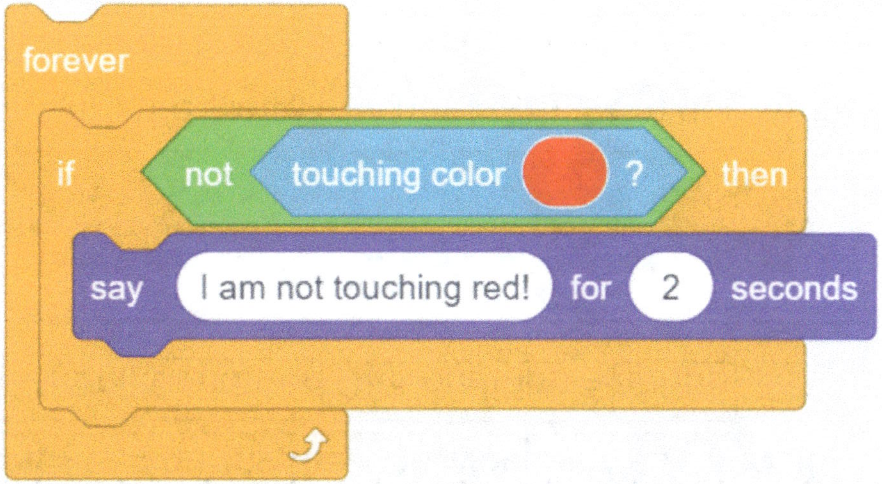
forever
if not touching color ? then
say I am not touching red! for 2 seconds

The condition is enclosed within a continuous loop so it is checked over and over.

Boolean OR

OR means that out of two or more conditions only one needs to be met to start something.

Everyday Boolean OR If you sleep during the day OR sleep during the night you will be rested. If you walk OR travel by bus OR take a car you will get to school. Condition OR Condition = Action

OR - Only one condition needs to be met to start something.

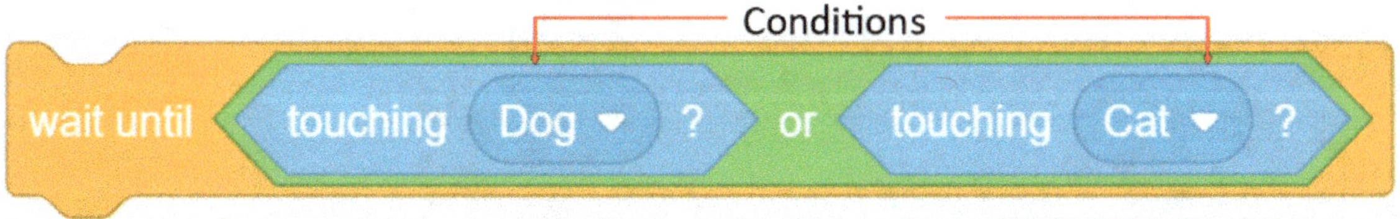
Conditions
wait until
touching Dog ?
or
touching Cat ?

The program can't continue until the sprite touches **EITHER** the dog sprite or the cat sprite Only **ONE** conditions need to be met.

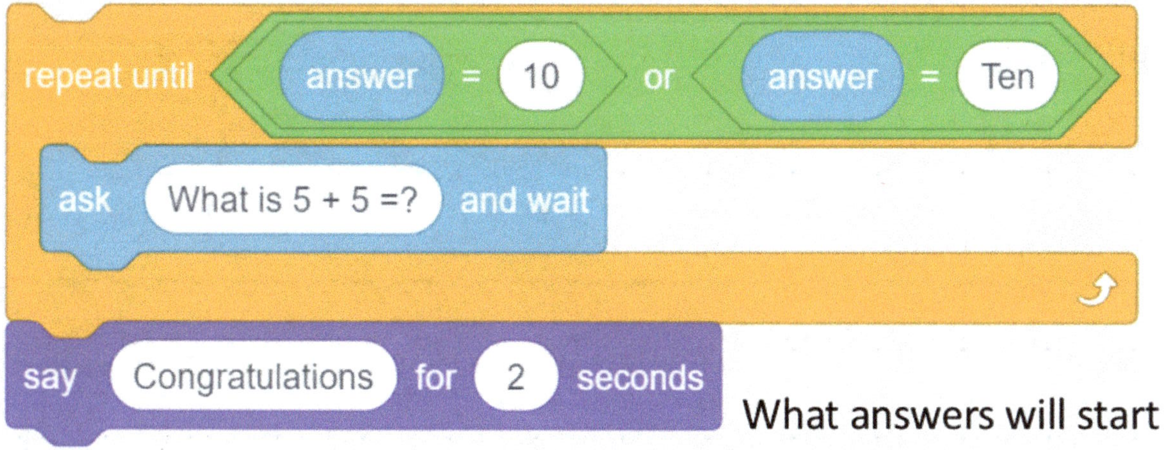
repeat until
answer = 10
or
answer = Ten
ask What is 5 + 5 =? and wait
say Congratulations for 2 seconds

What answers will start the congratulations?

OR - Many conditions can be combined using OR. Only one of them would have to be met to start something.

MET	OR	MET	=	TRUE
MET	OR	NOTMET	=	TRUE
NOTMET	OR	MET	=	TRUE
NOTMET	OR	NOTMET	=	FALSE

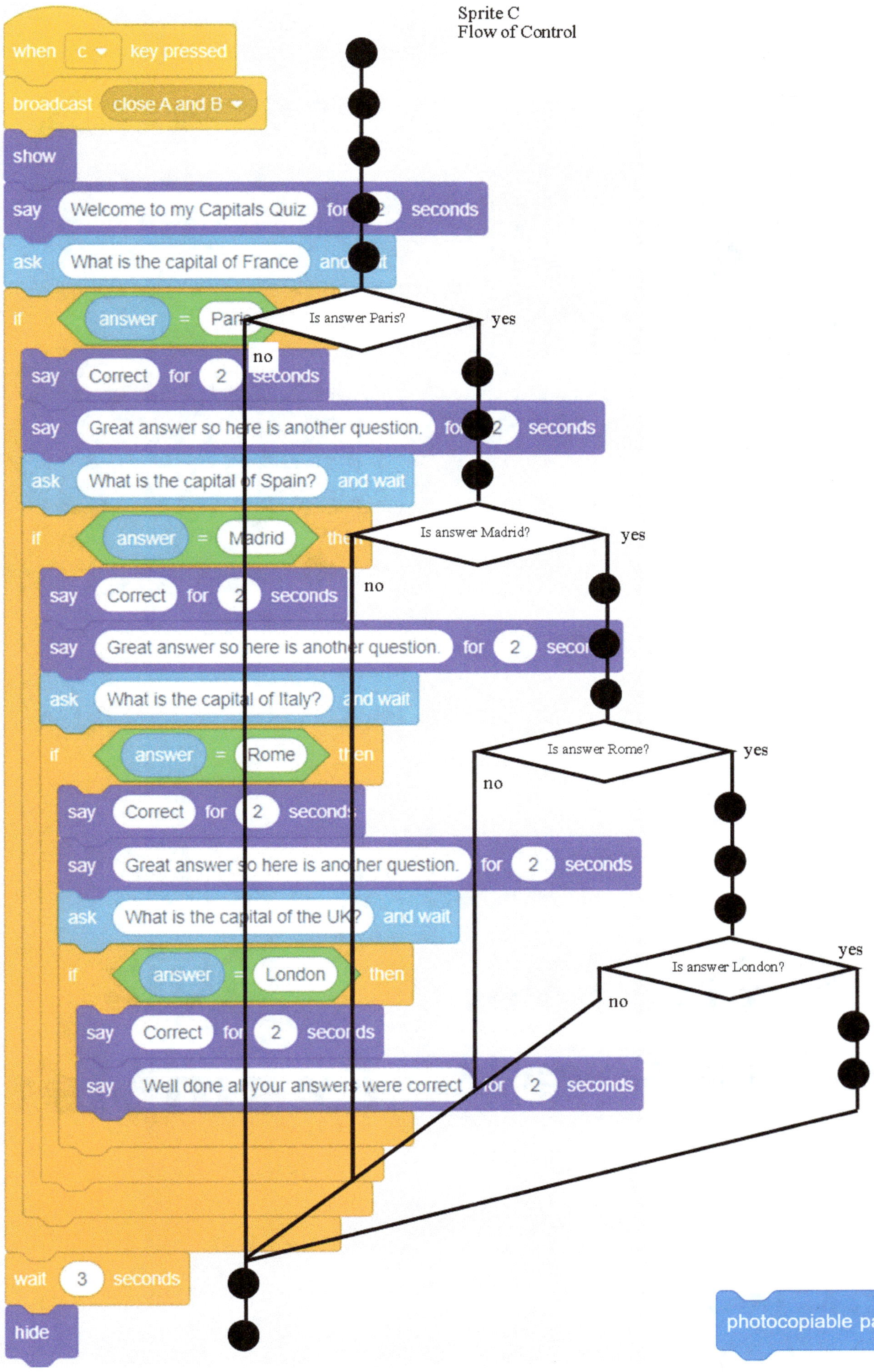

when c key pressed
broadcast close A and B
show
say Welcome to my Capitals Quiz for 2 seconds
ask What is the capital of France and wait
if answer = Paris then
say Correct for 2 seconds
say Great answer so here is another question. for 2 seconds
ask What is the capital of Spain? and wait
if answer = Madrid then
say Correct for 2 seconds
say Great answer so here is another question. for 2 seconds
ask What is the capital of Italy? and wait
if answer = Rome then
say Correct for 2 seconds
say Great answer so here is another question. for 2 seconds
ask What is the capital of the UK? and wait
if answer = London then
say Correct for 2 seconds
say Well done all your answers were correct for 2 seconds
wait 3 seconds
hide
Sprite C
Flow of Control
Is answer Paris?
yes
no
Is answer Madrid?
yes
no
Is answer Rome?
yes
no
Is answer London?
yes
no

photocopiable page

Ask 3x3=?
If answer is same as 9
Say correct
Else
Say wrong

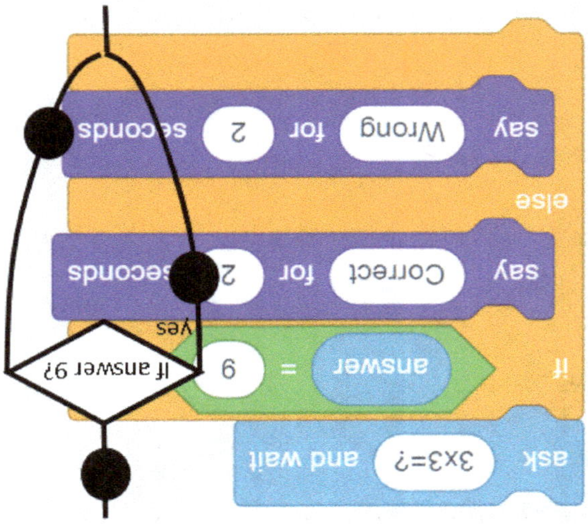

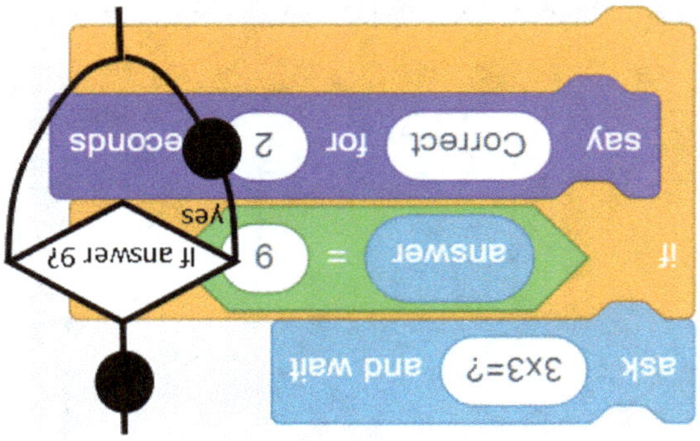

= means the same as

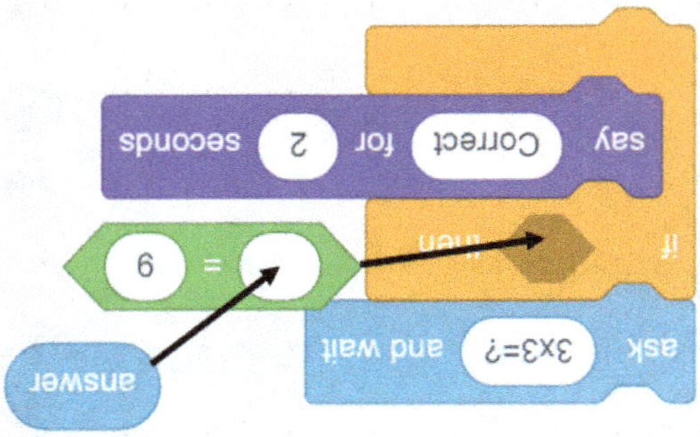

Quiz Examples Back Cover

Quiz Examples

PROGRAMMING MODULES THAT USE CONDITION-SWITCHES-BETWEEN-ACTIONS

CHAPTER 6 Wizards Choice Two

Overview

Pupils identify where conditions that switch between actions can be found in their everyday lives before roleplaying and writing everyday conditions. They then examine code that uses conditions that switch between actions before building their own programming that uses conditions.

To do before the session

1. Look at the grid below and decide which optional and SEN/ABLE activities you are going to include and exclude.
2. Print pupil worksheets for each activity chosen and staple into a booklet, one for each pupil.
3. Print marksheets for activities chosen to be placed where pupils can access them.
4. Download the code needed and place in a templates folder on your school network or add to a Scratch Studio or link on your learning platform.
5. Download the slides that go with the concept introduction.
6. Study the notes that go with the slides.
7. Examine the teacher help notes that are provided alongside every activity.
8. Photocopy some support cards for OR, AND & NOT for more ABLE (found at end of Making Choices activity).

To do at the start of the session

If you have not introduced **condition-switches-between-actions** with this class before, do this as a whole class activity.

To do after the concept has been introduced

Each activity has whole class notes to help you explain what is needed if it is the first time pupils have carried out this type of activity. There are also core instructions underneath in case you are sticking to the core activities only.

How this module fits into a programming progression

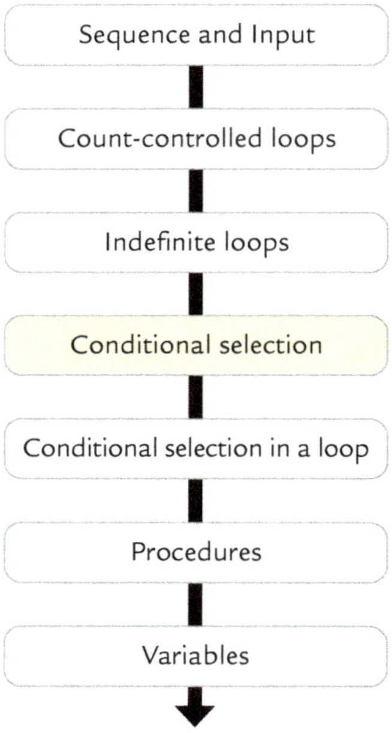

Vocabulary

Condition, selection, true, false, condition met, pathway, decomposition, , input ask block, answer block, equals means same as, choice

Resource Name	Core Optional SEN	Teacher	Pupil Grouping	How Assessed	SCRATCH ACCESS
CONCEPT condition-switches-between-actions	**CORE**	Leads Session	Solo Whole Class Activity	Formative	NO
PARSONS	OPTIONAL SEN OPTIONAL ALL (predict or parsons not both)	Support Poor Readers	Solo or Paired (Teacher choice)	Pupil Marked Marksheet Provided	YES Wizards Choice Parsons Two
PREDICT	OPTIONAL ALL (predict or parsons not both)	Support Poor Readers	Paired	Pupil Marked Marksheet Provided	NO
INVESTIGATE	**CORE**	Support Poor Readers	Paired	Pupil Marked Marksheet Provided	YES Wizards Choice Two
CHANGE	**CORE**	Support Poor Readers	Paired	Pupil Marked Marksheet Provided	YES Wizards Choice Two
FLOW	OPTIONAL ALL OPTIONAL ABLE	Support Poor Readers	Solo or Paired (Teacher Choice)	Pupil Marked Marksheet Provided	NO
CREATE	**CORE**	Assesses pupil work and checks pupil self-assessment	Solo	Pupil Assessed & Teacher Assessed	YES Wizards Choice Two

Core activities general instructions

1. Group pupils in roughly same ability pairs. For **investigate** and **change** worksheets pupils will work in pairs, for **create** they will work separately.
2. Give out the pupil booklets and explain that pupils need to follow the instructions on the sheets to explore how **count-controlled loops** work.
3. Explain that each pupil will record separately whilst working alongside their partner and keeping to the same pace as their partner.
4. Demonstrate where they can find the template code and explain that pupils will share one device for investigate and change.
5. Explain that during each question only one person should touch the shared device and they should swap who that person is when there is a new question.
6. Encourage them to discuss their answers with their partner. If they disagree with their partner they can record a different answer in their own booklet.
7. Show pupils where it says they should mark their work on the sheet where the answer sheets are in the classroom.
8. Remind pupils to return marksheets after marking, because there are not enough for every pair to have their own.

Key Programming Knowledge

A condition is a state we can check to see if it is true or false
Conditions starts with an if
Conditions are only checked once unless they are in a loop
Conditions lead to two possible pathways True and False
Conditions are only checked when reached in the flow of control
An algorithm is any set of instructions to carry out a task that can be understood by another human
Decomposition is breaking up a project into parts to solve separately

Resources

Wizards Choice Parsons Two https://scratch.mit.edu/projects/579039492/
Wizards Choice Two https://scratch.mit.edu/projects/578800428/

	On the sheet, if it says no Scratch, they must work only on the sheet.
	If it says Scratch with a green tick, they can use one device between the pair.
	If it says work with a partner, they must work at the same speed as their partner.
	If it says work on their own, they must do this using a separate device each working alone.

English Computing National Curriculum Programs of Study

Pupils should be taught to:

- **design, write and debug programs that accomplish specific goals**, including controlling or simulating physical systems; **solve problems by decomposing them into smaller parts.**
- **use sequence, selection** and **repetition in programs;** work with variables **and various forms of input and output.**
- **use logical reasoning to explain how some simple algorithms work and to detect and correct errors in algorithms and programs.**

Scottish Curriculum for Excellence Technologies

I understand the instructions of a visual programming language and can predict the outcome of a program written using the language. TCH 1-14a

I can explain core programming language concepts in appropriate technical language. TCH 2-14a

I can demonstrate a range of basic problem solving skills by building simple programs to carry out a given task, using an appropriate language. TCH 1-15a

I can create, develop and evaluate computing solutions in response to a design challenge. TCH 2-15a

Welsh National Curriculum Relevant Strands

Progression Step 3.

- I can use conditional statements to add control and decision-making to algorithms.
- I can explain and debug algorithms.

WIZARDS CHOICE TWO PARSONS

Work with a partner

Start Scratch and Load
Wizards Choices Parsons Two

If happy
Say Boo
Else
Say No
condition-switches-between-actions

Use the algorithm below to connect the code correctly in Darla

Algorithm

Start when the sprite is clicked
Make the sprites size 100% (initialisation to restore the sprite back to its starting size)
Say that Darla will grow in power if get question right
Say that Darla will lose power if get answer wrong

Ask 3×3=?
If answer is same as 9
    Increase size by 20%
Else
    Decrease size by –20%

Ask 25+76=?
If answer is same as 101
    Increase size by 20%
Else
    Decrease size by –20%

Ask 85–30=?
If answer is same as 55
    Increase size by 20%
Else
    Decrease size by –20%

Pause for 2 seconds
If size is same as 160%
    Say you got them all right
    Say My powers grow
Else
    Say better luck next time

Now mark the code using the **PARSONS** ANSWER SHEET

photocopiable page

Parsons teacher help notes wizards choice two

Whole class advice

Load Wizards Choice Parsons code and then use the algorithm on this page to build the code. When you have completed it, run the code and check your answer with the marking sheet.

Able advice

Parsons problems can be made more complex by separating more blocks in the example Scratch code and saving that version as a new template.

Send advice

Parsons problems can be made less complex by connecting more blocks in the example Scratch code and saving that version as a new template.

Understanding programming

You can find out more about Parsons problems in the teacher book.

Notes on the activity

This allow pupils to build part of the code first before investigating, modifying and creating code of their own. The algorithm is written in language similar but also different to the code. This helps pupils by enabling them to see an example of planning which will help them when they come to plan their own project. On its own it is not enough deep thinking about the code to enable agency, but as a starter activity it is useful to see how complex conditions can be built up.

Send advice

Some pupils may struggle with the more complex words in the planning such as increase and decrease. Pointing out that these mean changing the size to be larger or smaller may help some pupils.

Send advice

Covering up most of the algorithm so pupils can focus on a section at a time will help some pupils.

Individual advice

Pointing out that the code affected by the condition is indented once it is in the if block and it is indented in the planning algorithm can help some pupils.

Use the algorithm below to connect the code correctly in Darla

Algorithm

Start when the sprite is clicked
Make the sprites size 100%
Say that Darla will grow in power if get question right
Say that Darla will lose power if get answer wrong

Ask 3x3=?
If answer is same as 9
→ Increase size by 20%
Else
Decrease size by -20%

Ask 25+76=?
If answer is same as 101
Increase size by 20%
Else
Decrease size by -20%

Ask 85–30=?
If answer is same as 55
Increase size by 20%
Else
Decrease size by –20%

Pause for 2 seconds
If size is same as 160%
Say you got them all right
Say My powers grow
Else
Say better luck next time

when this sprite clicked
set size to 100 %
ask 3x3=? and wait
if answer = 9 then
change size by 20
else
change size by -20
ask 25+76=? and wait
if answer = 101 then
change size by 20
else
change size by -20
ask 85-30=? and wait
if answer = 55 then
change size by 20
else
change size by -20
wait 2 seconds
if size = 160 then
say You got them all right for 2 seconds
say My powers GROW! for 2 seconds
else
say Better luck next time! for 2 seconds

photocopiable page

WIZARDS CHOICE TWO PREDICT

Work with a partner

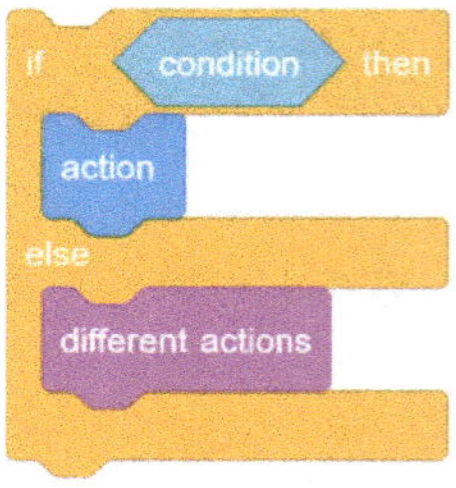
if
condition
then
action
else
different actions

condition-switches-between-actions

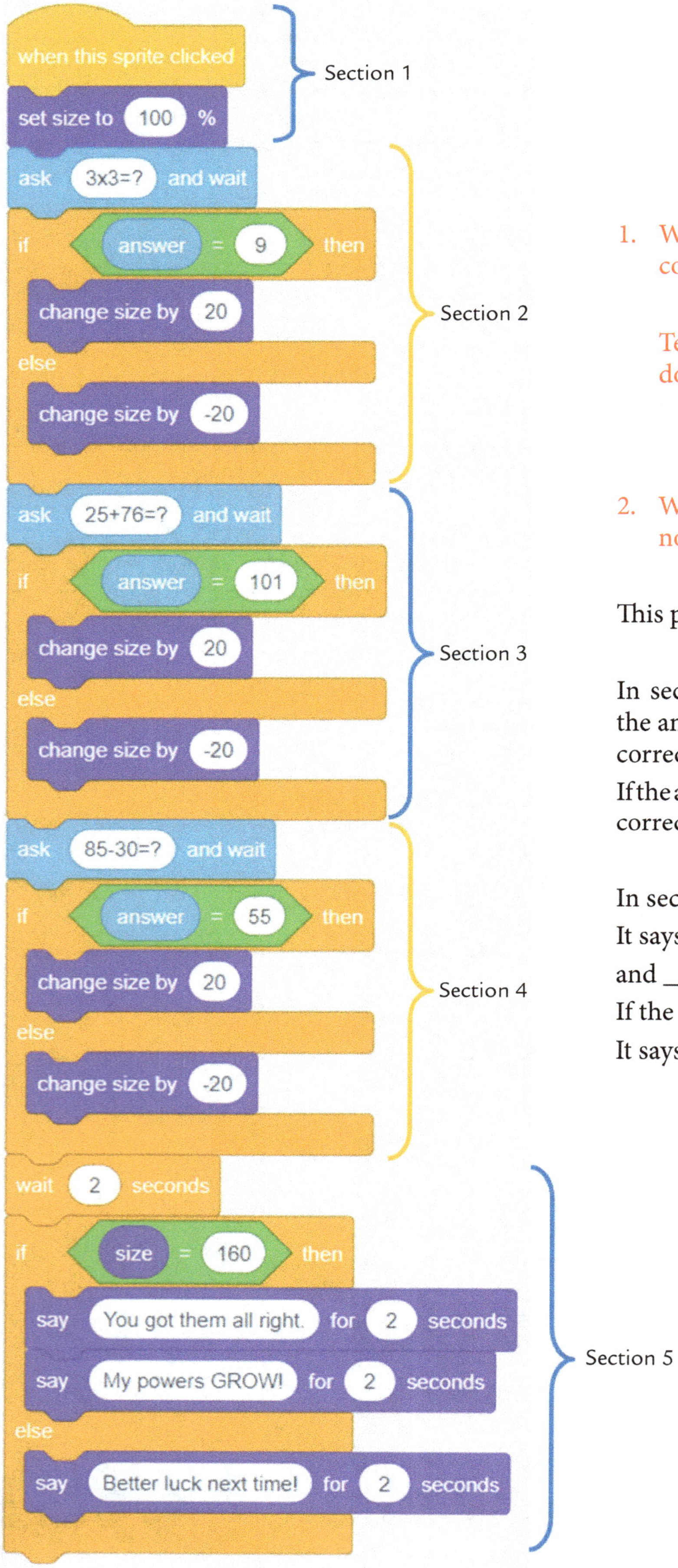
when this sprite clicked
set size to 100 %
Section 1
ask 3x3=? and wait
if answer = 9 then
change size by 20
else
change size by -20
Section 2
ask 25+76=? and wait
if answer = 101 then
change size by 20
else
change size by -20
Section 3
ask 85-30=? and wait
if answer = 55 then
change size by 20
else
change size by -20
Section 4
wait 2 seconds
if size = 160 then
say You got them all right. for 2 seconds
say My powers GROW! for 2 seconds
else
say Better luck next time! for 2 seconds
Section 5

1. With your partner take it in turns to read the code out loud a section at a time.

   Tell your partner what you think your section does.

2. With your understanding of the code sections now fill in the blanks.

This program is a Maths ___________

In sections 2, 3 & 4, a maths question is asked. If the answer typed in by the user is **the same as** = the correct answer, the sprite will_________________

If the answer typed in by the user is **not the same as** the correct answer, the sprite will_________________

In section 5 if the size ______________

It says____________________

and ______________________

If the size is not equal to _________

It says ______________________

photocopiable page

PREDICT TEACHER HELP NOTES WIZARDS CHOICE TWO

Whole class advice

Make sure you work with your partner on this sheet. Take it in turns to read a section and tell your partner what you think it does. Then fill in the gaps using your understanding of the code.

Send advice

While they or you are reading and explaining what the code section does, cover up the previous and past code sections.

Able advice

Cover up the fill in the blanks section and ask them to explain in their own words what the code in section 2, 3 & 4 does and what the code in section 5 does.

Notes on the activity

This optional activity helps pupils to think about the bigger purpose of the program before they start looking at parts of it in later sections.

Before you let pupils complete this activity, it can help to drag out and make one quiz question if they have not used the ask and answer blocks before. Make sure you explain how the answer block has whatever the user types in assigned to it. You can do this by clicking on the answer block as shown or by ticking next to it to show the contents on screen. Also remind pupils that = means the same as.

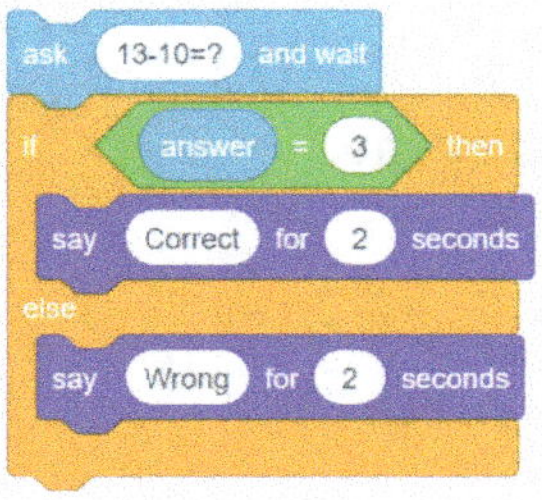

ask 13-10=? and wait
if answer = 3 then
say Correct for 2 seconds
else
say Wrong for 2 seconds

Question to Demonstrate

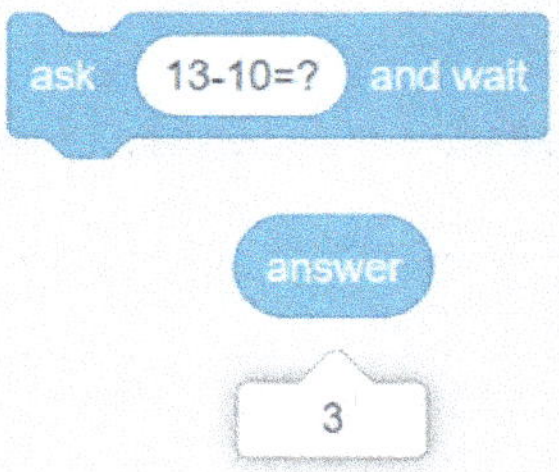

ask 13-10=? and wait
answer
3

Viewing the value assigned by the users by clicking on answer box

answer

Viewing the value assigned by the users by ticking next to the answer block in sensing

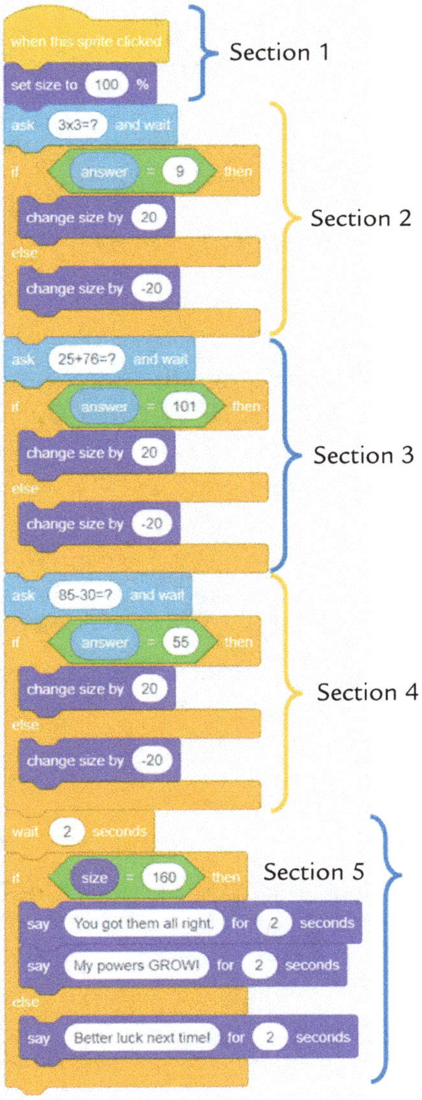

when this sprite clicked
set size to 100 %
Section 1
ask 3x3=? and wait
if answer = 9 then
change size by 20
else
change size by -20
Section 2
ask 25+76=? and wait
if answer = 101 then
change size by 20
else
change size by -20
Section 3
ask 85-30=? and wait
if answer = 55 then
change size by 20
else
change size by -20
Section 4
wait 2 seconds
if size = 160 then
say You got them all right. for 2 seconds
say My powers GROW! for 2 seconds
else
say Better luck next time! for 2 seconds
Section 5

1. With your partner take it in turns to read the code out loud a section at a time.

   Tell your partner what you think your section does.

2. With your understanding of the code sections now fill in the blanks.

   This program is a maths quiz or questions (1 mark)

   In sections 2, 3 & 4, a maths question is asked. If the answer typed in by the user is **the same as** the correct answer, the sprite

   Gets bigger or larger or similar increase in size or changes size by 20 (1 mark)

   If the answer typed in by the user is **not the same as** the correct answer the sprite

   Gets smaller or shrinks or similar decrease in size or changes size by -20 (1 mark)

   In section 5 if the size is the same as 160 or equal to 160 or = to 160 (1 mark)

   It says You got them all right! (1 mark)

   and says My powers GROW! (1 mark)

   If the size is not equal to 160 (1 mark)

   It says Better luck next time (1 mark)

Individual advice

If pupils are struggling with Part 2, check that they completed Part 1 by pointing at a section and asking what they thought it did.

Send advice

As you or they read a line from the fill in the blanks, point to part of the code it could be summing up.

Individual advice

Ask pupils if section 2, 3 and 4 look the same. If they can see that they do, say that if they can work out what is happening in one of these sections they will have cracked all three.

Individual advice

Remind pupils what each block did from your build a question demonstration. If you did not carry that part out, do a demo now.

Understanding programming

Answer and size are fixed name variables. The answer variable is assigned a value by typing into the ask input block.

The size variable is assigned a value by using the set size to block. Just like a user named variable it can be overwritten by another set size block or increased/decreased by change size to. In the absence of better evidence I avoid mentioning them as variables at this stage.

WIZARDS CHOICE TWO INVESTIGATE

Work with a partner

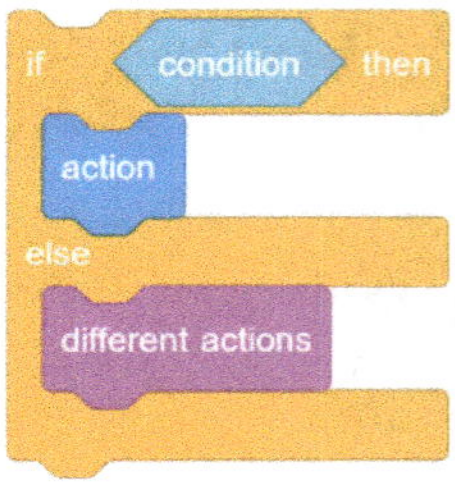

condition-switches-between-actions

Start Scratch and load **Wizards Choices Two** or Continue with **Wizard Choices Two Parsons**

Investigate

Run the code inside **Darla** and answer these questions.

Darla

1. How many **condition-switches-between-actions (if else)** blocks are there?

2. If you answer the questions correctly what will happen?

3. If you answer the questions incorrectly what will happen?

4. Look at the last **condition-switches-between-action (if else)** block. What do you need to do in the rest of the program to make sure than the size is = (the same as) 160% after the last question?

Gustav

Run the code inside **Gustav** and answer these questions.

5. How many **count-controlled loops (repeat x)** are there?

6. In the 4x4 question. How many times is the ***change whirl effect by 2*** block run? *HINT It is in a loop*

7. Which block is there for initialization purposes? Initialization is to make sure the program always runs in the same way every time, clearing away the effects of previous program changes. *HINT Often found near the start of programming*

Run the code inside **Maurice** and answer these questions.

Maurice

8. How many **condition-switches-between-actions (if-else)** blocks are there?

9. What happens if you input something other than yes on the first question?

10. How many questions do you have to answer yes to for Maurice to say Magicus, magicus, Magicus Moo?

Now mark the questions using the INVESTIGATE ANSWERS

INVESTIGATE ANSWERS TEACHERS HELP SHEET WIZARDS CHOICE TWO

Run the code inside **Darla** and answer these questions.

1. How many **condition-switches-between-actions (if else)** blocks are there?

   4 (1 mark)

2. If you answer the questions correctly what will happen?

   Darla get larger by 20% (1 mark for any answer which refers to getting bigger in size)

3. If you answer the questions incorrectly what will happen?

   Darla get smaller by 20% (1 mark for any answer which refers to getting smaller in size)

4. Look at the last **condition-switches-between-action (if else)** block. What do you need to do in the rest of the program to make sure than the size is = (the same as) 160% after the last question?

   Get all the questions correct (1 mark) Darla starts at 100% and adds 20% every time you get an answer right. After getting three questions right Darla is 160%.

Run the code inside **Gustav** and answer these questions.

5. How many **condition-switches-between-actions (if else)** blocks are there?

   3 (1 mark)

6. How many **count-controlled loops (repeat x)** are there?

   3 (1 mark)

7. Which block is there for initialisation purposes? *Initialisation is to make sure the program always runs in the same way every time, clearing away the effects of previous program changes.*

   Clear graphics effects (1 mark)

Run the code inside **Maurice** and answer these questions.

8. How many **condition-switches-between-actions** blocks are there?

   3 (1 mark)

9. What happens if you input something other than yes on the first question?

   Maurice says nothing left for it, I will just have to vanish. OR He vanishes or disappears (1 mark)

10. How many questions do you have to answer yes to for Maurice to say Magicus, magicus, Magicus Moo?

    3 questions have to have yes answers (1 mark). If you would like to understand more about how the code works inside Maurice ask your teacher for the flow of control sheet.

Notes on the activity

Investigating the code encourages pupils to think deeply about how it works. The Maurice code and questions are more complex. If pupils are significantly behind their peers in completing this activity, removing the Maurice section by crossing it out will allow pupils to catch up without impacting their understanding of the basics. Sometimes one pupil in a pair decides to work faster than their partner; check that this is not happening and that every pupil is filling in and marking the questions individually but at the pace of the slowest in the pair. Sometimes a pair decides not to mark to speed up their efforts. Marking gives valuable information, so I recommend sending them back to mark their work if this is the case. A class instruction to come and talk to you if they have over half of the questions wrong or they do not understand the answer after they have marked it helps to check progress is being made correctly. There is real value in collecting these scores to build up a summative picture of pupil progress.

Q4 Individual advice

Ask pupils what the size is of Darla when the code starts. Then ask how big she is after getting the question right. You might want to point out that 100 + 20 =120. How big is she after getting two questions right? 100+20+20=140 Ask them if they can see the pattern. How will she become 160%?

Whole class advice

Work in pairs, one device between the pair. Take it in turns every question to swap who runs code. You must work at the same pace as your partner and not move on to the next question until you have both written your answer down. If you disagree, write a different answer. You must mark your work before moving on to the next section.

Q6 Individual advice

If you are following this scheme, these were covered in Year 4, so this part is revision. Ask pupils about using repeat blocks in Year 4. What did they make with them?

Q7 Individual advice

Programs are designed to be run many times. Initialisation gets them ready to be run again. Your kitchen at home is designed to be used many times. Washing up and cleaning the sides is kitchen initialisation.

Send advice

See comment about Maurice section in **notes on the activity** above.

Understanding programming

You can find out more about initialisation in the teacher book.

Notes on the activity

If you have not used it before, print some copies of the flow of control sheet so that pupils who want to know more can examine it alongside the working code.

WIZARDS CHOICE TWO
CHANGE

Work with a partner

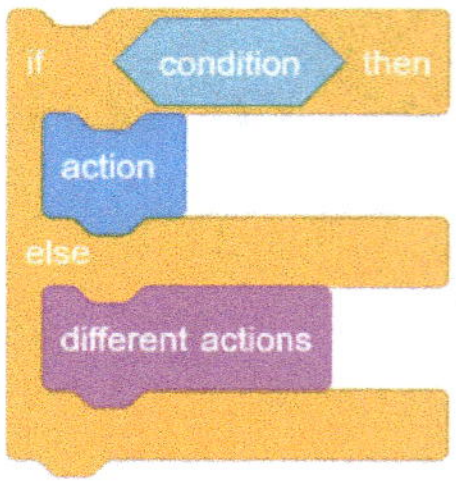
if
condition
then
action
else
different actions

condition-switches-between-actions

Change Code in Darla

Darla

Make small changes or small additions to the code

1. Adapt the code to make Darla grow even bigger when the user gets an answer correct. What did you change?

2. Adapt the code to make Darla grow even smaller when the user gets an answer wrong. What did you change?

3. Add an additional effect to question one if someone gets the answer right. What did you add? Draw an arrow on the code to the right to show where you added your effect.

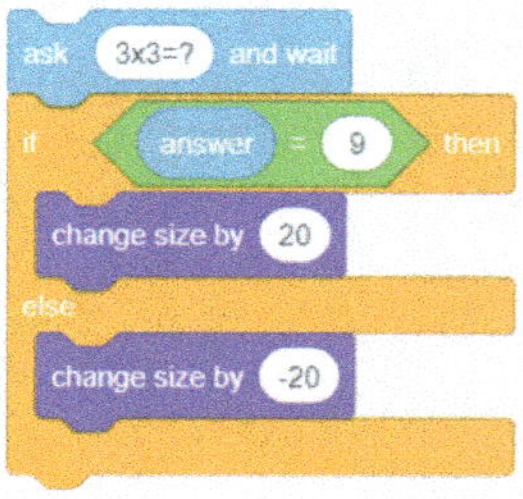
ask
3x3=?
and wait
if
answer
=
9
then
change size by
20
else
change size by
-20

Change Code in Gustav

Gustav

Make small changes or small additions to the code

4. Modify the code to make Gustav whirl quicker if the answer is wrong. What did you change?

5. Slow down Gustav's whirl. What did you change?

6. Can you make Gustav whirl counterclockwise? What did you change?

7. Change Gustav's whirl for a different graphical effect? What did you change it to? Did it work as well?

Change Code in Maurice

Maurice

Make small changes or small additions to the code

8. Modify the code to make Maurice spin round slowly after he says the magic words (*Magicus, Magicus Magicus Moo*), but before he disappears. What did you add? Where did you add it?

Now mark the these questions using the CHANGE ANSWERS sheet

CHANGE ANSWERS TEACHER'S HELP SHEET WIZARDS CHOICE TWO

Change Code in Darla

1. Adapt the code to make Darla grow even bigger when the user gets an answer correct. What did you change?

   Change size by more than 20 (1 mark)

2. Adapt the code to make Darla grow even smaller when the user gets an answer wrong. What did you change?

   Change size by less than –20 (1 mark)

3. Add an additional effect to Question 1 if someone gets the answer right. What did you add? Draw an arrow on the code to the right to show where you added your effect.

   Lots of possible additional effects (1 mark for any that work). (1 mark) for any indication that it needed to be added below the if and above the else as shown

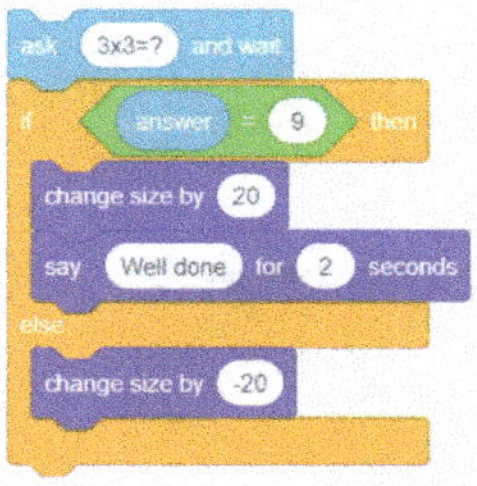

ask 3x3=? and wait
if answer = 9 then
change size by 20
say Well done for 2 seconds
else
change size by -20

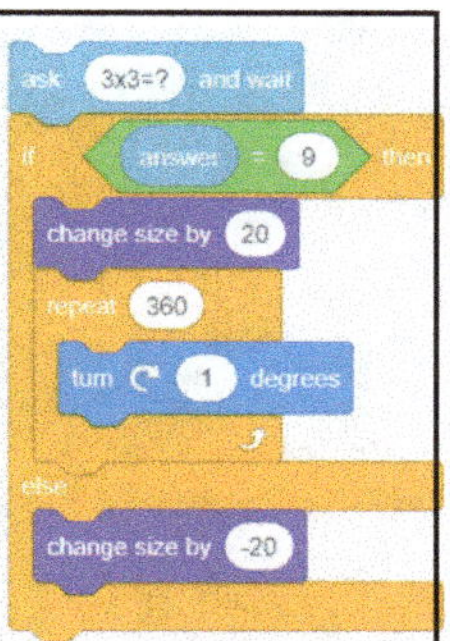

ask 3x3=? and wait
if answer = 9 then
change size by 20
repeat 360
turn 1 degrees
else
change size by -20

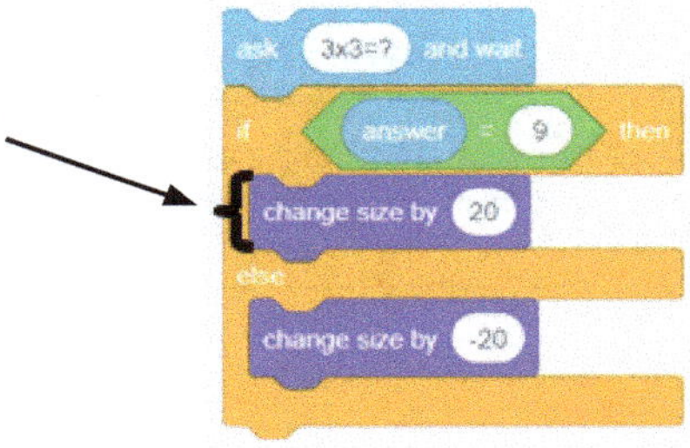

ask 3x3=? and wait
if answer = 9 then
change size by 20
else
change size by -20

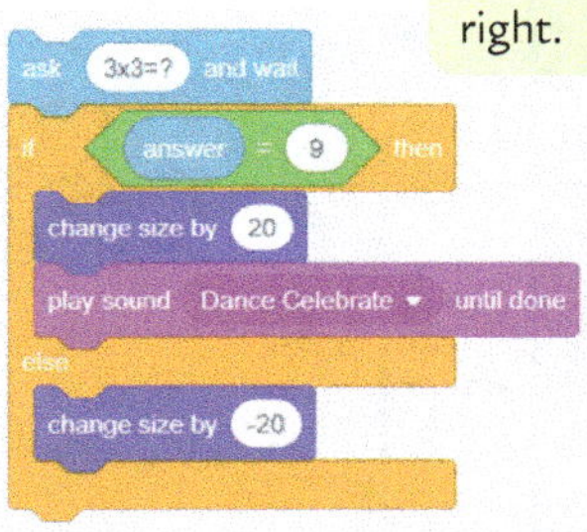

ask 3x3=? and wait
if answer = 9 then
change size by 20
play sound Dance Celebrate until done
else
change size by -20

Change Code in Gustav

4. Modify the code to make Gustav whirl quicker if the answer is wrong. What did you change?

   Either reduce wait to less than 0.2 secs or change whirl effect by more than 2 or both (1 mark)

5. Slow down Gustav's whirl. What did you change?

   Either increase wait to more than 0.2 secs or change whirl effect by less than 2 or both (1 mark)

6. Can you make Gustav whirl counterclockwise? What did you change?

   Change whirl effect by –2 or another negative number (1 mark)

7. Change Gustav's whirl for a different graphical effect. What did you change it to? Did it work as well?

   Change to colour, pixelate, whirl, fisheye, brightness, mosaic or ghost (1 mark)

Change Code in Maurice

8. Modify the code to make Maurice spin round slowly after he says the magic words (Magicus, Magicus Magicus Moo), but before he disappears. What did you add? Where did you add it?

   Add a count-controlled loop with a turn right or turn left a number of degrees block inside. (1 mark)

Notes on the activity

Changing or modifying the code is a core part of this module, so I suggest you do not leave it out. It is an important step toward creation of their own code. Recording their marks can help with formative and summative assessment.

Whole class advice

Work in pairs, one device between the pair. Take it in turns every question to swap who runs code. You must work at the same pace as your partner and not move on to the next question until you have both written your answer down. If you disagree, write a different answer. You must mark your work before moving on to the next section.

Understanding programming

You can find out more about changing code in the teacher book.

Q3 Individual advice

Lots of possible options including simple things like those on the left, or more complex like those on the right.

Send advice

What simple effects did you learn to create in Year 3?

Q4+5 Individual advice

Ask pupils what numbers they could change in the whirl section? Repeat x, change whirl effect by x and wait x seconds.

Q6 Individual advice

Tell pupils that there is a hidden plus sign before the number to make it whirl clockwise. What would be the inverse of addition?

Q7 Individual advice

Point out that there is a drop-down next to whirl.

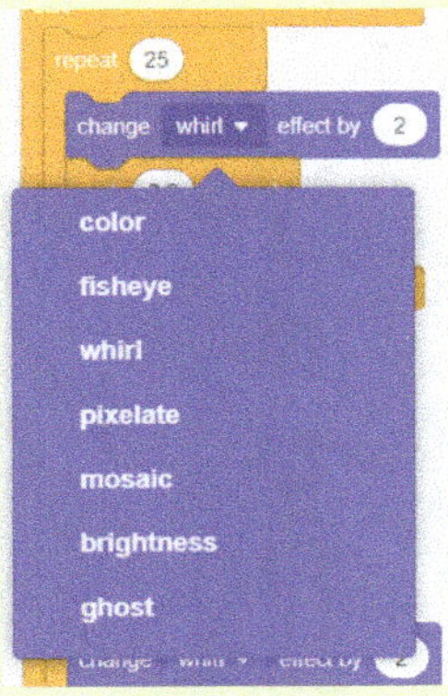

repeat 25
change whirl effect by 2
color
fisheye
whirl
pixelate
mosaic
brightness
ghost

Q7 Individual advice

Does it work as well? is a good question to ask if observing pupils progress formatively. Pupils who have a yes, no or sometimes answer with reasons have taken part fully in the task.

Q8 Individual advice

If pupils are struggling to decide where to put their code addition, ask them if there are keywords in the text that help them find where to put their new code.

WIZARDS CHOICE TWO FLOW

Read the code and look at the flow of control diagram

The key at the bottom will help you

Possible pathways the code can take

A. Say yes at first condition and **not** say yes at second condition

B. Say yes at all three conditions

C. **Not** say yes at 1st condition

D. Say yes at first two conditions and **not** say yes at third condition

Now mark on the correct pathway letters. One has been done for you.

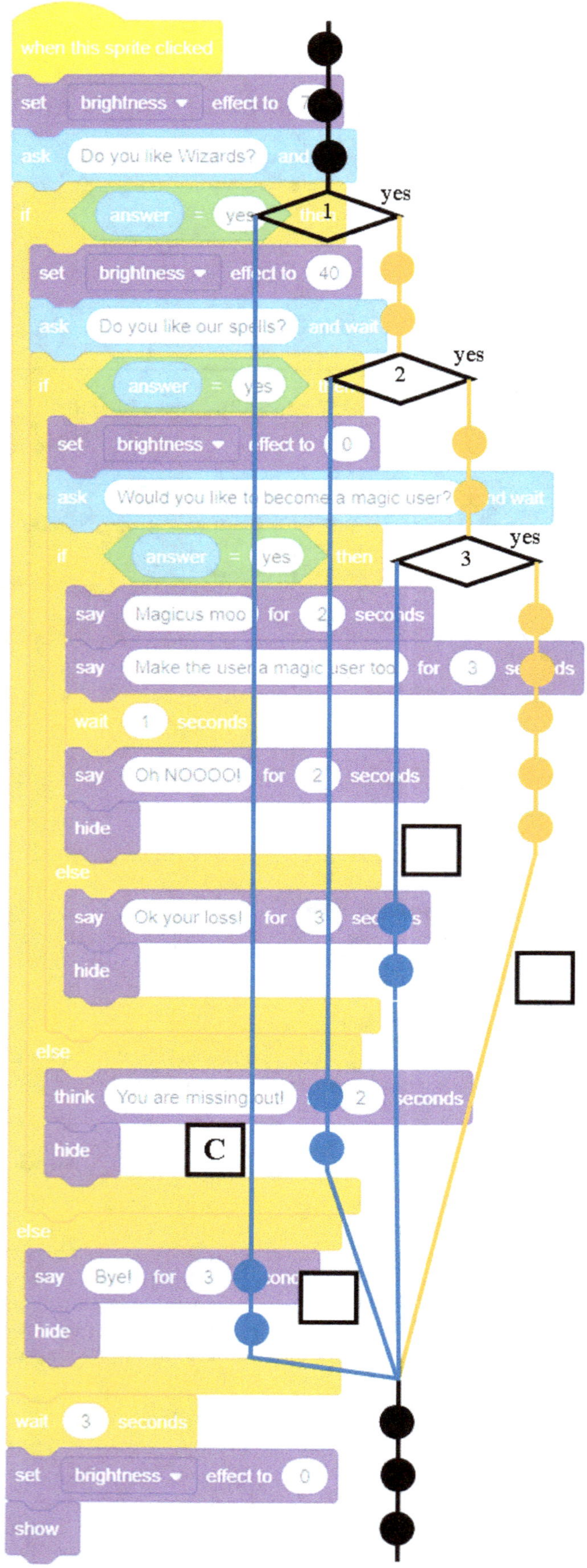

Pathways not affected by a condition	
Pathways where condition is FALSE	
Pathways where condition is TRUE	
Actions where condition is TRUE	
Actions where condition is FALSE	
Actions not affected by a condition	
Condition	

Key

E

FLOW TEACHER'S HELP NOTES WIZARDS CHOICE TWO

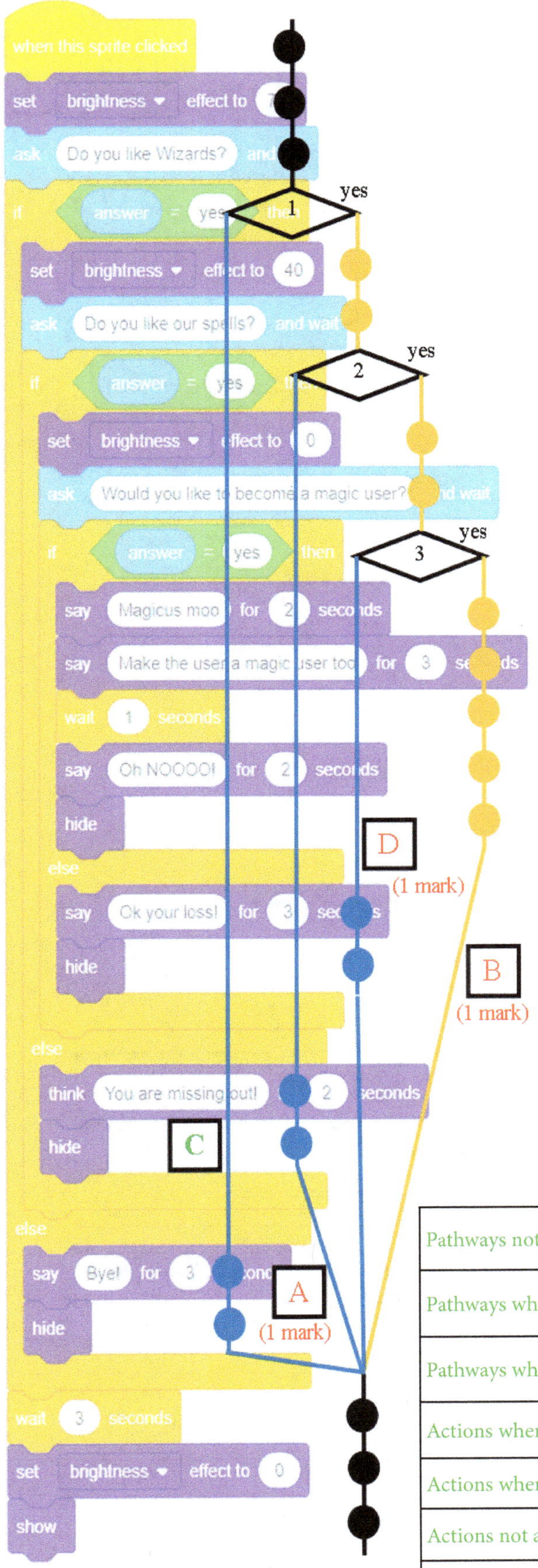

Pathways not affected by a condition	
Pathways where condition is FALSE	
Pathways where condition is TRUE	
Actions where condition is TRUE	
Actions where condition is FALSE	
Actions not affected by a condition	
Condition	

Key

Notes on the activity

The section that this is based on is the most complex section, so this activity could be reserved for your more ABLE pupils. It could also be printed out and used when pupils are working on the code for Maurice, or you could give the challenge to your whole class.

Whole class advice

Have a look at the key. What colour is the pathway not affected by a condition? Answer Black. What colour is a pathway where the condition is TRUE? Answer orange. What colour is a pathway where the condition is FALSE? Answer blue. Point to a condition in the code and on the diagram. Good it is an irregular hexagon shape in code and a rhombus on the flow of control diagram.

Take it in turns to read the code carefully while the other partner traces the flow of control on the diagram. If you are reading the code, make sure you say if you type in YES or NOT YES every time you reach a condition, so your partner knows which path to go down. Then answer the questions together.

Send advice

Point out that each dot is alongside an action and each rhombus is alongside a condition.

Individual advice

If pupils are struggling, trace a pathway with them only reading out the actions and conditions that are dots on your pathway. Now encourage them to go down a different pathway and only read the actions and conditions on that pathway.

Understanding Programming

Complex pathways are very common in programming. An automated telephone answering system is an example of this. When the user presses a number they are choosing a different path.

Understanding Programming

You can find out more about flow of control in the teacher book.

Read the code and look at the flow of control

The key at the bottom will help you

Possible pathways the code can take

A. Say yes at first condition and **not** say yes at second condition
B. Say yes at all three conditions
C. **Not** say yes at first condition
D. Say yes at first two conditions and **not** say yes at third condition

Now mark on the correct pathway letters. One has been done for you.

CREATE
WIZARDS CHOICE TWO

Work on your own

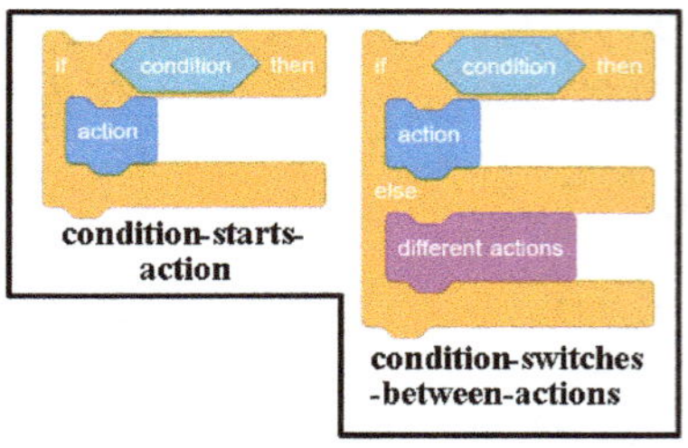

Make First (Choose one of these ideas first)

1. Add another question that uses **condition-switches-between-action (if else)** to the maths quiz in Darla. Make sure you adjust the size condition at the end to cope with four rather than three questions.

2. Add a question that uses **condition-switches-between-action (if else)** to the Maths quiz in Gustav. Make sure it does totally new things if the answer is right or wrong.

Make Second (Choose one of these ideas second)

1. Create your own quiz about a recently studied school topic that uses **condition-switches-between-action blocks**. Either choose a new sprite or start a new program.

2. Create your own quiz about a topic that you know a lot about. Use **condition-switches-between-action and condition-starts-action** blocks. Either choose a new sprite or start a new program.

3. Create a maths quiz where you get harder questions if you get the answer right and easier questions if you get the answer wrong. Either choose a new sprite or start a new program.

Use the space on the right to plan your make second choice creations

Task level (what will my program do?)

My design (questions, initialisation, algorithms)

Teacher & Pupil Assessment

Circle one column on each row to show what you think you have achieved so far

condition-switches-between-actions	Not used condition-switches-between-action (if else) blocks	Used a condition-switches-between-action (if else) block simply	AS 1 mark & used condition-starts-action blocks **OR** effects not in template program **OR** nested conditions (like Maurice)	AS 2 marks **&** used either <, >, OR, AND or NOT in any condition
	0 marks	1 mark	2 marks	3 marks

Used previous programming concept such as count-controlled or indefinite loops correctly	Not used previous programming concepts for real purpose	Used previous programming concepts for real purpose
	0 marks	1 mark

Has workable planning for some elements of their project	No planning	planning
	0 marks	1 mark

F

CREATE TEACHER'S HELP SHEET WIZARDS CHOICE TWO

Make First (Choose one of these ideas first)

1. Add another question that uses **condition-switches-between-action (if else)** to the maths quiz in Darla. Make sure you adjust the size condition at the end to cope with four rather than three questions.
2. Add a question that uses **condition-switches-between-action (if else)** to the maths quiz in Gustav. Make sure it does totally new things if the answer is right and wrong.

Make Second (Choose one of these ideas second)

1. Create your own quiz about a recently studied school topic that uses **condition-switches-between-action blocks.** Either choose a new sprite or start a new program.
2. Create your own quiz about a topic that you know a lot about. Use **condition-switches-between-action** and **condition-starts-action blocks** . Either choose a new sprite or start a new program.
3. Create a maths quiz where you get harder questions if you get the answer right and easier questions if you get the answer wrong. Either choose a new sprite or start a new program.

Use the space below to plan your make second choice creations

Notes on the activity

The make part of a project is really important, and teachers should always make sure that pupils have time to make their own project, even if that means reducing the time spent on other stages for pupils who work slowly. It helps if pupils work on their own for this while supporting their partner.

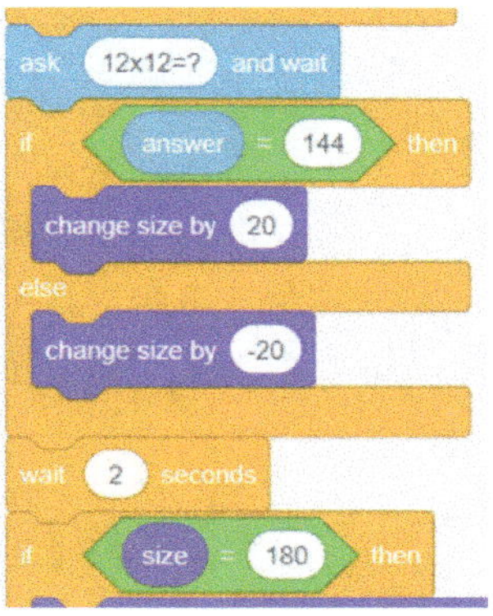

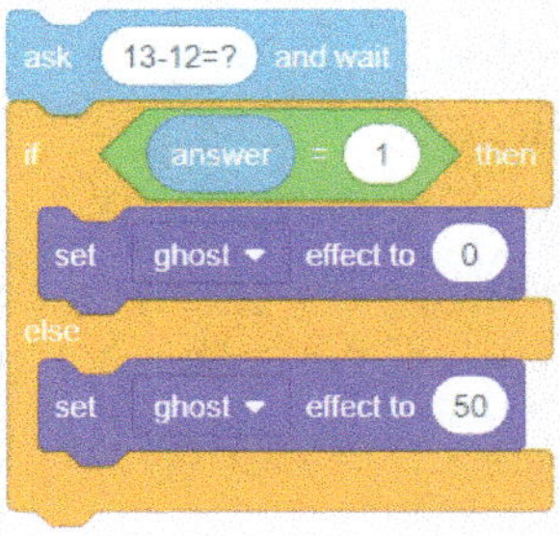

Whole class advice

Work on your own, one device each. You can discuss the work with your former partner, but you are responsible for creating your own projects. Save your work regularly. Read the instructions carefully. Assess your own work by circling where you think you are in the assessment grid at the bottom of the page.

Individual advice

If you are providing hints at this point, then it should be reflected in your summative assessment

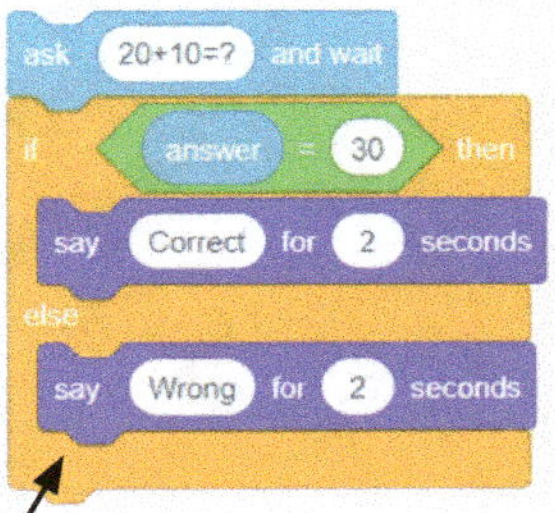

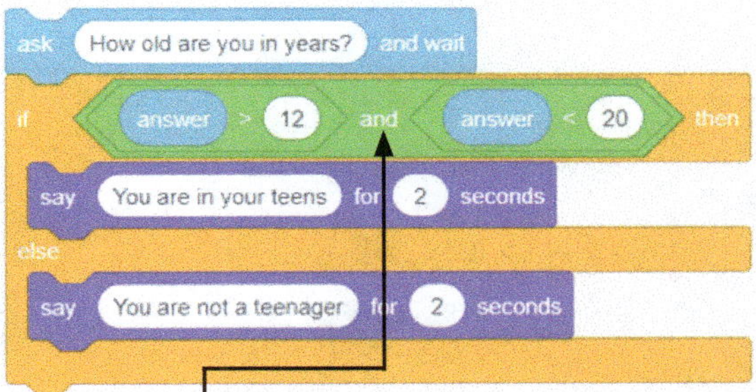

Teacher & Pupil Assessment

Circle one column on each row to show what you think you have achieved so far

condition-switches-between-actions	Not used condition-switches-between-action (if else) blocks	Used a condition-switches-between-action (if else) block simply (effects shown in template or simple text)	AS 1 mark & used condition-starts-action blocks **OR** effects not in template program **OR** nested conditions (like Maurice)	AS 2 marks **&** used either <, >, OR, AND or NOT in any condition
	0 marks	1 mark	2 marks	3 marks

Used previous programming concept such as count-controlled or indefinite loops correctly	Not used previous programming concepts for real purpose	Used previous programming concepts for real purpose
	0 marks	1 mark

Has workable planning for some elements of their project	No planning	planning
	0 marks	1 mark

Task level (what will my program do?)

A basic outline of what their program will do.

E.G. An Ancient Greeks quiz. If you get the answers right the background changes.

My design (questions, initialization, algorithms)

Who lived in a labyrinth?
If answer = minotaur
    Show labyrinth backdrop
Else
    Tell them right answer

PARSONS ANSWERS
WIZARDS CHOICE TWO

Use the algorithm below to connect the code correctly in Darla

Algorithm

Start when the sprite is clicked
Make the sprites size 100%
Say that Darla will grow in power if get question right
Say that Darla will lose power if get answer wrong

Ask 3x3=?
If answer is same as 9
    Increase size by 20%
Else
    Decrease size by –20%

Ask 25+76=?
If answer is same as 101
    Increase size by 20%
Else
    Decrease size by –20%

Ask 85–30=?
If answer is same as 55
    Increase size by 20%
Else
    Decrease size by –20%

Pause for 2 seconds
If size is same as 160%
    Say you got them all right
    Say My powers grow
Else
    Say better luck next time

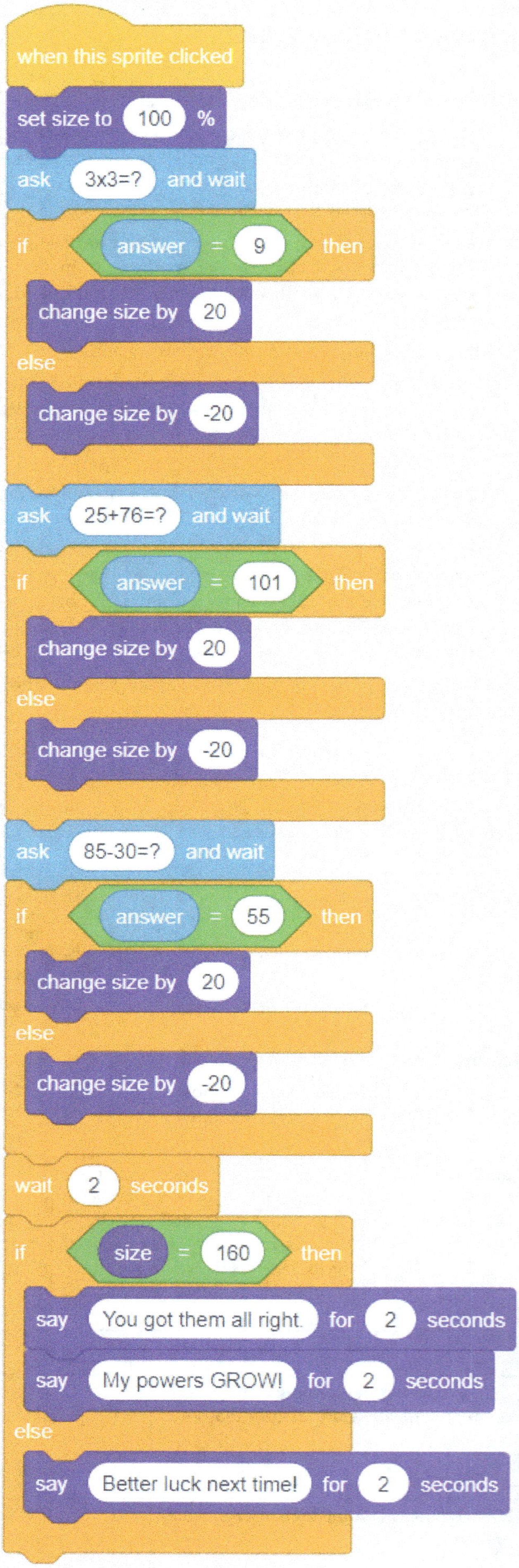
when this sprite clicked
set size to 100 %
ask 3x3=? and wait
if answer = 9 then
change size by 20
else
change size by -20
ask 25+76=? and wait
if answer = 101 then
change size by 20
else
change size by -20
ask 85-30=? and wait
if answer = 55 then
change size by 20
else
change size by -20
wait 2 seconds
if size = 160 then
say You got them all right. for 2 seconds
say My powers GROW! for 2 seconds
else
say Better luck next time! for 2 seconds

PREDICT ANSWERS WIZARDS CHOICE TWO

Work with a partner

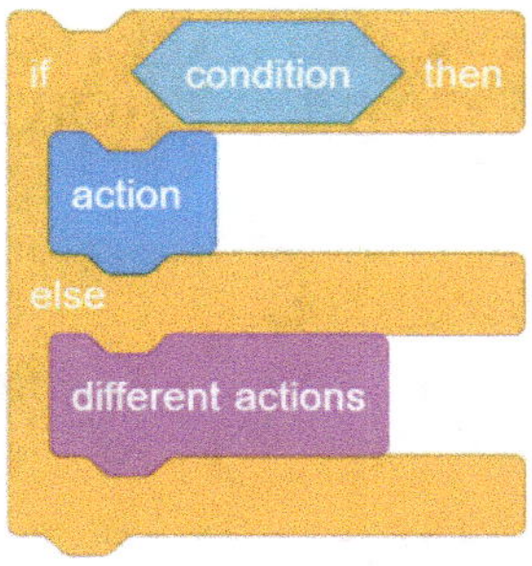
if condition then
action
else
different actions

condition-switches-between-actions

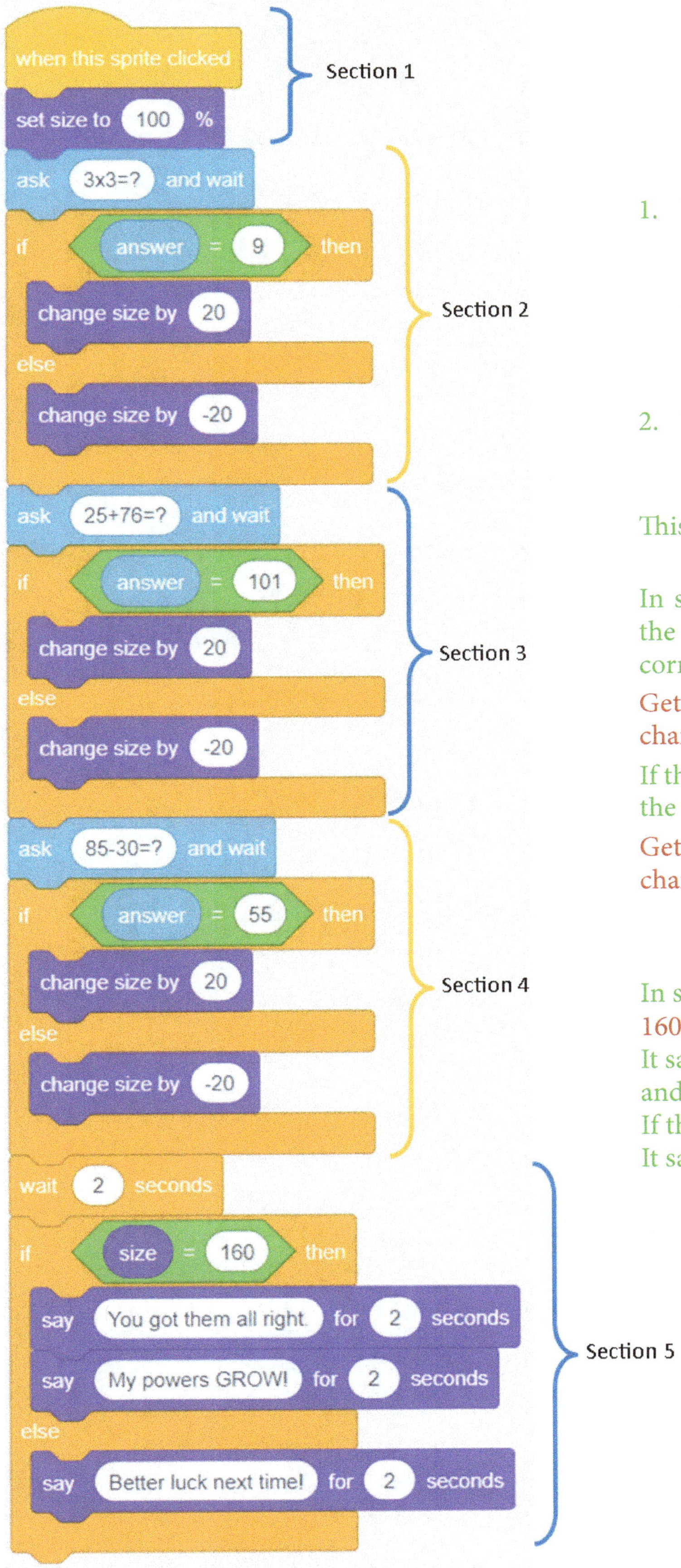
when this sprite clicked
set size to 100 %
Section 1
ask 3x3=? and wait
if answer = 9 then
change size by 20
else
change size by -20
Section 2
ask 25+76=? and wait
if answer = 101 then
change size by 20
else
change size by -20
Section 3
ask 85-30=? and wait
if answer = 55 then
change size by 20
else
change size by -20
Section 4
wait 2 seconds
if size = 160 then
say You got them all right for 2 seconds
say My powers GROW! for 2 seconds
else
say Better luck next time! for 2 seconds
Section 5

1. With your partner, take it in turns to read the code out loud a section at a time.

   Tell your partner what you think your section does.

2. With your understanding of the code sections now fill in the blanks.

This program is a maths quiz or questions (1 mark)

In sections 2, 3 & 4, a maths question is asked. If the answer typed in by the user is **the same as** the correct answer the sprite

Gets bigger or larger or similar increase in size or changes size by 20 (1 mark)

If the answer typed in by the user is **not the same as** the correct answer the sprite

Gets smaller or shrinks or similar decrease in size or changes size by -20 (1 mark)

In section 5 if the size is the same as 160 or equal to 160 or = to 160 (1 mark)
It says You got them all right! (1 mark)
and says My powers GROW! (1 mark)
If the size is not equal to 160 (1 mark)
It says Better luck next time (1 mark)

INVESTIGATE ANSWERS
WIZARDS CHOICE TWO

Run the code inside **Darla** and answer these questions.

1. How many **condition-switches-between-actions (if else)** blocks are there?

   4 (1 mark)

2. If you answer the questions correctly what will happen?

   Darla gets larger by 20% (1 mark for any answer which refers to getting bigger in size)

3. If you answer the questions incorrectly what will happen?

   Darla gets smaller by 20% (1 mark for any answer which refers to getting smaller in size)

4. Look at the last **condition-switches-between-action (if else)** block. What do you need to do in the rest of the program to make sure than the size is = (the same as) 160% after the last question?

   Get all the questions correct (1 mark) Darla starts at 100% and adds 20% every time you get an answer right. After getting three questions right Darla is 160%.

Run the code inside **Gustav** and answer these questions.

5. How many **condition-switches-between-actions (if else)** blocks are there?

   3 (1 mark)

6. How many **count-controlled loops** are there?

   3 (1 mark)

7. Which block is there for initialization purposes? *Initialization is to make sure the program always runs in the same way every time, clearing away the effects of previous program changes.*

   Clear graphics effects (1 mark)

Run the code inside **Maurice** and answer these questions.

8. How many **condition-switches-between-actions** blocks are there?

   3 (1 mark)

9. What happens if you input something other than yes on the first question?

   Maurice says, Nothing left for it, I will just have to vanish. OR He vanishes or disappears (1 mark)

10. How many questions do you have to answer yes to for Maurice to say Magicus, magicus, Magicus Moo?

    3 questions have to have yes answers (1 mark). If you would like to understand more about how the code works inside Maurice ask your teacher for the flow of control sheet.

CHANGE ANSWERS
WIZARDS CHOICE TWO

Change Code in Darla (Make small changes or small additions to the code)

1. Adapt the code to make Darla grow even bigger when the user gets an answer correct. What did you change?

   Change size by more than 20 (1 mark)

2. Adapt the code to make Darla grow even smaller when the user gets an answer wrong. What did you change?

   Change size by less than -20 (1 mark)

3. Add an additional effect to question one if someone gets the answer right. What did you add? Draw an arrow on the code to the right to show where you added your effect.

   Lots of possible additional effects (1 mark for any that work). (1 mark) for any indication that it needed to be added below the if and above the else as shown

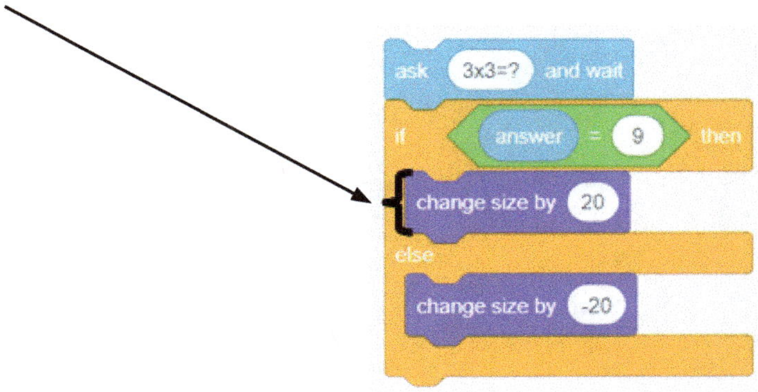
ask
3x3=?
and wait
if
answer
=
9
then
change size by
20
else
change size by
-20

Change Code in Gustav (Make small changes or small additions to the code)

4. Modify the code to make Gustav whirl quicker if the answer is wrong. What did you change?

   Either reduce wait to less than 0.2 secs or change whirl effect by more than 2 or both (1 mark)

5. Slow down Gustav's whirl. What did you change?

   Either increase wait to more than 0.2 secs or change whirl effect by less than 2 or both (1 mark)

6. Can you make Gustav whirl counterclockwise? What did you change?

   Change whirl effect by –2 or another negative number (1 mark)

7. Change Gustav's whirl for a different graphical effect? What did you change it to? Did it work as well?

   Change to colour, pixelate, whirl, fisheye, brightness, mosaic or ghost (1 mark)

Change Code in Maurice (Make small changes or small additions to the code)

8. Modify the code to make Maurice spin round slowly after he says the magic words (Magicus, Magicus Magicus Moo), but before he disappears. What did you add? Where did you add it?

   Add a count-controlled loop with a turn right or turn left a number of degrees block inside. (1 mark)

FLOW OF CONTROL ANSWERS
WIZARDS CHOICE TWO

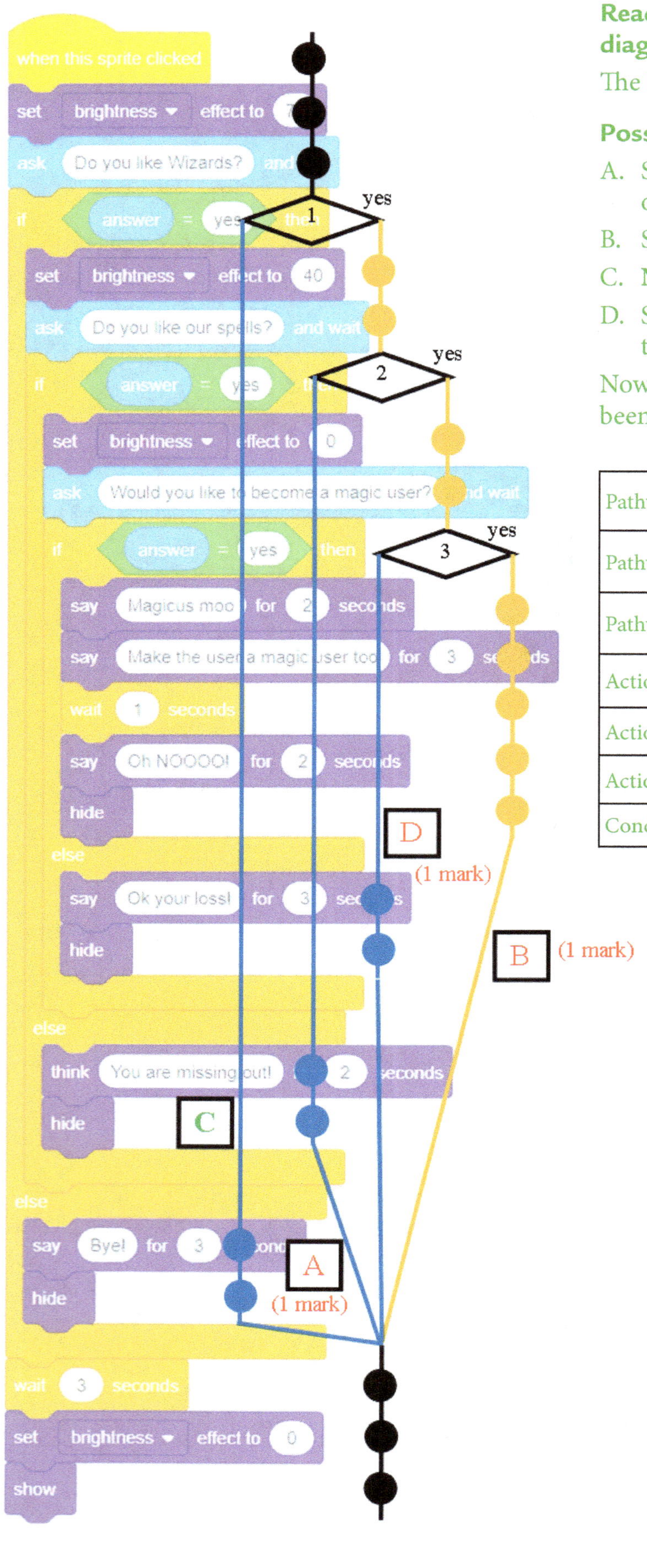

Read the code and look at the flow of control diagram

The key at the bottom will help you.

Possible pathways the code can take

A. Say yes at first condition and **not** say yes at second condition

B. Say yes at all three conditions

C. **Not** say yes at 1st condition

D. Say yes at first two conditions and **not** say yes at third condition

Now mark on the correct pathway letters. One has been done for you.

Pathways not affected by a condition	
Pathways where condition is FALSE	
Pathways where condition is TRUE	
Actions where condition is TRUE	
Actions where condition is FALSE	
Actions not affected by a condition	
Condition	

Key

PROGRAMMING MODULES THAT USE CONDITION CHECKED IN A LOOP

CHAPTER 7 Butterfly Fun

Overview

Pupils explore how Scratch can use conditions inside indefinite (forever) loops in a simple Butterfly game. Pupils then use these ideas to plan and make their own game.

To do before the session

1. Look at the grid below and decide which optional and SEN activities you are going to include and exclude.
2. Print pupil worksheets for each activity chosen and staple into a booklet, one for each pupil.
3. Print marksheets for activities chosen to be placed where pupils can access them.
4. Download the code needed and place in a templates folder on your school network or add to a Scratch Studio or link on your learning platform.
5. Download the slides that go with the concept introduction.
6. Study the notes that go with the slides.
7. Examine the teacher help notes that are provided alongside every activity.

To do at the start of the session

If you have not introduced **conditions-start-action-in-a-loop** with this class before, do this first as a whole class activity.

To do after the concept has been introduced

Each activity has whole class notes to help you explain what is needed if it is the first time pupils have carried out this type of activity. There are also core instructions underneath, in case you are sticking to the core activities only.

How this module fits into a programming progression

- Sequence and Input
- Count-controlled loops
- Indefinite loops
- Conditional selection
- Conditional selection in a loop
- Procedures
- Variables

Vocabulary

Condition, selection, true, false, condition met, pathway, decomposition, condition in a loop

Examine plan is a resources that we recommend pupils have access to while they plan their own game, as it shows a plan for Butterfly Fun.

Resource Name	Core Optional SEN	Teacher	Pupil Grouping	How Assessed	SCRATCH ACCESS
CONCEPT condition-starts-action-in-a-loop	**CORE**	Leads Session	Solo Whole Class Activity	Formative	NO
PARSONS	OPTIONAL SEN OPTIONAL ALL (predict or parsons not both)	Support Poor Readers	Solo or Paired (Teacher choice)	Pupil Marked Marksheet Provided	YES
FLOW	OPTIONAL ALL OPTIONAL ABLE	Support Poor Readers	Solo or Paired (Teacher Choice)	Pupil Marked Marksheet Provided	NO
PREDICT	OPTIONAL ALL (predict or parsons not both)	Support Poor Readers	Paired	Pupil Marked Marksheet Provided	NO
INVESTIGATE	**CORE**	Support Poor Readers	Paired	Pupil Marked Marksheet Provided	YES
CHANGE	**CORE**	Support Poor Readers	Paired	Pupil Marked Marksheet Provided	YES
EXAMINE PLAN	**CORE**		Paired or Solo		YES
CREATE	**CORE**	Assesses Pupil Work and Checks Pupil Self-Assessment	Solo	Pupil Assessed & Teacher Assessed	YES

Core activities general instructions

1. Group pupils in roughly same ability pairs. For **investigate** and **change** worksheets pupils will work in pairs, for **create** they will work separately.
2. Give out the pupil booklets and explain that pupils need to follow the instructions on the sheets to explore how **count-controlled loops** work.
3. Explain that each pupil will record separately whilst working alongside their partner and keeping to the same pace as their partner.
4. Demonstrate where they can find the template code and explain that pupils will share one device for investigate and change.
5. Explain that during each question only one person should touch the shared device and they should swap who that person is when there is a new questions.
6. Encourage them to discuss their answers with their partner. If they disagree with their partner, they can record a different answer in their own booklet.
7. Show pupils where it says they should mark their work on the sheet where the answer sheets are in the classroom.
8. Remind pupils to return marksheets after marking, because there are not enough for every pair to have their own.

Key programming knowledge

A condition is a state we can check to see if it is true or false

Conditions starts with an if

Conditions are only checked once unless they are in a loop

Conditions lead to two possible pathways True and False

Conditions are only checked when reached in flow of control

An algorithm is any set of instructions to carry out a task that can be understood by another human

Decomposition is breaking up a project into parts to solve separately

Resources

Butterfly Fun	https://scratch.mit.edu/projects/572222000/
Parsons Butterfly Fun	https://scratch.mit.edu/projects/619853348/

	On the sheet, if it says no Scratch, they must work only on the sheet.
	If it says Scratch with a green tick, they can use one device between the pair.
	If it says work with a partner, they must work at the same speed as their partner.
	If it says work on their own, they must do this using a separate device each working alone.

The First Software Loop

The scholarly consensus is that the first instance of a software loop was the loop **Ada Lovelace** used to calculate Bernoulli numbers using **Charles Babbage's** Analytical Engine mechanical computer

Scottish Curriculum for Excellence Technologies

I understand the instructions of a visual programming language and can predict the outcome of a program written using the language. TCH 1-14a

I can explain core programming language concepts in appropriate technical language TCH 2-14a

I can demonstrate a range of basic problem solving skills by building simple programs to carry out a given task, using an appropriate language. TCH 1-15a

I can create, develop and evaluate computing solutions in response to a design challenge. TCH 2-15a

English Computing National Curriculum Programs of Study

Pupils should be taught to:

- **design, write and debug programs that accomplish specific goals**, including controlling or simulating physical systems; solve problems by decomposing them into smaller parts.
- **use sequence,** selection and **repetition in programs;** work with variables **and various forms of input and output**.
- **use logical reasoning to explain how some simple algorithms work and to detect and correct errors in algorithms and programs.**

Welsh National Curriculum Relevant Strands

Progression Step 3.

- I can use conditional statements to add control and decision-making to algorithms.
- I can explain and debug algorithms.

Butterfly Fun
PARSONS

Work with a partner

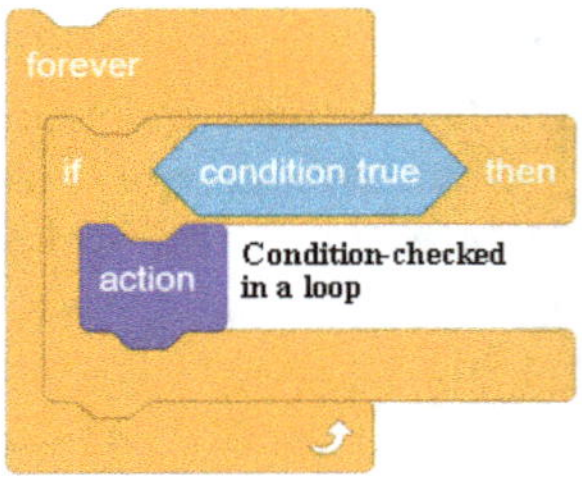
forever
if
condition true
then
action
Condition-checked in a loop

Load Parsons Butterfly Fun

Use the algorithms below to build the code. Then run the game to test your code.

Green flag Go to y and y Rotation all around Loop always Move 1 step	Green flag Loop always If press right arrow key Turn right 15 degrees
Green flag Loop always If press left arrow key Turn left 15 degrees	Green flag Loop always If touch cloud Change colour effect Else Clear graphics effects
Green flag Loop always If touch purple Turn right 10 degrees	

Supporting parsons

Whole class advice

Load Parsons Butterfly Fun code and then use the algorithm on this page to build the code. When you have completed it, run the code and check your answer with the marking sheet.

Send advice

Parsons problems can be made less complex by connecting more blocks in the example Scratch code and saving that version as a new template.

Understanding programming

You can find out more about Parsons problems in the teacher book.

Notes on the activity

This allow pupils to build part of the code first before investigating, modifying and creating code of their own. The algorithm is written in language similar but also different to the code. This helps pupils by enabling them to see an example of planning which will help them when they come to plan their own project. On its own, it is not enough deep thinking about the code to enable agency, but as a starter activity it is useful to see how conditions can be built inside loops. It can also be a useful SEN starter activity.

Send advice

Covering up most of the algorithm so pupils can focus on a section at a time will help some pupils.

Individual advice

Pointing out that the code affected by the condition or within a loop is indented in both algorithm and code can help some pupils.

Able advice

Parsons problems can be made more complex by separating more blocks in the example Scratch code and adding a few not needed blocks and saving that version as a new template.

Load Parsons Butterfly Fun

Use the algorithms below to build the code. Then run the game to test your code.

Green flag
Go to y and y
Rotation all around
Loop always
    Move 1 step
	Green flag
	Loop always
	    If press right arrow key
	        Turn right 15 degrees

Green flag
Loop always
    If press left arrow key
        Turn left 15 degrees
	Green flag
	Loop always
	    If touch cloud
	        Change colour effect
	    Else
	        Clear graphics effects

Green flag
Loop always
    If touch purple
        Turn right 10 degrees
	(See code examples from the marking sheet on page 91)

Butterfly Fun
FLOW

Don't load Scratch

Work with a partner

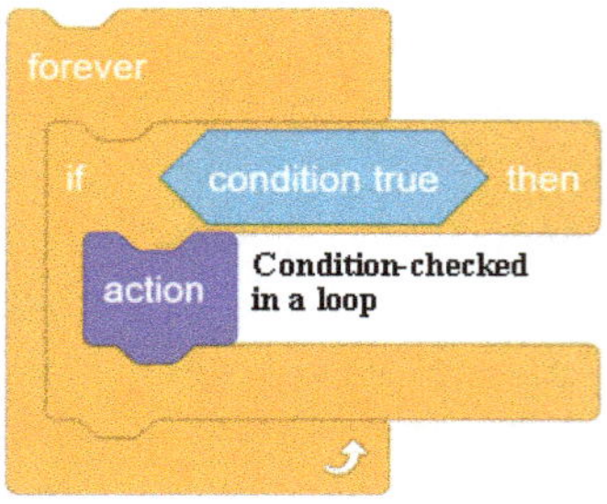

1. Trace your finger over the order the code will be run in the rainbow home sprite. Make sure you go through the loop when the butterfly is touched (orange path) and when it is not being touched (blue path).

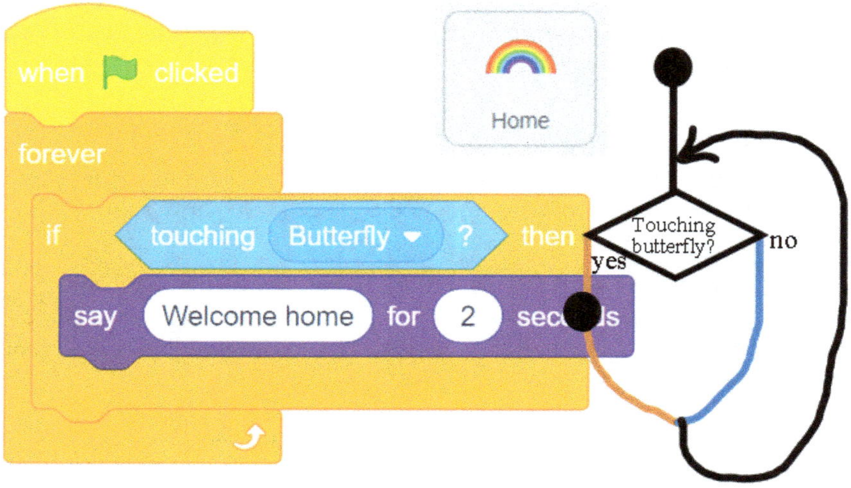

2. Draw a line to show the order the code will be run in this code. Draw dots to show actions. You do not need to draw coloured lines.

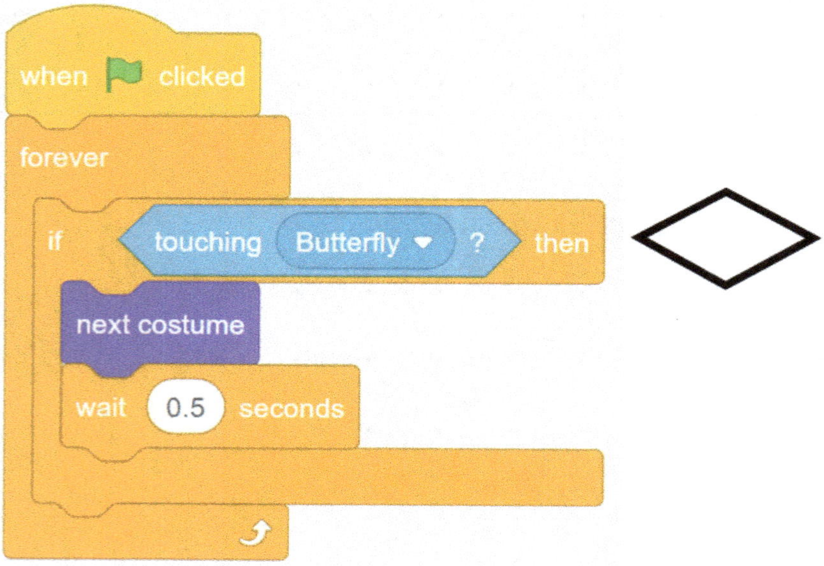

Now mark this sheet using the answer sheet

A

Supporting FLOW

Notes on the activity

This could be a lesson starter type activity or part of the predict or investigate process or saved for pupils who struggled to answer questions about conditions within loops.

If using it as a lesson starter, you could get all pupils to trace the flow of control over the top example with you. Say is it touching the butterfly when you get to the decision diamond. If it is, go down the orange path and say welcome home. If it is not, go down the blue path and back round the loop to start again. Go through the loop at least four times. You can touch or not touch the butterfly on the right of the page.

1. Trace your finger over the order the code will be run in the rainbow home sprite. Make sure you go through the loop when the butterfly is touched (orange path) and when it is not being touched (blue path).

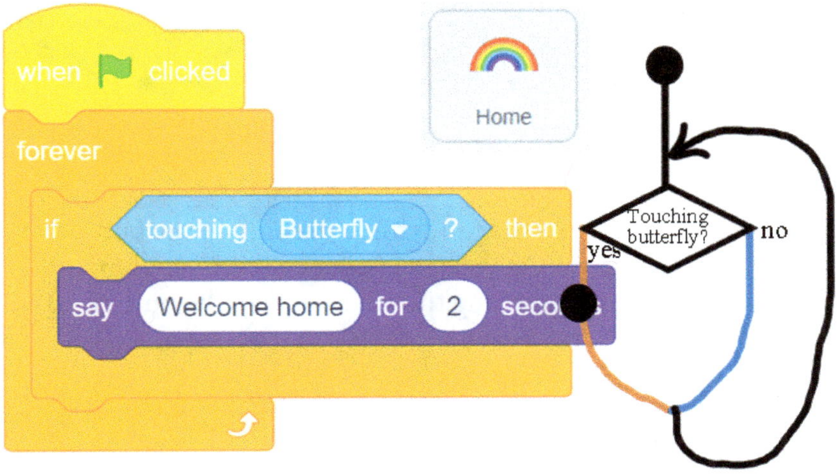

Did you say?
Green flag
Am I touching the butterfly (yes)
Say welcome home (orange path)
Am I touching the butterfly (no)
(blue path)
Am I touching the butterfly (no)
(blue path)
Am I touching the butterfly (yes)
Say welcome home (orange path)
etc.
(2 marks if you did)

2. Draw a line to show the order the code will be run in this code. Draw dots to show actions. You do not need to draw coloured lines.

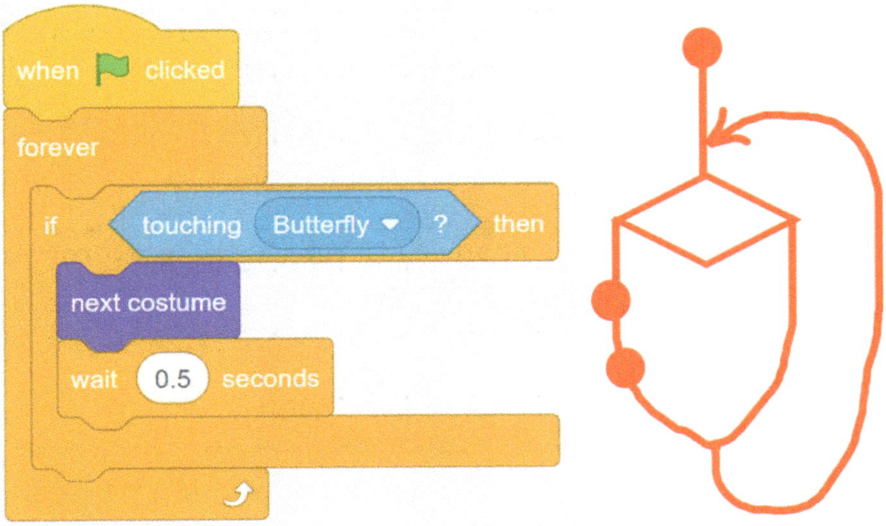

1 mark if you drew the top line and green flag dot

1 mark if you drew in two pathways and put actions dots on one pathway

1 mark if you drew a pathway back up the top of the forever loop.

Whole class advice

Say

Remember the line shows the order that the code will run in and the dots mark actions that will happen. There is an example at the top and we drew some when we introduced conditions inside indefinite loop algorithms

Individual advice

Most pupils can draw the flow of control for these, but making sure they really understand how the condition inside the loop works is harder.

Ask them to say both the actions and the condition as a question. Such as: Am I touching the butterfly?

Individual advice

Remind pupils to mark this sheet before moving on and to tell you if they got them all wrong so you can help.

SEN advice

For some SEN pupils, it can help to blank out the second question until they have completed the first using piece or paper or exercise book. This reduces the amount of information on the page.

Now mark this sheet using the answer sheet

BUTTERFLY FUN
PREDICT

Read the code. Draw a line from the correct Prediction to the correct code.

Don't load Scratch

Work with a partner

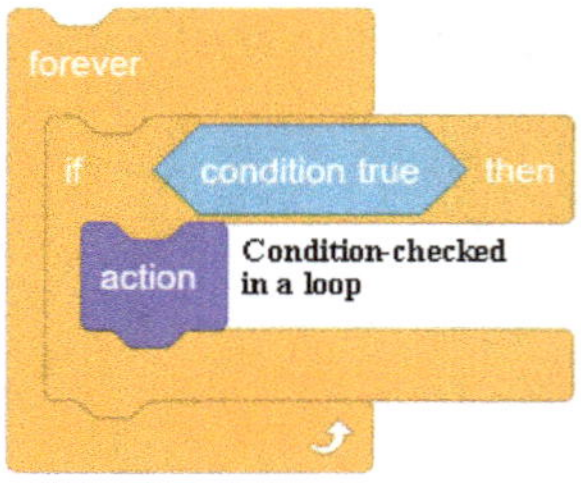
forever
if
condition true
then
action
Condition-checked in a loop

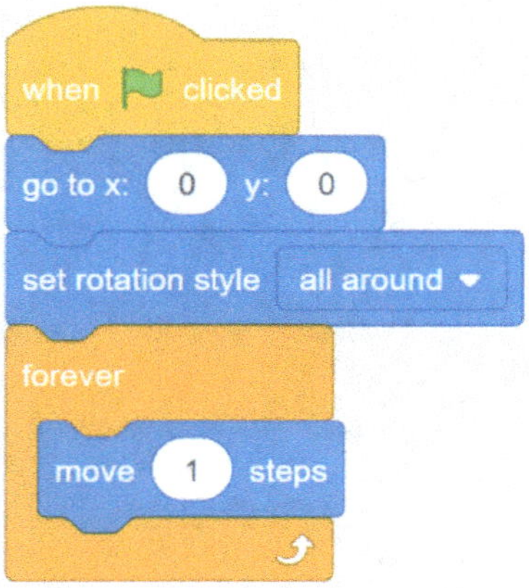
when clicked
go to x: 0 y: 0
set rotation style all around
forever
move 1 steps

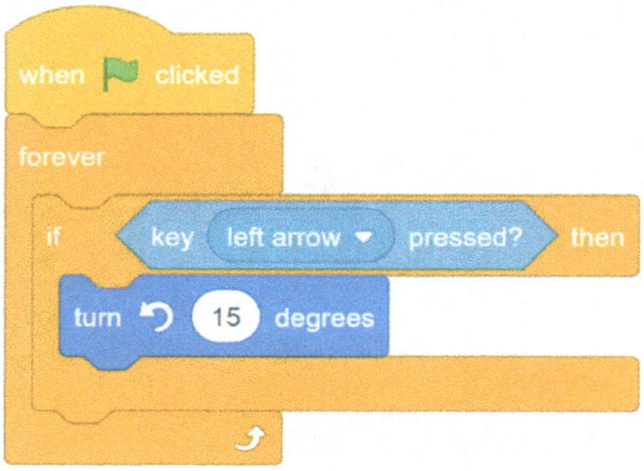
when clicked
forever
if key left arrow pressed? then
turn 15 degrees

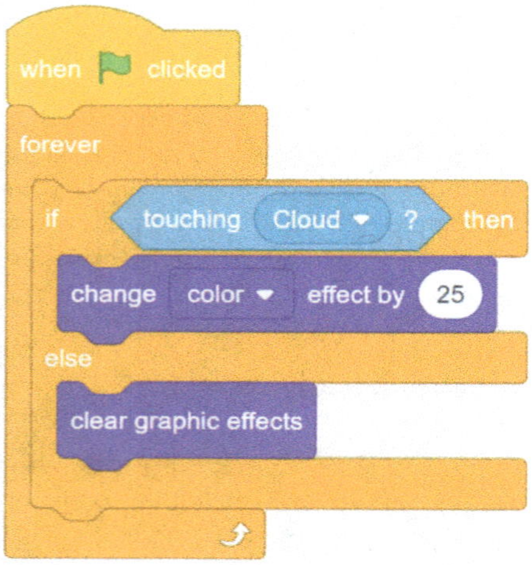
when clicked
forever
if touching Cloud ? then
change color effect by 25
else
clear graphic effects

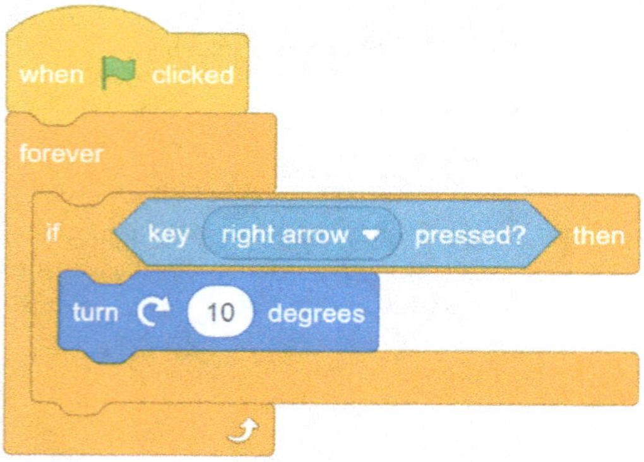
when clicked
forever
if key right arrow pressed? then
turn 10 degrees

While the program is running, if the butterfly is touching a cloud change its colour. Once it is not touching the cloud, return the butterfly to its normal colour.
While the program is running, if the right arrow is pressed turn right.
Send the butterfly back to centre of the screen and then start it moving continuously.
While the program is running, if the left arrow is pressed turn left.

Supporting PREDICT

Notes on the activity

Normally predicting helps pupils to think about the bigger purpose of the program before they start looking at parts of it in later sections. However, as all gaming modules have many decomposed parts to the whole program, prediction is often about identifying what some parts might do.

Read the code and any pictures near it. Draw a line from the correct prediction to the correct code.

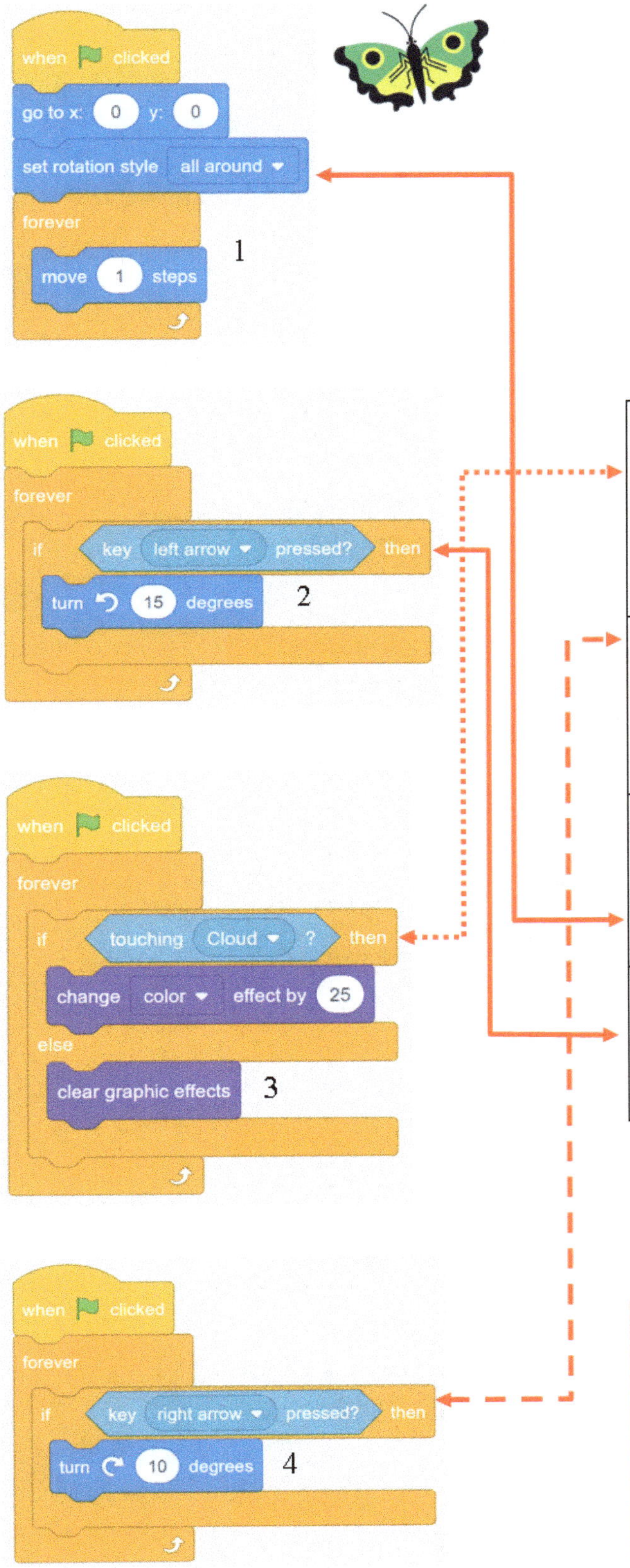
when clicked
go to x: 0 y: 0
set rotation style all around
forever
move 1 steps
1
when clicked
forever
if key left arrow pressed? then
turn 15 degrees
2
when clicked
forever
if touching Cloud ? then
change color effect by 25
else
clear graphic effects
3
when clicked
forever
if key right arrow pressed? then
turn 10 degrees
4

Supporting Top Prediction

Can pupils find keywords?

If touching cloud or change colour

Supporting second prediction

What is the condition? Remember the condition starts with if

Supporting third prediction

What block sends something somewhere?

What is the keyword? ANSWER Moving or continuously

While the program is running, if the butterfly is touching a cloud change its colour. Once it is not touching the cloud, return the butterfly to its normal colour. (A)
While the program is running, if the right arrow is pressed turn right (B)
Send the butterfly back to centre of the screen and then start it moving continuously. (C)
While the program is running, if the left arrow is pressed turn left. (D)

Supporting fourth prediction

What is the condition? Remember the condition starts with if

SUPPORTING SEN PUPILS

You might want to remove some of the choices, so there is only a choice between two descriptions and two bits of code

1 & 2 C & D

3 & 4 A & B

Cover the rest with some paper

BUTTERFLY FUN
Investigate

Work with a partner

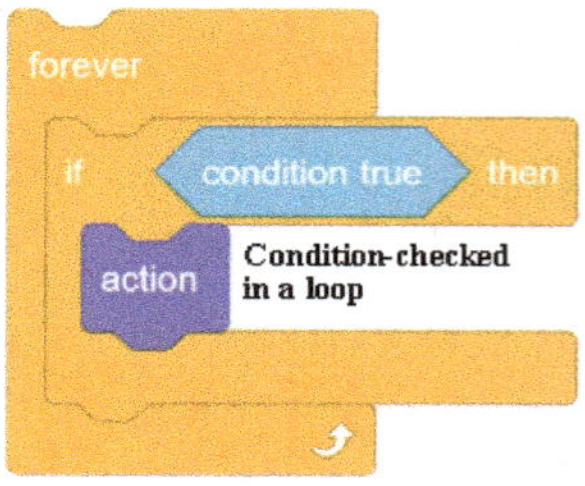
forever
if
condition true
then
action
Condition-checked in a loop

Start Scratch and Load
BUTTERFLY FUN

Investigate the Code

Look at the code inside the butterfly

Run the programs lots of times to help you answer the questions but don't change the code

1. How many conditions (starts with if) are checked inside forever loops?

2. List all three conditions? *HINT Start with if*

   A

   B

   C

3. What code block is run if the butterfly is **NOT touching the cloud**?

4. What two blocks working together make the butterfly move?

5. In the sections of code that start with a green flag two blocks are initialization. Name these two blocks.
   HINT Initialization makes a sprite behave the same way every time it is started

   A

   B

Look at the code inside the bell

6. When the butterfly touches the bell, for how many seconds does the bell swing for?
   HINT Count-controlled-loop/repeat loop
   HINT 0.5 seconds is half a second

Now mark the investigate questions using the answer sheet

SUPPORTING
Investigate

Notes on the activity

Investigating the code encourages pupils to think deeply about how it works. Sometimes one pupil in a pair decides to work faster than their partner; check that this is not happening and that every pupil is filling in and marking the questions individually but at the pace of the slowest in the pair. Sometimes a pair decides not to mark to speed up their efforts. Marking gives valuable information, so I recommend sending them back to mark their work if this is the case. A class instruction to come and talk to you if they have over half of the questions wrong or they do not understand the answer after they have marked it helps to check progress is being made correctly. There is real value in collecting these scores to build up a summative picture of pupil progress.

Send advice

Hide questions that you are not working on with a book or piece of paper.

Investigate the Code

Look at the code inside the butterfly

Run the programs lots of times to help you answer the questions, but don't change the code

1. How many conditions (starts with if) are checked inside forever loops?

   3 (1 mark)

2. List all three conditions? *HINT Start with if*

   A if key right arrow pressed (1 mark)

   B if key left arrow pressed (1 mark)

   C if touching Cloud (1 mark)

3. What code block is run if the butterfly is **NOT touching the cloud?**

   Clear graphic effects (1 mark)

4. What two blocks working together make the butterfly move?

   Forever loop and move 1 step (1 mark)

5. In the sections of code that start with a green flag, two blocks are initialization. Name these two blocks. *HINT Initialization makes a sprite behave the same way every time it is started*

   A go to x and y (1 mark)

   B set rotation style all around (1 mark)

6. When the butterfly touches the bell, for how many seconds does the bell swing for?

   HINT Count-controlled-loop/repeat loop

   HINT 0.5 seconds is half a second

   6 seconds (1 mark)

   $6 \times 0.5 + 0.5 = 6 \times 1$ *second*

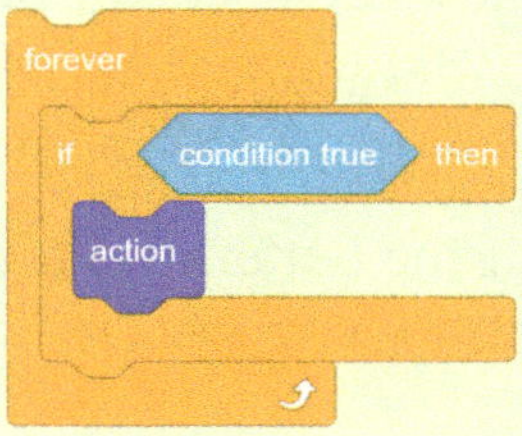
forever
if
condition true
then
action

Q1 support

Point pupils towards the code theme in top right-hand side of the page.

Q2 support

Use your fingers to indicate a <   > shape similar to the condition shape in code.

Q3 support

If pupils have not encountered the condition switches block before, then a quick explanation that the else part is triggered if the condition is false or not met.

Q4 support

This is a revision question about how loops work. You might want to ask them about what they studied in Year 4.

Q5 support

Remind pupils that initialization often comes near the top of code, so the code can be set back to what it was like when it was run the first time.

Q6 support

This is a revision question about how loops work. You might want to ask them about what they studied in Year 4. Can they point out the loop? Ask how that will affect the waits.

Whole class support

Check that pupils are marking work, as it is easier to help pupils soon after they have completed work than in later weeks.

BUTTERFLY FUN
Change

Work with a partner

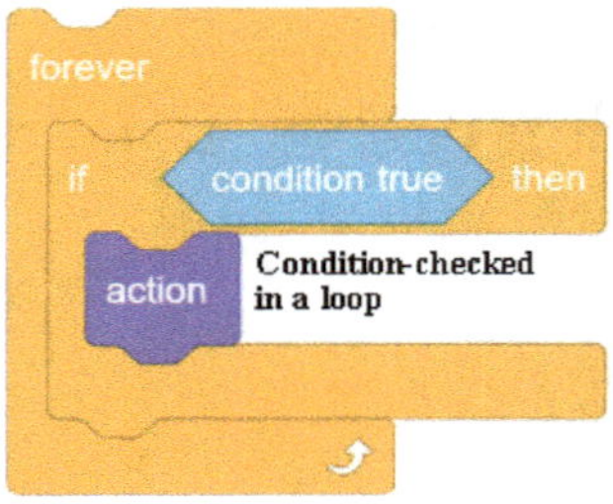
forever
if
condition true
then
action
Condition-checked in a loop

Start Scratch and Load the BUTTERFLY FUN program

Make small changes to the code

Look at the code inside the butterfly

1. Change the code to make the butterfly travel twice as fast. What did you change? *HINT This is revision question on loops*

2. Change the code so that the **a** key steers the butterfly left.
   What did you change? *Hint If key left...*

3. Change the code so that if the butterfly is touching the cloud it stops changing colour, but if it is not touching the cloud it changes colour. What did you change? *HINT Time for a swap*

Look at the code inside home

4. Change the code so that if home touches the butterfly, home spins round slowly instead of saying anything. What did you change?

Look at the code inside balloon 1

5. Change the code so the colour of the balloon changes faster. What did you change?

Look at the code inside bell

6. Change the code so if the butterfly touches the bell it ends the game. What did you remove? What did you add? *HINT Control*

Now mark the changing code questions using the answer sheet

SUPPORTING
Change

Send advice

Cover up questions you have no need to see yet.

Whole class advice

Work in pairs, one device between the pair. Take it in turns every question to swap who runs code. You must work at the same pace as your partner and not move on to the next question until you have both written your answer down. If you disagree, write a different answer. You must mark your work before moving on to the next section.

Notes on the activity

Changing or modifying the code is a core part of this module, so I suggest you do not leave it out. It is an important step towards creation of their own code. Recording their marks can help with formative and summative assessment.

Make small changes to the code

Look at the code inside the butterfly

1. Change the code to make the butterfly travel twice as fast. What did you change? *HINT This is revision question on loops*

   Change move 1 to move 2 (1 mark)

2. Change the code so that the a key steers the butterfly left. What did you change? *Hint If*

   Change if key left arrow pressed to if key a pressed (1 mark)

3. Change the code so that if the butterfly is touching the cloud it stops changing colour, but if it is not touching the cloud it changes colour. What did you change?

   Move change colour affect into else part of the block and clear graphics effect into if part of block. Any answer that indicates that these blocks swap places (1 mark)

Individual advice Q2

Ask pupils what code steers left. Can they find the conditions which starts with if key...

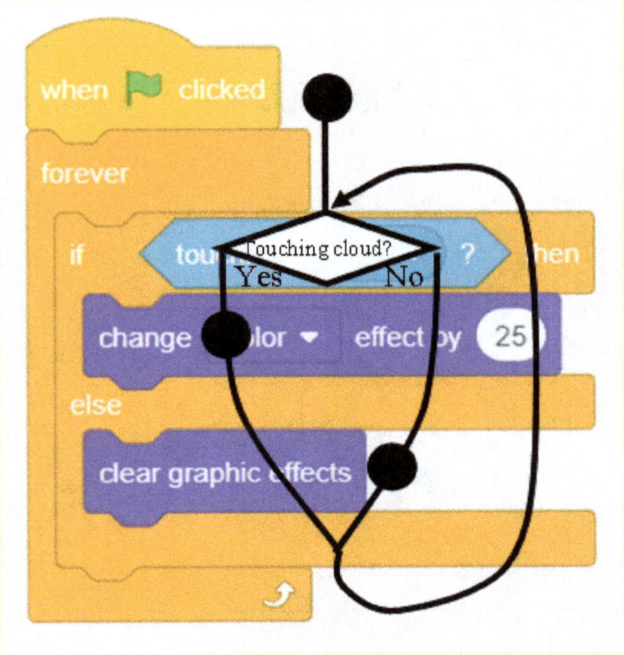
when clicked
forever
if
tou
Touching cloud?
Yes
No
?
hen
change
lor
effect
by
25
else
clear graphic effects

Individual advice Q3

Talk pupils through the flow of control as shown above.

Look at the code inside home

4. Change the code so that if home touches the butterfly, home spins round slowly instead of saying anything. What did you change? Remove say block and replace it with any turn right so many degrees or turn left so many degrees (1 mark)

Look at the code inside balloon 1

5. Change the code so the colour of the balloon changes faster. What did you change?

   Change wait 0.5 seconds to any smaller decimal fraction such as 0.1 or 0.01 or remove the wait block completely (1 mark)

Individual advice Q5

HINT key word is faster.

Look at the code inside bell

6. Change the code so if the butterfly touches the bell it ends the game. What did you remove? What did you add? *HINT Control*

   Either remove the sounds or repeat 6 loop and add a stop all block or build new code that forever if touching butterfly stops all (1 mark)

Individual advice Q6

HINT stop code found in control blocks.

Now mark the changing code questions using the answer sheet

BUTTERFLY FUN
CREATE

Work on your own

Show your plan to your teacher before you start to make anything

Look at how Butterfly Fun was planned first before writing your own plan

Idea Level

Design Level 1: What will your sprites do?

Design Level 2: Draw what will happen and take some Design Level 2 ideas and turn them into planning algorithms.

Teacher & Pupil Assessment

Circle the stage that you think you have reached in each row, your teacher will check it.

	Not used a condition checked in a loop	Copied a condition checked in a loop from butterfly game	Copied and changed condition checked in a loop from butterfly game	Found own use for a condition checked in a loop
Indefinite (forever) loops	0 marks	1 mark	2 marks	3 marks

	Not used previous programming concepts for real purpose	Used previous programming concepts for real purpose
Used previous programming concept such as count-controlled loops	0 marks	1 mark

	No theme in planning or code	Has a theme in planning or code
Has a project theme in planning or code	0 marks	1 mark

You can check your progress using the planning and making code marksheet

SUPPORTING CREATE

Idea Level

Design Level 1: What will your sprites do?

Design Level 2: Draw what will happen and include algorithms.

Supporting Assessment

It is fine to copy ideas from the example project in fact almost all code is copied and adapted. However, it is worth pointing out to pupils what score they would get and how they can improve the score as many will then look for their own ideas or greater adaptations.

Notes on the activity

The make part of a project is really important, and teachers should always make sure that pupils have time to make their own project, even if that means reducing the time spent on other stages for pupils who work slowly. It helps for assessment purposes if pupils work on their own for this.

Supporting idea level

Have pupils written a simple idea? What characters will they use? What will these characters do? Is there a clear aim to the game? Focus pupils back on the example planner if they are stuck. Can they adapt that aim?

Supporting design level 1

Check that pupils have broken up every action and determined what will control that action. It is not enough to talk about general steering, it should be: Steer right how? Steer left how? etc.

Supporting design level 2

Make sure pupils have taken at least two or three Design Level 1 ideas and turned them into detailed algorithms before they start coding. It is fine if pupils plan a bit and then make it before returning to plan more.

Whole class support

Make sure pupils have looked at the example planner. Make sure they have planned carefully with an Ideas Level, Design Level 1 and part of Design Level 2 before coding.

Idea Level
A butterfly will more around steered by the user. when it touches different sprites things will happen to it.

Design Level
Butterfly 1. move automatically. 2. steer right with right arrow. 2. steer left left arrow 3. touch purple spin to right more 4. touch cloud change colour 5. touch rainbow say something

Loop always Move 1 step	Loop always If press right arrow turn right	Loop always If press left arrow turn left

Whole class support

You can plan with the whole class or a group using the last four slides in condition-starts-action-in-a-loop slides.

Teacher & Pupil Assessment

Circle the stage that you think you have reached in each row, your teacher will check it.

	Not used a condition checked in a loop	Copied a condition checked in a loop from butterfly game	Copied and changed condition checked in a loop from butterfly game	Found own use for a condition checked in a loop
Indefinite (forever) loops	0 marks	1 mark	2 marks	3 marks

	Not used previous programming concepts for real purpose	Used previous programming concepts for real purpose
Used previous programming concept such as count-controlled loops	0 marks	1 mark

	No theme in planning or code	Has a theme in planning or code
Has a project theme in planning or code	0 marks	1 mark

BUTTERFLY FUN
EXAMINE PLAN

Examine the butterfly game plan below before planning your own game

Idea Level A butterfly will more around steered by the user. When it touches different sprites things will happen to it.

Design Level Butterfly 1, move automatically, 2, steer right with right arrow, 2, steer left left arrow 3, touch purple spin to right more, 4, touch cloud change colour 5, touch rainbow say something

Loop always Move 1 step	Loop always If press right arrow turn right	Loop always If press left arrow turn left
Loop always If touch purple turn right	Loop always If touch cloud Change colour Else Stop changing colour	Loop always If touch rainbow Say I am home
Loop always If touch dark cloud Say end of game End game		

Loop always
If key b is pressed
Hide

algorithm examples

Loop always
If touching orange
Stop game

This method was fine in Year 3 but will not work in any other programming language

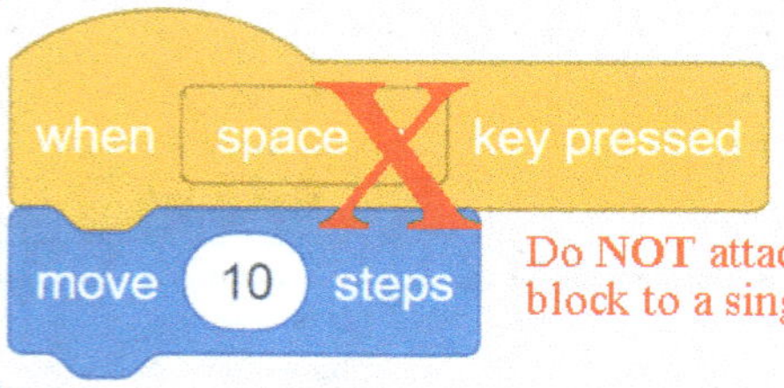

Do NOT attach a starting block to a single block of code

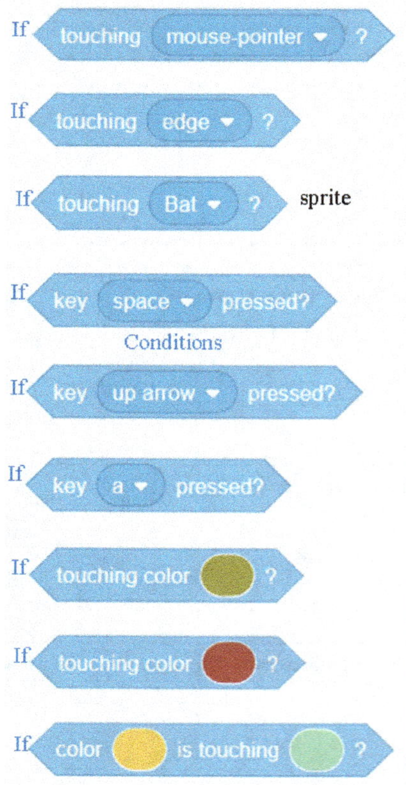

Useful conditions

Butterfly Fun
PARSONS MARKING SHEET

Load Parsons Butterfly Fun

Use the algorithms below to build the code. Then run the game to test your code.

Green flag
Go to y and y
Rotation all around
Loop always
    Move 1 step

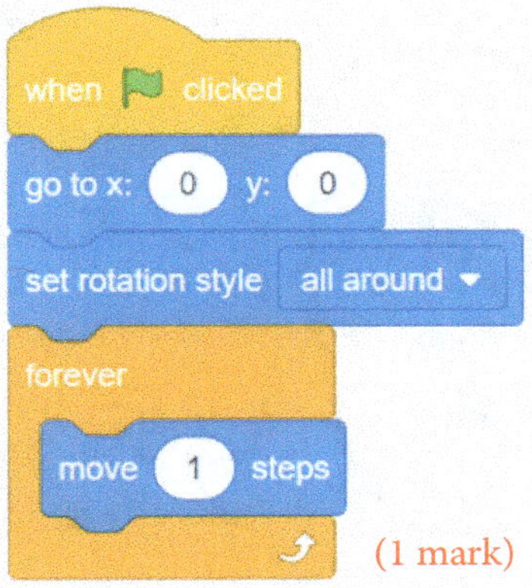
when clicked
go to x: 0 y: 0
set rotation style all around
forever
move 1 steps

(1 mark)

Green flag
Loop always
    If press right arrow key
        Turn right 15 degrees

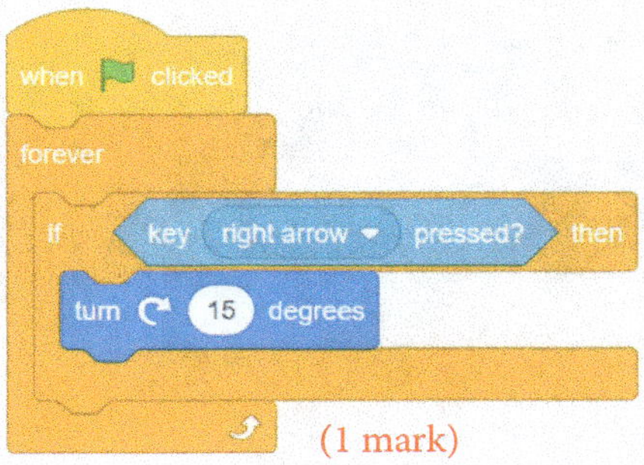
when clicked
forever
if key right arrow pressed? then
turn 15 degrees

(1 mark)

Green flag
Loop always
    If press left arrow key
        Turn left 15 degrees

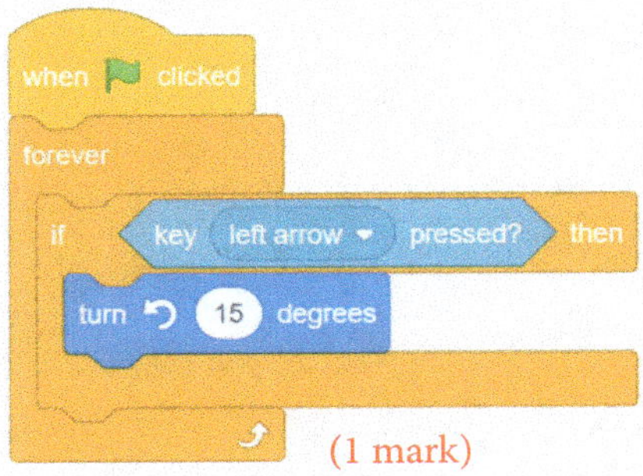
when clicked
forever
if key left arrow pressed? then
turn 15 degrees

(1 mark)

Green flag
Loop always
    If touch cloud
        Change colour effect
    Else
        Clear graphics effects

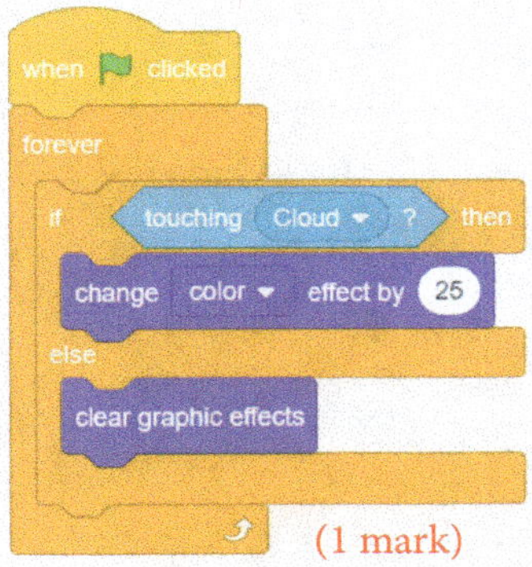
when clicked
forever
if touching Cloud ? then
change color effect by 25
else
clear graphic effects

(1 mark)

Green flag
Loop always
    If touch purple
        Turn right 10 degrees

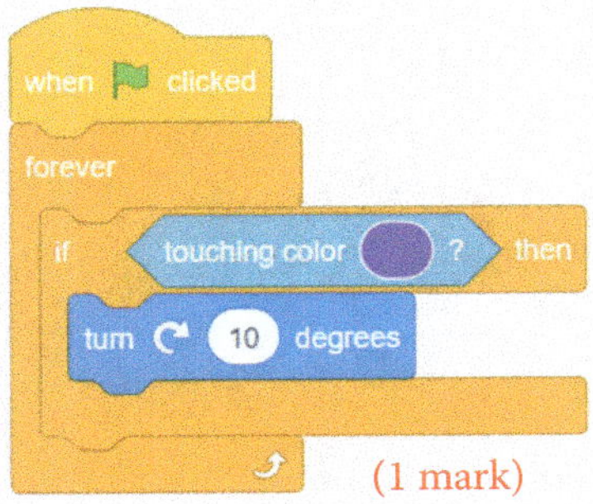
when clicked
forever
if touching color ? then
turn 10 degrees

(1 mark)

Butterfly Fun

Reading code and predicting what it will do
Draw the Flow of Control Marksheet

1. Trace your finger over the order the code will be run in the rainbow home sprite. Make sure you go through the loop when the butterfly is touched (orange path) and when it is not being touched (blue path). Say what happens when you get to each action and condition.

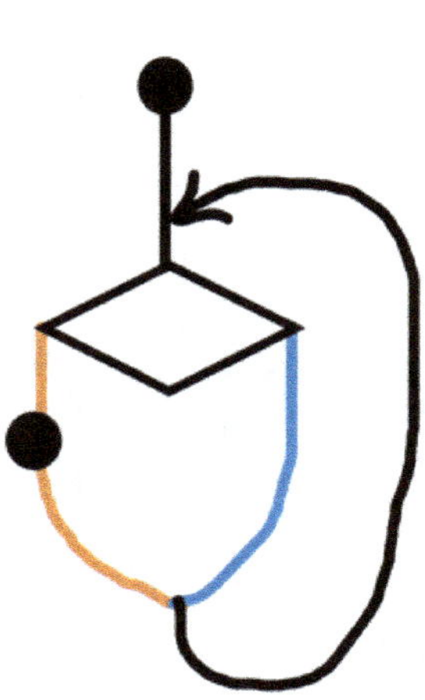

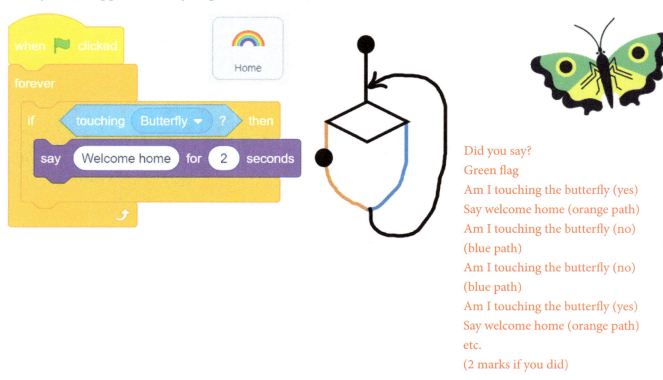

Did you say?
Green flag
Am I touching the butterfly (yes)
Say welcome home (orange path)
Am I touching the butterfly (no)
(blue path)
Am I touching the butterfly (no)
(blue path)
Am I touching the butterfly (yes)
Say welcome home (orange path)
etc.
(2 marks if you did)

2. Draw a line to show the order the code will be run in this code. Draw dots to show actions. You do not need to draw coloured lines.

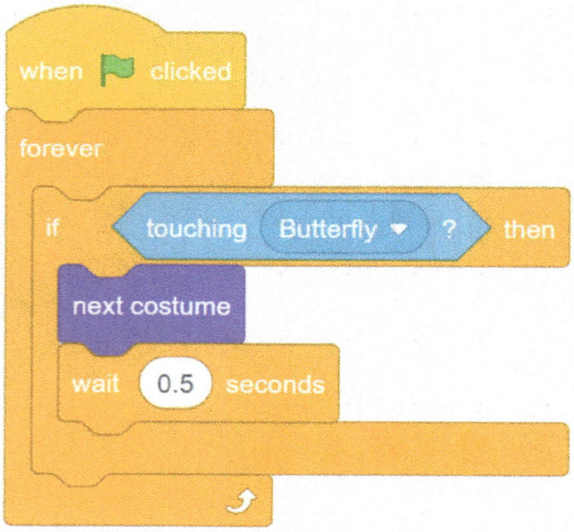

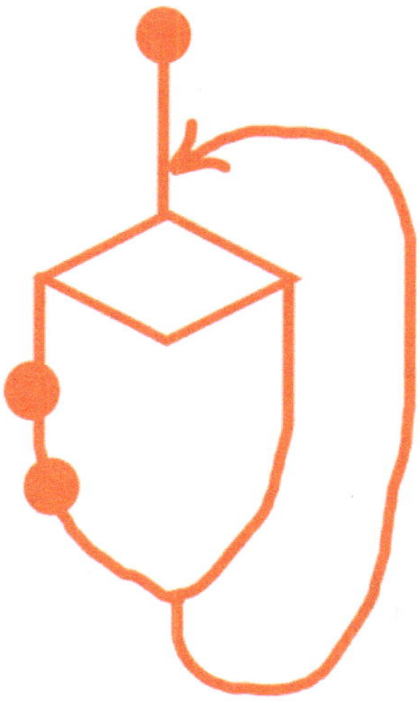

1 mark if you drew the top line and green flag dot

1 mark if you drew in two pathways and put actions dots on one pathway

1 mark if you drew a pathway back up the top of the forever loop.

MARKING Reading code and predicting what it will do

Read the code and any pictures near it. Draw a line from the correct prediction to the correct code.

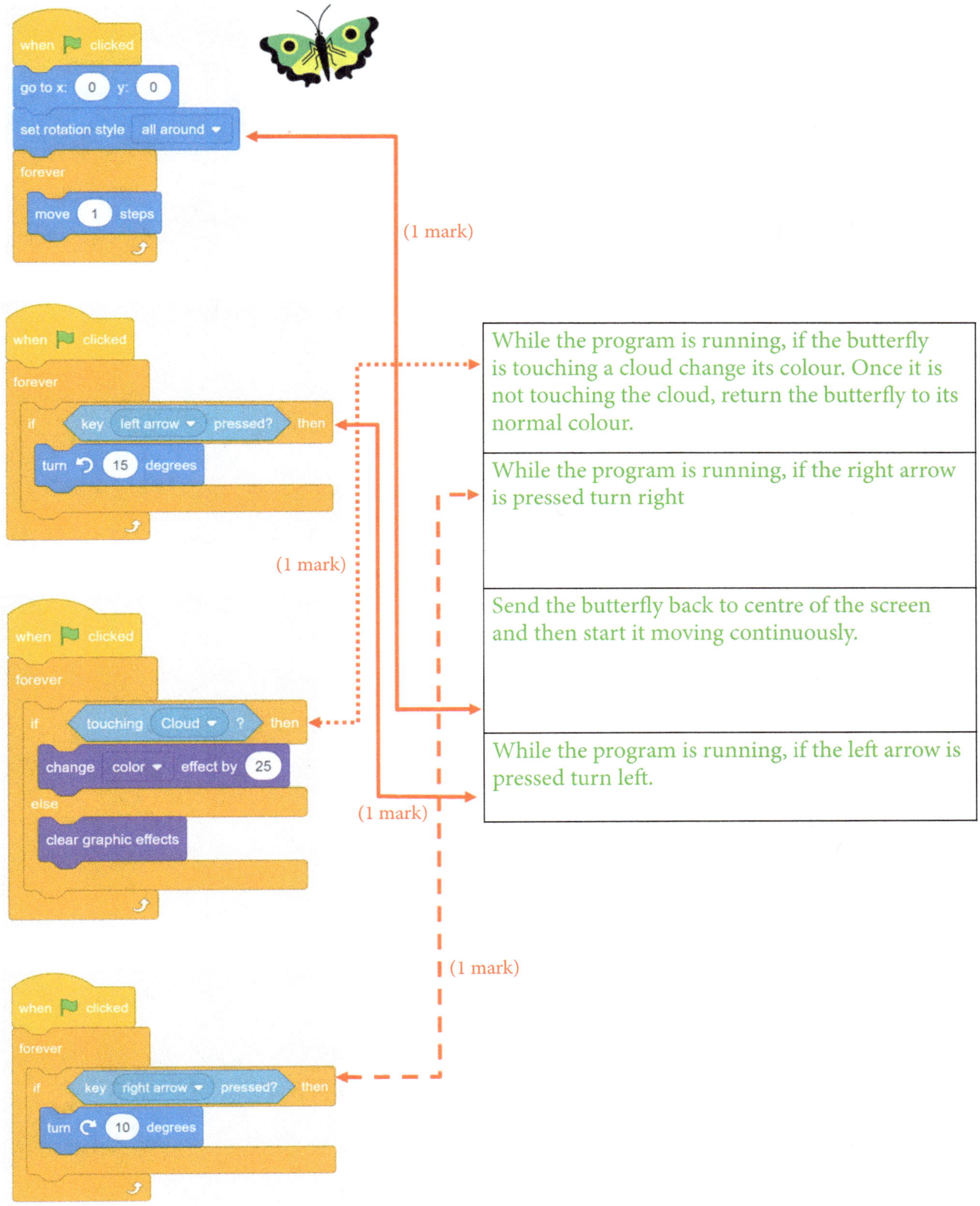
when clicked
go to x: 0 y: 0
set rotation style all around
forever
move 1 steps
(1 mark)
when clicked
forever
if key left arrow pressed? then
turn 15 degrees
(1 mark)
when clicked
forever
if touching Cloud ? then
change color effect by 25
else
clear graphic effects
(1 mark)
when clicked
forever
if key right arrow pressed? then
turn 10 degrees
(1 mark)
While the program is running, if the butterfly is touching a cloud change its colour. Once it is not touching the cloud, return the butterfly to its normal colour.
While the program is running, if the right arrow is pressed turn right
Send the butterfly back to centre of the screen and then start it moving continuously.
While the program is running, if the left arrow is pressed turn left.

BUTTERFLY FUN
Running & Investigating Code Marksheet

Investigate the code

Look at the code inside the butterfly

Run the programs lots of times to help you answer the questions, but don't change the code.

1. How many conditions (starts with if) are checked inside forever loops?

   3 (1 mark)

2. List all three conditions? *HINT Start with if*

   A of key right arrow pressed (1 mark)

   B if key left arrow pressed (1 mark)

   C if touching Cloud (1 mark)

3. What code block is run if the butterfly is **NOT touching the cloud**?

   Clear graphic effects (1 mark)

4. What two blocks working together make the butterfly move?

   Forever loop and move 1 step (1 mark)

5. In the sections of code that start with a green flag two blocks are initialisation. Name these two blocks.
   HINT Initialisation makes a sprite behave the same way every time it is started

   A go to x and y (1 mark)

   B set rotation style all around (1 mark)

Look at the code inside the bell

6. When the butterfly touches the bell, how many seconds is the bell rung for?

   HINT Count-controlled-loop/repeat loop

   HINT 0.5 seconds is half a second

   6 seconds (1 mark)

   $6 \times 0.5 + 0.5 = 6 \times 1$ second

Now mark the investigate questions using the answer sheet

BUTTERFLY FUN
MARKING
Changing Code

Make small changes to the code

Look at the code inside the butterfly

1. Change the code to make the butterfly travel twice as fast. What did you change? *HINT This is revision question on loops*

   Change move 1 to move 2 (1 mark)

2. Change the code so that the a key steers the butterfly left.

   What did you change? *Hint If*

   Change if key left arrow pressed to if key a pressed (1 mark)

3. Change the code so that if the butterfly is touching the cloud it stops changing colour, but if it is not touching the cloud it changes colour. What did you change?

   Move change colour effect into else part of the block and clear graphics effect into if part of block. Any answer that indicates that these blocks swap places (1 mark)

Look at the code inside home

4. Change the code so that if home touches the butterfly, home spins round slowly instead of saying anything. What did you change? Remove say block and replace it with any turn right so many degrees or turn left so many degrees (1 mark)

Look at the code inside balloon 1

5. Change the code so the colour of the balloon changes faster. What did you change?

   Change wait 0.5 seconds to any smaller decimal fraction such as 0.1 or 0.01 (1 mark)

Look at the code inside bell

6. Change the code so if the butterfly touches the bell it ends the game. What did you remove? What did you add? *HINT Control*

   Either remove the sounds or repeat 6 loop and add a stop all block or build new code that forever if touching butterfly stops all (1 mark)

Now mark the changing code questions using the answer sheet

CHAPTER 8 Ocean Pollution

Overview

Pupils learn about how conditions within loops work away from the computer. They then explore how Scratch can use conditions inside indefinite (forever) loops in an Ocean Pollution game before using these ideas to plan and make their own game.

To do before the session

1. Look at the grid below and decide which optional and SEN activities you are going to include and exclude.
2. Print pupil worksheets for each activity chosen and staple into a booklet, one for each pupil.
3. Print marksheets for activities chosen to be placed where pupils can access them.
4. Download the code needed and place in a templates folder on your school network or add to a Scratch Studio or link on your learning platform.
5. Download the slides that go with the concept introduction.
6. Study the notes that go with the slides.
7. Examine the teacher help notes that are provided alongside every activity.

To do at the start of the session

If you have not introduced **conditions-start-action-in-a-loop** with this class before do this first as a whole class activity.

To do after the concept has been introduced

Each activity has whole class notes to help you explain what is needed if it is the first time pupils have carried out this type of activity. There are also core instructions underneath, in case you are sticking to the core activities only.

How this module fits into a programming progression

Sequence and Input
↓
Count-controlled loops
↓
Indefinite loops
↓
Conditional selection
↓
Conditional selection in a loop
↓
Procedures
↓
Variables
↓

Vocabulary

Condition, selection, true, false, condition met, pathway, decomposition, condition in a loop

Examine plan is a resource that we recommend pupils have access to while they plan their own game, as it shows a plan for Ocean Pollution

Resource Name	Core Optional SEN	Teacher	Pupil Grouping	How Assessed	SCRATCH ACCESS
CONCEPT condition-starts-action-in-a-loop	**CORE**	Leads Session	Solo Whole Class Activity	Formative	NO
PARSONS	OPTIONAL SEN OPTIONAL ALL (predict or parsons not both)	Support Poor Readers	Solo or Paired (Teacher choice)	Pupil Marked Marksheet Provided	YES Ocean Pollution Plan Parsons
FLOW	OPTIONAL ALL	Support Poor Readers	Solo or Paired (Teacher Choice)	Pupil Marked Marksheet Provided	NO
PREDICT	OPTIONAL ALL (predict or parsons not both)	Support Poor Readers	Paired	Pupil Marked Marksheet Provided	NO
EXAMINE PLAN	**CORE**		Paired	Pupil Marked Marksheet Provided	NO
INVESTIGATE	**CORE**	Support Poor Readers	Paired	Pupil Marked Marksheet Provided	YES Ocean Pollution Plan
CHANGE	**CORE**	Support Poor Readers	Paired	Pupil Marked Marksheet Provided	YES Ocean Pollution Plan
CREATE	**CORE**	Assesses Pupil Work and Checks Pupil Self-Assessment	Solo	Pupil Assessed & Teacher Assessed	YES Ocean Pollution Plan

Core activities general instructions

1. Group pupils in roughly same ability pairs. For **investigate** and **change** worksheets pupils will work in pairs, for **create** they will work separately.
2. Give out the pupil booklets and explain that pupils need to follow the instructions on the sheets to explore how **count-controlled loops** work.
3. Explain that each pupil will record separately while working alongside their partner and keeping to the same pace as their partner.
4. Demonstrate where they can find the template code and explain that pupils will share one device for investigate and change.
5. Explain that during each question only one person should touch the shared device and they should swap who that person is when there is a new questions.
6. Encourage them to discuss their answers with their partner. If they disagree with their partner, they can record a different answer in their own booklet.
7. Show pupils where it says they should mark their work on the sheet where the answer sheets are in the classroom.
8. Remind pupils to return marksheets after marking, because there are not enough for every pair to have their own.

Key Programming Knowledge

A **condition** is a state we can check to see if it is true or false
Conditions starts with an if
Conditions are only checked once unless they are in a loop
Conditions lead to two possible pathways True and False
Conditions are only checked when reached in the flow of control
An **algorithm** is any set of instructions to carry out a task that can be understood by another human
Decomposition is breaking up a project into parts to solve separately

Resources

Ocean Pollution Plan	https://scratch.mit.edu/projects/598885579/
Ocean Pollution Plan Parsons	https://scratch.mit.edu/projects/622023960/

	On the sheet, if it says no Scratch, they must work only on the sheet.
	If it says Scratch with a green tick, they can use one device between the pair.
	If it says work with a partner, they must work at the same speed as their partner.
	If it says work on their own, they must do this using a separate device each working alone.

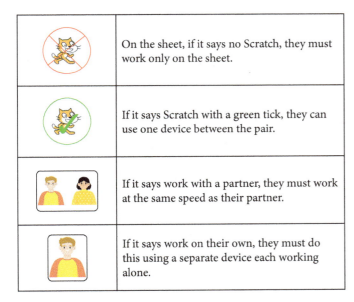

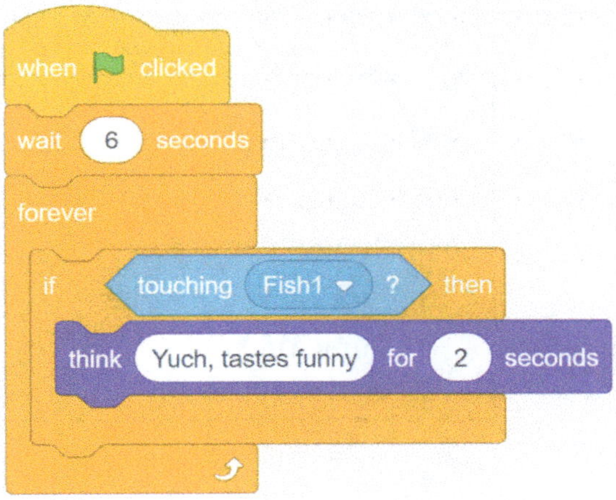

English Computing National Curriculum Programs of Study

Pupils should be taught to:

- **design, write and debug programs that accomplish specific goals,** including controlling or simulating physical systems; solve problems by decomposing them into smaller parts
- **use sequence,** selection and **repetition in programs;** work with variables **and various forms of input and output**
- **use logical reasoning to explain how some simple algorithms work and to detect and correct errors in algorithms and programs**

Scottish Curriculum for Excellence Technologies

I understand the instructions of a visual programming language and can predict the outcome of a program written using the language. TCH 1-14a

I can explain core programming language concepts in appropriate technical language TCH 2-14a

I can demonstrate a range of basic problem solving skills by building simple programs to carry out a given task, using an appropriate language. TCH 1-15a

I can create, develop and evaluate computing solutions in response to a design challenge. TCH 2-15a

Welsh National Curriculum Relevant Strands

Progression Step 3.

- I can use conditional statements to add control and decision-making to algorithms.
- I can explain and debug algorithms.

OCEAN POLLUTION PARSONS

Work with a partner

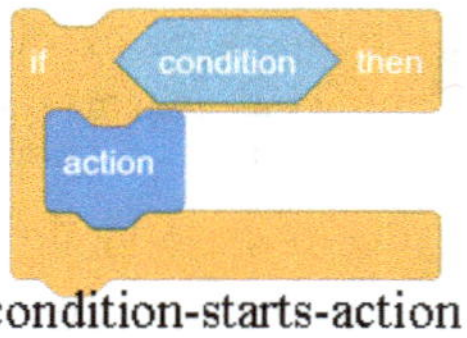

condition-starts-action

Start Scratch and Load
Ocean Pollution Game Parsons

Look inside the diving beetle sprite
The code has been collected but not assembled in the right order.
Use the algorithms below to help you complete the code.

Start on green flag
Pause 6 secs
Loop always
    If touching light grey
        Stop everything
	Start of green flag
	Go x219 y153
	Pause 6 seconds
	Point down
	Loop always
	    Move 1 step
	    Bounce if hit sides
		Start on green flag
		Pause 6 seconds
		Loop always
		    If left arrow key pressed
		        Turn left 15 degrees

Start on green flag
Wait 6 seconds
Loop always
    If touching Fish1 sprite
        Think Yuch
	Start on green flag
	Pause 6 secs
	Loop always
	    If right arrow key touched
	        Turn right 15 degrees

Now use the Parsons marksheet to check your code is correct

SUPPORT PARSONS

Start Scratch and load Ocean Pollution game Parsons

Whole class advice

Load Ocean Pollution game Parsons code and then use the algorithm on this page to build the code. When you have completed it, run the code and check your answer with the marking sheet.

Send advice

Parsons problems can be made more complex by separating more blocks in the example Scratch code and saving that version as a new template.

Notes on the activity

This allow pupils to build part of the code first before investigating, modifying and creating code of their own. The algorithm is written in language similar but also different to the code. This helps pupils by enabling them to see an example of planning which will help them when they come to plan their own project. On its own, it is not enough deep thinking about the code to enable agency, but as a starter or SEN activity it is useful to see how code can be built.

Send advice

Parsons problems can be made less complex by connecting more blocks in the example Scratch code and saving that version as a new template.

Look inside the diving beetle sprite

The code has been collected but not assembled in the right order.

Use the algorithms below to help you complete the code.

Individual advice

Pointing out that the code affected by a condition or in a loop is indented can help some pupils.

Start on green flag
Pause 6 secs
Loop always
  If touching light grey
    Stop everything
	Start of green flag
	Go x219 y153
	Pause 6 seconds
	Point down
	Loop always
	  Move 1 step
	  Bounce if hit sides
		Start on green flag
		Pause 6 seconds
		Loop always
		  If left arrow key pressed
		    Turn left 15 degrees

Start on green flag
Wait 6 seconds
Loop always
  If touching Fish1 sprite
    Think Yuch
	Start on green flag
	Pause 6 secs
	Loop always
	  If right arrow key touched
	    Turn right 15 degrees

Understanding programming

You can find out more about Parsons problems in the teacher book, Chapter 19.

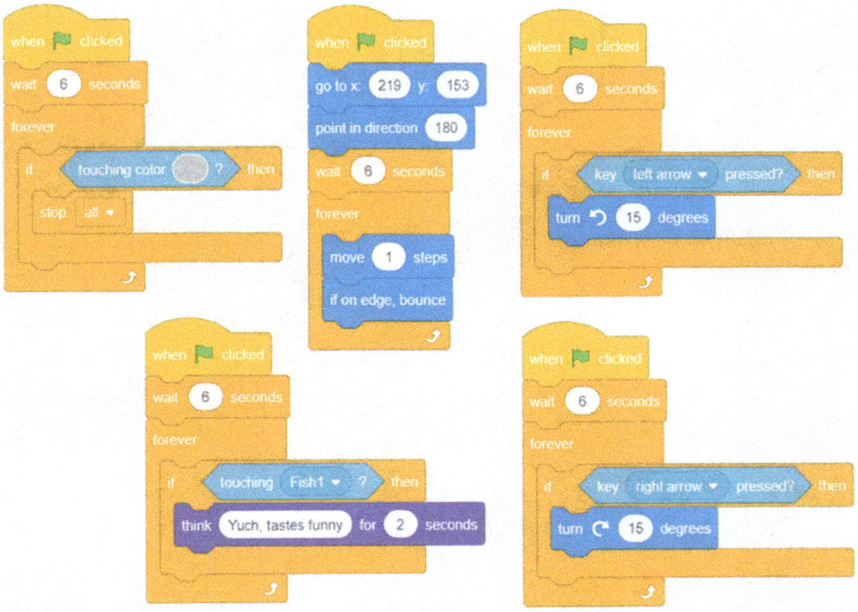

OCEAN POLLUTION FLOW

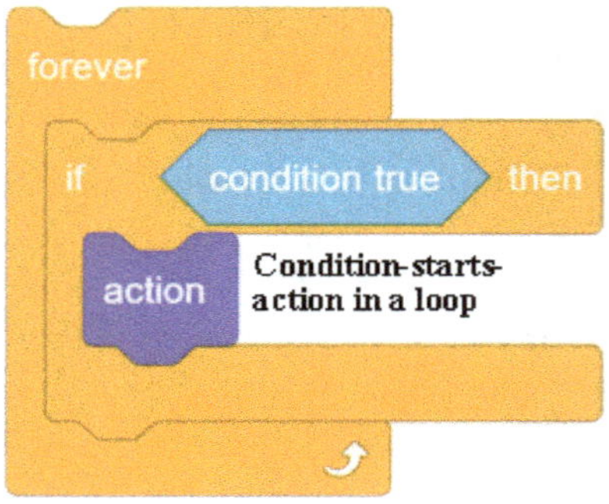

Complete the flow of control pathways for these programming sections. Dots to show actions. Arrows back to show loops. Pathways to show where conditions take two paths. Write in each condition as a question and mark yes and no on the pathways.

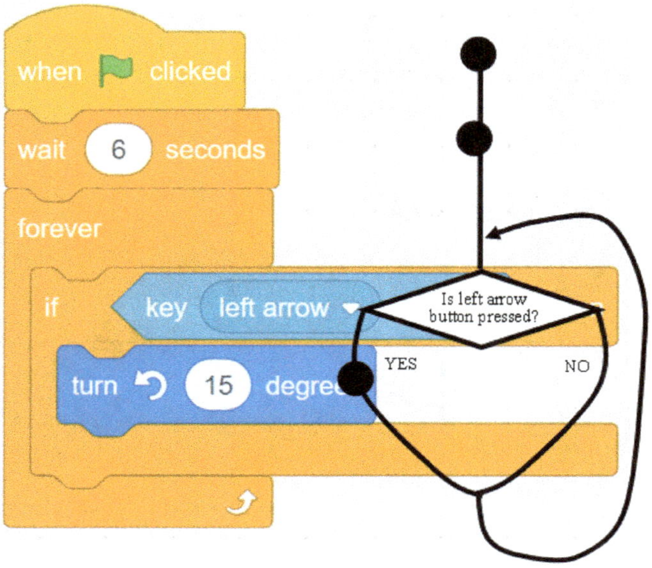

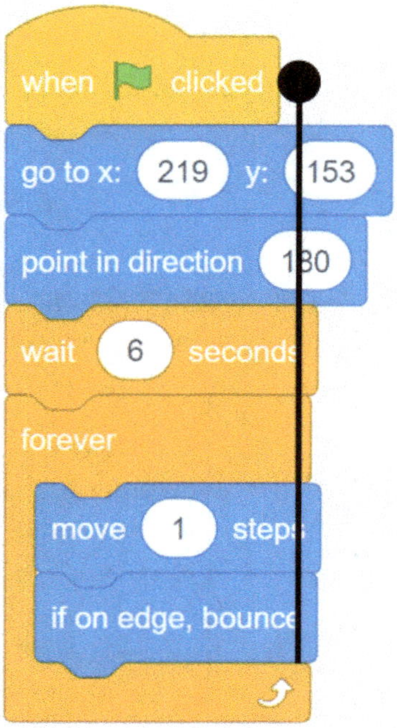

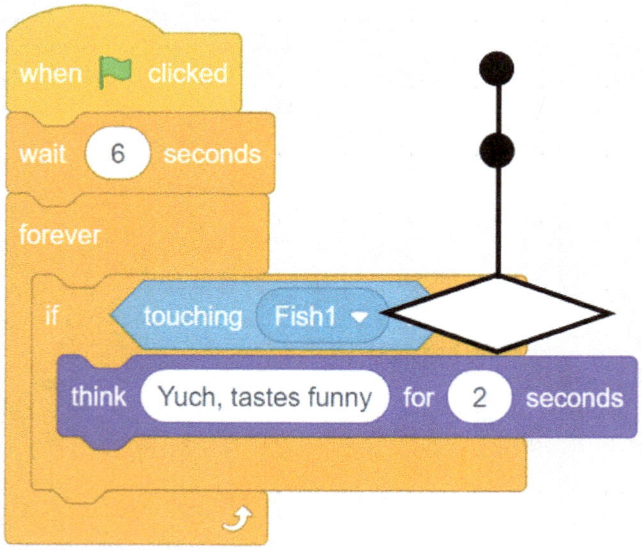

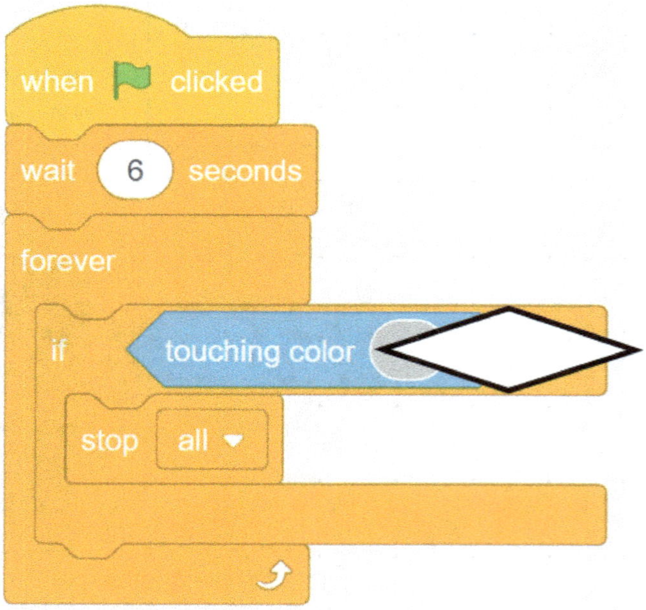

SUPPORTING FLOW

Complete the flow of control pathways for these programming sections. Dots to show actions. Arrows back to show loops. Pathways to show where conditions take two paths. Write in each condition as a question and mark yes and no on the pathways.

Individual advice

Go through the top left example and role-play it with pupils as you have done during the concept introduction

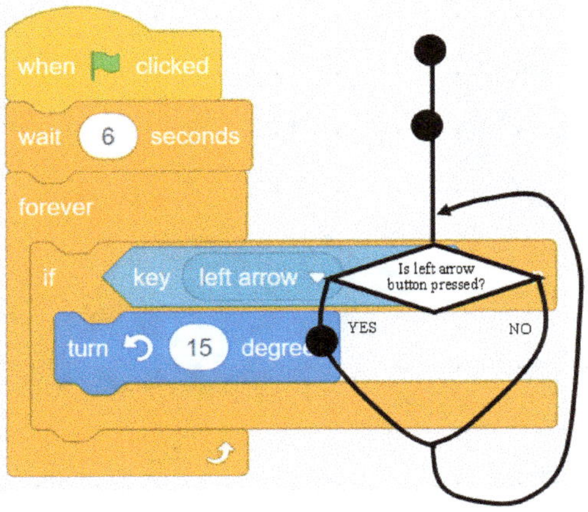

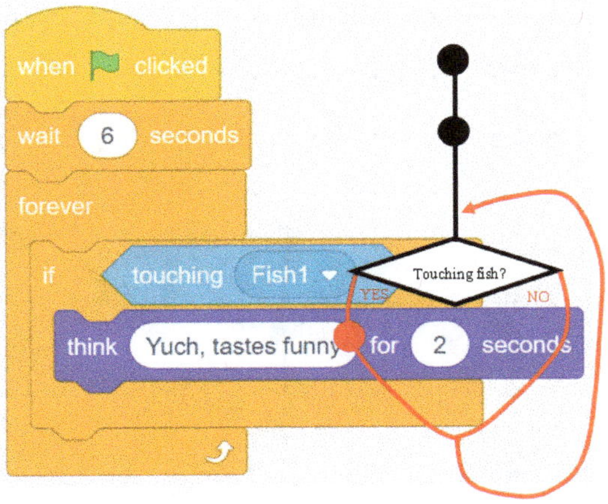

1 mark for the two paths

1 mark for the loop which must go back to forever

1 mark for one dot inside the loop

1 mark for question inside condition

1 mark for yes and no

Notes on the activity

This activity builds on the concept introduction. It could also be used to work with SEN pupils or individual pupils who struggle with the key concept.

Whole class advice

Look at this code carefully. Now draw the flow of control on top of the code as a line and each action as a dot. The top left one has been done for you.

Send advice

Support pairs of pupils who are poor readers by reading questions, reading code samples and covering up questions until they get to them.

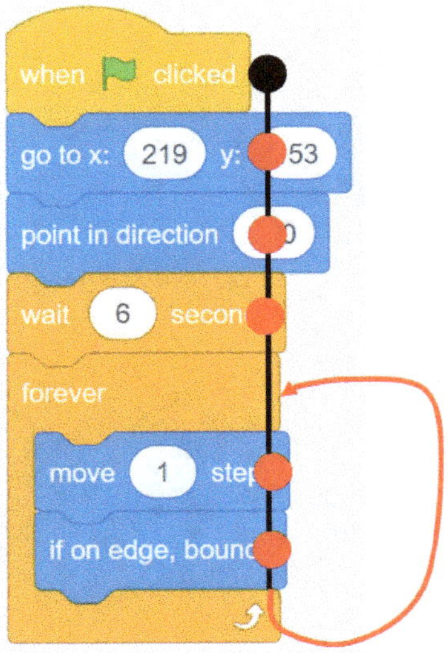

1 mark for dots above the loop

1 mark for the loop which must go back to forever

1 mark for two dots inside the loop

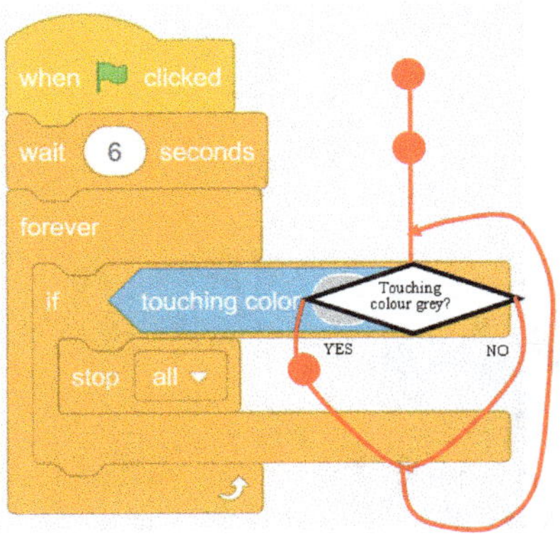

1 mark for the two paths

1 mark for the loop which must go back to forever

1 mark for one dot inside the loop

1 mark for two dots before the condition

1 mark for question inside condition

1 mark for yes and no

OCEAN POLLUTION PREDICT

Tick the correct prediction for each code block

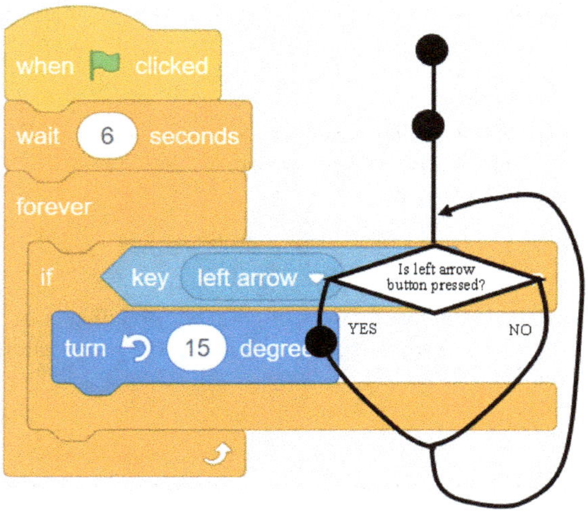

Tick the correct prediction

- ☐ Steer right
- ☐ Explain how to play
- ☐ Steer left
- ☐ Move continuously
- ☐ End game if touching grey pollution
- ☐ Say something if touch a fish
- ☐ Go to next level

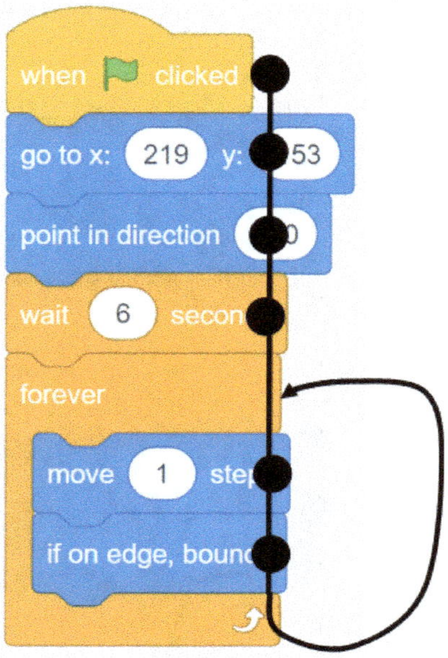

Tick the correct prediction

- ☐ Steer right
- ☐ Explain how to play
- ☐ Steer left
- ☐ Move continuously
- ☐ End game if touching grey pollution
- ☐ Say something if touch a fish
- ☐ Go to next level

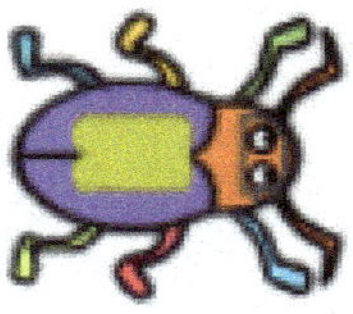

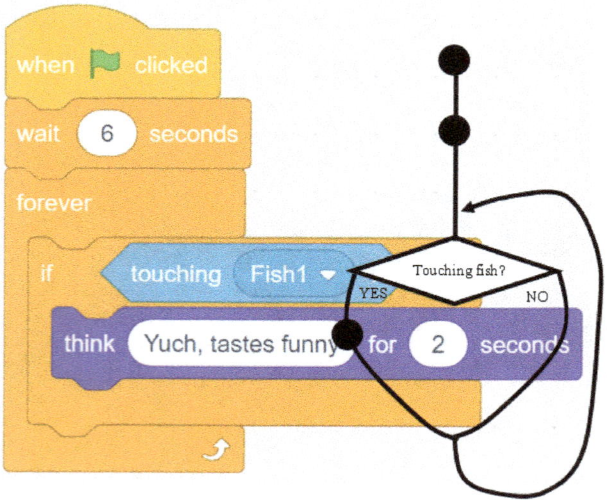

Tick the correct prediction

- ☐ Steer right
- ☐ Explain how to play
- ☐ Steer left
- ☐ Move continuously
- ☐ End game if touching grey pollution
- ☐ Say something if touch a fish
- ☐ Go to next level

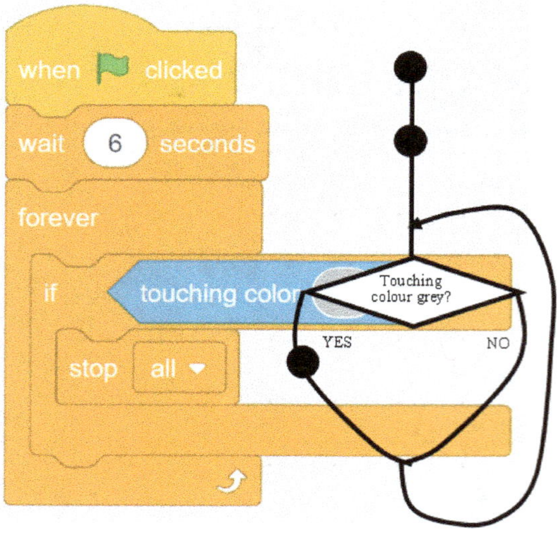

Tick the correct prediction

- ☐ Steer right
- ☐ Explain how to play
- ☐ Steer left
- ☐ Move continuously
- ☐ End game if touching grey pollution
- ☐ Say something if touch a fish
- ☐ Go to next level

SUPPORTING PREDICT

Whole class advice

Make sure you work with your partner on this sheet. Take it in turns to read a section and tell your partner what you think it does. Then answer the questions using your understanding of the code.

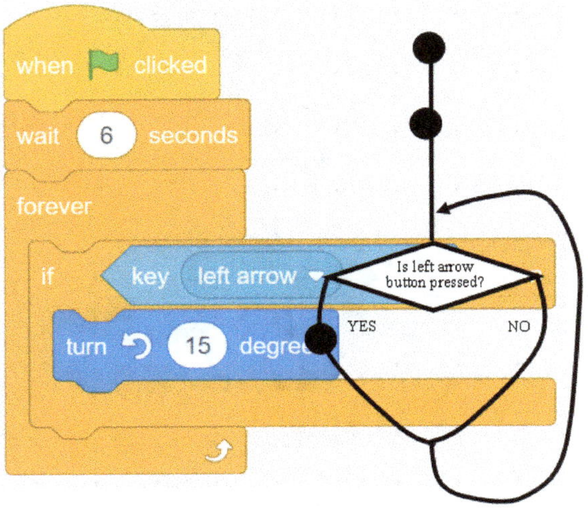

Tick the correct prediction

- ☐ Steer right
- ☐ Explain how to play
- ☐ Steer left (1 mark)
- ☐ Move continuously
- ☐ End game if touching grey pollution
- ☐ Say something if touch a fish
- ☐ Go to next level

Individual Pupil Support

Role-play a question with pupils as you have done during the concept introduction.

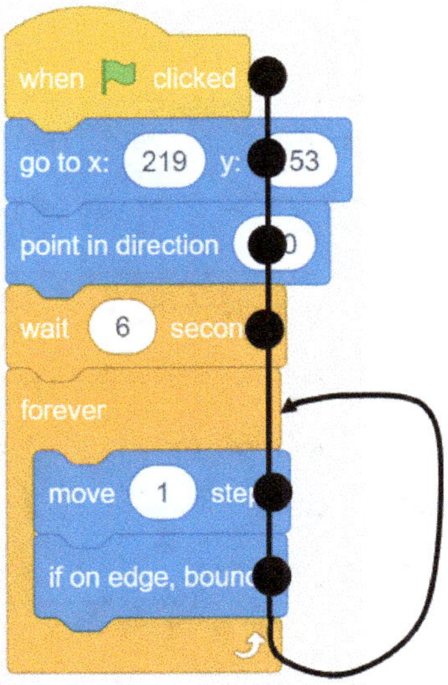

Notes on the activity

This optional activity helps pupils to think about the bigger purpose of the program before they start looking at parts of it in later sections.

Send advice

Support pairs of pupils who are poor readers by reading questions, reading code samples and covering up questions until they get to them.

Individual advice

Keywords helps in this activity.

Tick the correct prediction

- ☐ Steer right
- ☐ Explain how to play
- ☐ Steer left
- ☐ Move continuously (1 mark)
- ☐ End game if touching grey pollution
- ☐ Say something if touch a fish
- ☐ Go to next level

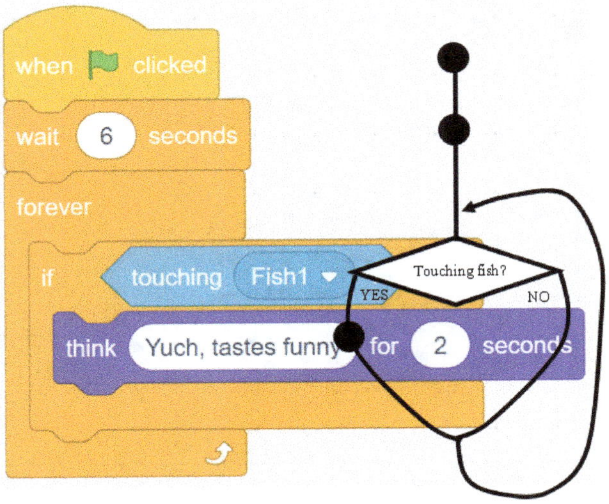

Tick the correct prediction

- ☐ Steer right
- ☐ Explain how to play
- ☐ Steer left
- ☐ Move continuously
- ☐ End game if touching grey pollution
- ☐ Say something if touch a fish (1 mark)
- ☐ Go to next level

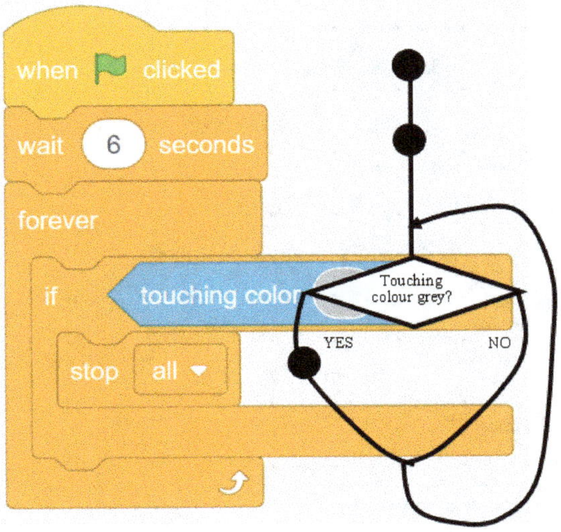

Tick the correct prediction

- ☐ Steer right
- ☐ Explain how to play
- ☐ Steer left
- ☐ Move continuously
- ☐ End game if touching grey pollution (1 mark)
- ☐ Say something if touch a fish
- ☐ Go to next level

Ocean Pollution
EXAMINE PLAN

Work with a partner

Condition-starts-action in a loop.

Loop always
    If touch fish
        End game

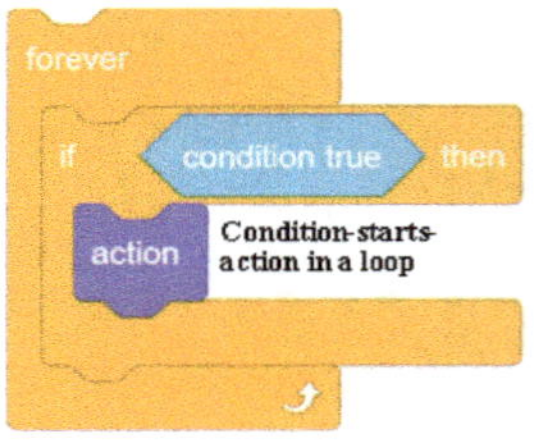
forever
if
condition true
then
action
Condition-starts-action in a loop

EXAMINE PLAN

Have a look at the design of this game. Answer the questions below.

Idea Level *My game will... My characters will be... The aim of the game will be....*

A beetle tries to catch a small fish whilst avoiding clouds of pollution.

Design Level What will your characters do?

Beetle – Move ① – Touch pollution end game
②–Turn right right arrow key
③–Turn left left arrow key
④ –Touch fish end game

Fish – touch beetle hide ⑤
– Move + bounce ⑥
– Touch pollution move faster ⑦

Pollution – Start anywhere
– Move any direction

Design Level (Draw your game simply and use **condition-starts-action** in your algorithms)

① Beetle Move
Loop always
    move ½ step
    Bounce on edge

② Loop always
    If press right arrow
        turn right 20°

③ Loop always
    If press left arrow
        turn left 20°

④ Loop always
    If touch fish sprite
        end game

⑤ Loop always
    If touch beetle
        hide

⑥ Loop always
    Move 2 step
    Bounce

⑦ Loop always
    If touch colour of pollution
        Move more steps

Beetle start (x+y)

Fish start (x + y)

Pollution Random

Initialisation Jot down how your sprites will always start in the same place

x+y blocks for start of fish and Beetle.

1. Circle all the **conditions-starts-action inside loops** that you can see.
2. Underline all the **initialisation** (thinking about start positions or clearing old program effects) you can see.

Now mark your work using the answer sheet provided

Supporting EXAMINE PLAN

EXAMINE PLAN

Have a look at the design of this game. Answer the questions below.

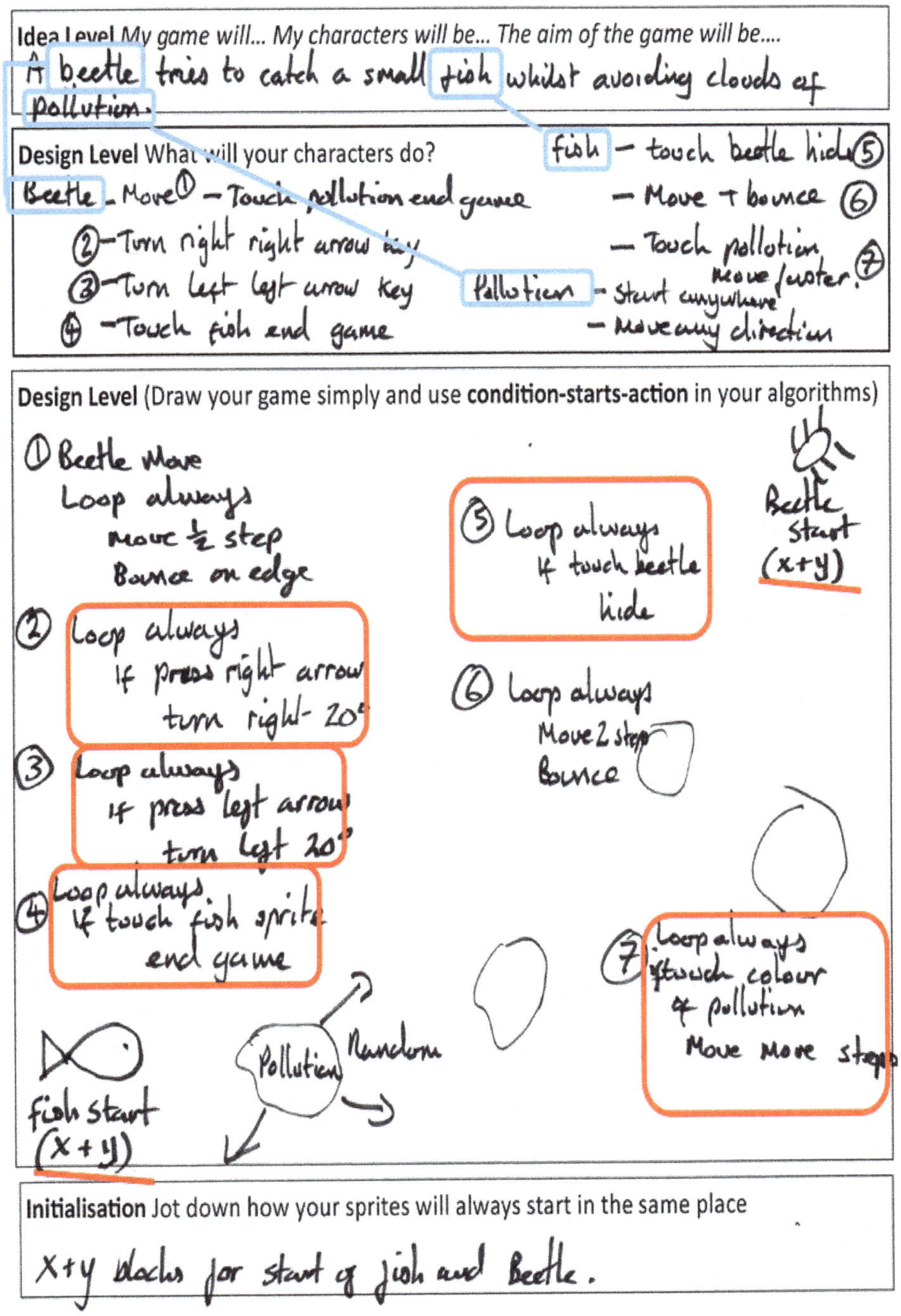

1. Circle all the conditions inside loops that you can see. (Max 5 marks)
2. Underline all the initialisation (thinking about start positions or clearing old program effects) you can see. (2 marks)

About the activity

In the last phase of this module, pupils will be asked to design and create their own game. Without examining a good example they will struggle. This activity forces them to look carefully at a planning example before needing to write their own later.

Whole Class Support

Work with your partner to examine the game plan before you go and examine the Ocean Pollution code. Make sure you answer the two questions below. Do not run any code while doing this activity.

SEN Support

Cover the three bottom sections while you are looking at the ideas level then reveal the top design level. Can pupils see how the beetle, fish and pollution from the ideas level have been defined/expanded in the top design level? (Light Blue)

When you reveal the bottom design level, can pupils spot how the information on what the characters will do in the top design level have been turned into algorithms in the bottom design level? The numbers from both design levels match.

You may wish to read text as it is written rather than typed, making it harder to read.

Q1 Support

Remember conditions start with if and you can spot loops. Conditions are also indented.

Q2 Initialisation Support

Remember initialisation is about making each character work in the same way every time the code is run. In games, this is often about sending a character back to the same starting point and or pointing them in a common direction. What code sends things to specific places? Answer go to x & y.

Whole class Support

You can plan with the whole class or a group using the last four slides in condition-starts-action-in-a-loop slides.

OCEAN POLLUTION INVESTIGATE

Work with a partner

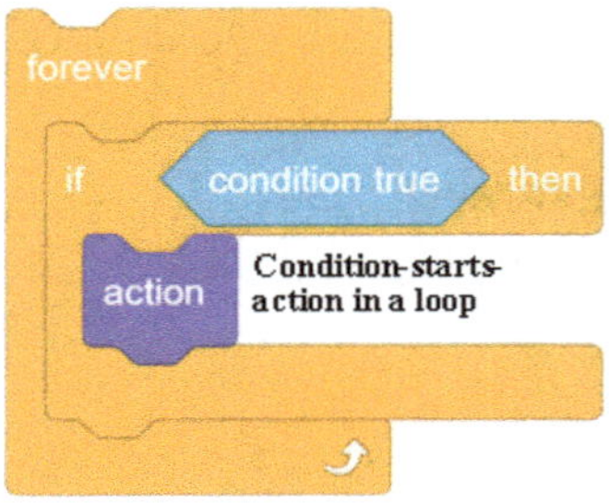
forever
if
condition true
then
action
Condition-starts-action in a loop

Start Scratch and Load Ocean Pollution Game

USE the code (Run the program lots of times but don't change the code)

Look at the code inside diving beetle sprite

1. What will happen if the diving beetle touches the Fish1 sprite (controlled diving beetle code)?

2. What loop are all the if then condition-starts-action blocks inside?

3. Which section of code hasn't got a condition? Write down what is inside the loop

4. What happens if you press the right arrow key?

Look at the code inside fish1 sprite (fish costumes may differ)

Fish1 Sprite Questions

5. What direction is the fish1 sprite pointing at the start of the game (initialisation code)?

6. What code block *creates* a fish1 clone (programmed copy or itself)?

7. How many sections of code start once a clone has been created? *HINT Starting block mentions clone*

8. If a fish1 clone touches the diving beetle, what two things happen (controlled by fish1 code)?

9. How many seconds before a new fish1 clone is created?

Look at the code inside pollution1 sprite

Pollution1 sprite Questions

10. What size does the pollution1 sprite start at (initialisation code)?

11. After one second, what size will the pollution1 sprite be?

12. How fast does the pollution1 sprite move?

Now mark your investigate work using the marksheet

Supporting Investigate

Whole class advice

Work in pairs, one device between the pair. Take it in turns every question to swap who runs code. You must work at the same pace as your partner and not move on to the next question until you have both written your answer down. If you disagree, write a different answer. You must mark your work before moving on to the next section.

USE the code (Run the programs lots of times but don't change the code)

Look at the code inside diving beetle sprite 

1. What will happen if the diving beetle touches the fish1 sprite *(diving beetle code)?*

   Think Yuch, tastes funny for 2 seconds (1 mark)

2. What loop are all the if then condition-starts-action blocks inside?

   Forever loops (1 mark)

3. Which section of code **hasn't** got a condition? *Write down what is inside the loop*

   Move 1 step, If on edge bounce (1 mark for either)

4. What happens if you press the right arrow key?

   Turn right 15 degrees (1 mark)

Look at the code inside Fish1 sprite 
(fish costumes may differ)

Fish1 Sprite Questions

5. What direction is the fish1 sprite pointing at the start of the game (initialisation code)?

   90 degrees or right (1 mark)

6. What code block *creates* a fish1 clone (programmed copy of itself)?

   Create clone of myself (1 mark)

7. How many sections of code start once a clone has been created? *HINT Starting block mentions clone*

   3 (all start with when I start as a clone) (1 mark)

8. If a fish1 clone touches the diving beetle, what two things happen (controlled by fish1 code)?

   Change score by 1 or one gets added to score and hide (1 mark for both). It does also say Yuch, but that is not controlled by fish1 code

9. How many seconds before a new fish1 clone is created? Between 3 and 5 seconds (1 mark)

Look at the code inside pollution1 sprite

Pollution1 Sprite Questions

10. What size does the pollution1 sprite start at (initialisation code)?

    100% (1 mark)

11. After one second what size will the pollution1 sprite be?

    110% (1 mark)

12. How fast does the pollution1 sprite move?

    0.2 steps (1mark)

Now mark your investigate work using the marksheet

Notes on the activity

Investigating the code encourages pupils to think deeply about how it works. Sometimes one pupil in a pair decides to work faster than their partner; check that this is not happening and that every pupil is filling in and marking the questions individually but at the pace of the slowest in the pair. Sometimes a pair decides not to mark to speed up their efforts. Marking gives valuable information ,so I recommend sending them back to mark their work if this is the case. A class instruction to come and talk to you if they have over half of the questions wrong or they do not understand the answer after they have marked it helps to check progress is being made correctly. There is real value in collecting these scores to build up a summative picture of pupil progress.

Q1 Support

It can be tempting to just look at the program effects rather than the code. Pupils need to look at the code to get this questions correct. Some of the effects are programmed elsewhere.

Q3 Support

Remind pupils that conditions start with if.

Q6 & 7 Support

Explain that the cloning effect creates copies of the same sprite that only run the code inside the when I start as a clone blocks

Q8 Support

It also thinks Yuch... but that is not programmed in this sprite. Remind pupils that the answer is only within the code in that sprite.

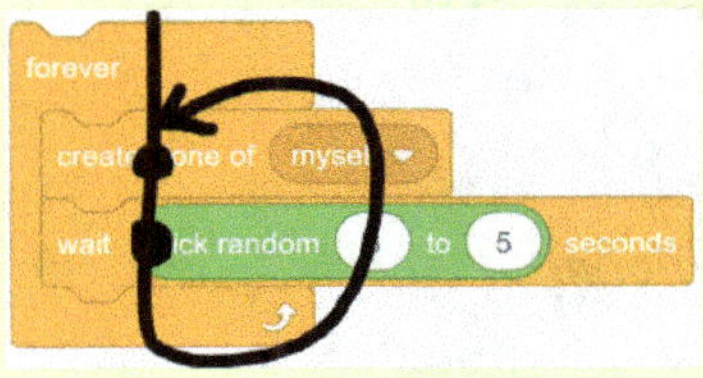

Q9 Support

Remind pupils of the flow of control, as shown above. What happens when it gets to the wait block?

Send advice

Hide questions that you are not working on with a book or piece of paper

Understanding Programming

Cloning allows many instances of a sprite to be run. They tend to all do the same type of thing, but there can be significant differences. Each clone fish chooses a random fish costume. They all also start on a random place in the Y axis. The pollution bubbles could also have been made as clones.

Whole class advice

Check that pupils are marking work, as it is easier to help pupils soon after they have completed work than in later weeks.

OCEAN POLLUTION CHANGE

Work with a partner

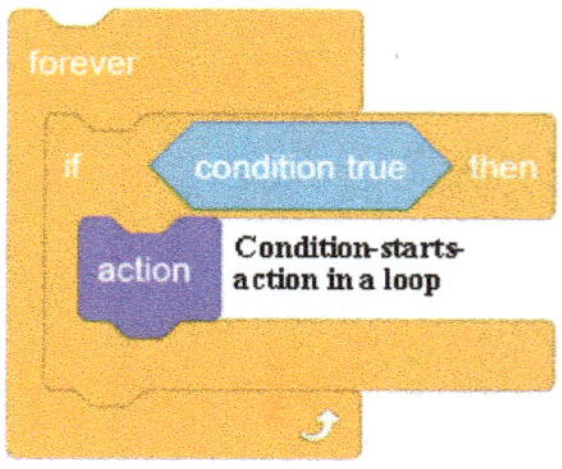
forever
if
condition true
then
action
Condition starts action in a loop

Change (Run the code and make small changes)

Diving Beetle Questions

1. Can you make the diving beetle move faster? What did you change?

2. Can you make the diving beetle turn slower? What did you change?

3. Can you make the diving beetle point to the left when it starts? What did you change?

Fish1 Sprite Questions

4. Can you make the fish1 clone move faster? What did you change?

5. Can you make the fish1 clone add two points to the score variable when it is caught?

6. Can you make the fish1 clones appear after 2 seconds rather than randomly?

Pollution1 Questions

7. Modify the code in pollution1. Can you make it start at 200%? What did you change? Is this a good idea? If yes or no why?

8. Modify the code in pollution1 so it starts at 300% and get smaller every second. What did you change to make it get smaller?

Pollution1 Optional Extension Question

9. Can you modify pollution1 so that it automatically generates 10 pollution sprite clones?
   A. You will need to delete all other pollution sprites
   B. You will need to add new code to create 10 clones *HINT Repeat 10 create clone of myself*
   C. You will need to change the green flag starting blocks for *when I start as a clone*
   D. You will need to hide the original pollution1
   HINT Examine fish1

Now mark this page using the marksheet

SUPPORTING CHANGE

Change (Run the code and make small changes)

Diving Beetle Questions 

1. Can you make the diving beetle move faster? What did you change?

   Change move 1 step to a higher number (1 mark)

2. Can you make the diving beetle turn slower? What did you change?

   Change both turn blocks to less than 15 degrees (1 mark)

3. Can you make the diving beetle point to the left when it starts? What did you change?

   Change point in direction 180 to –90 (1 mark)

Fish1 Sprite Questions 

4. Can you make the fish1 clone move faster? What did you change?

   Change move 0.5 steps to a higher number (1 mark)

5. Can you make the fish1 clone add two points to the score variable when it is caught?

   Modify change score by 1 to change score by 2 (1 mark)

6. Can you make a new fish1 clones appear after 2 seconds rather than randomly between 3 and 5 seconds?

   Either change pick random to 2 to 2 or remove the random block and adapt wait to 2 seconds (1 mark) for either solution

Pollution1 Questions 

7. Modify the code in pollution1. Xan you make it start at 200%? What did you change? Is this a good idea? If yes or no why?

   Change set size to 100% to set size to 200% (1 mark). It is not a good idea as the game is over even faster any similar answer (1 mark)

8. Modify the code in pollution1 so it starts at 300% and get smaller every second. What did you change to make it get smaller?

   Modify change size by 10 to change size by –10 or similar number (1 mark)

Pollution1 Optional Extension Question

9. Can you modify pollution1 so that it automatically generates 10 pollution sprite clones?

   A You will need to delete all other pollution sprites

   B You will need to add new code to create 10 clones HINT Repeat 10 *create clone of myself*

   C You will need to change the green flag starting blocks for *when I start as a clone*

   D You will need to hide the original pollution1

HINT Examine fish1

clone code

This is not the only way to create pollution 1 as a clone. If it works it is correct (5 marks)

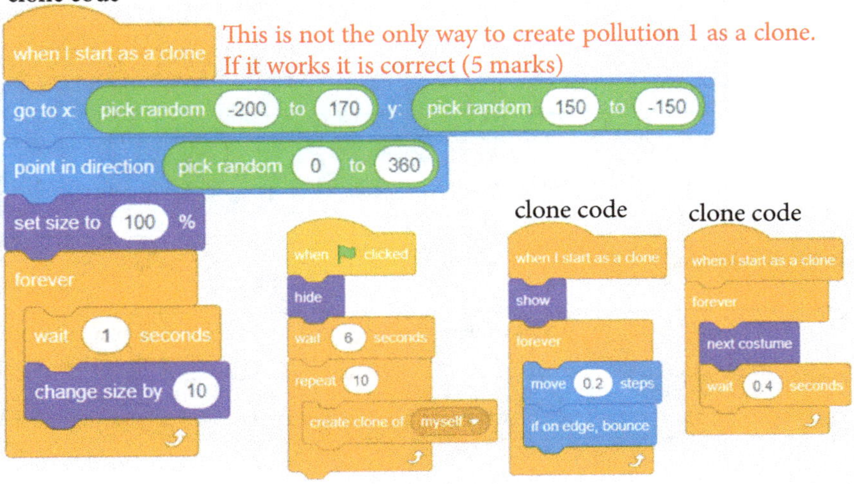

Notes on the activity

Changing or modifying the code is a core part of this module, so I suggest you do not leave it out. It is an important step towards creation of their own code.

Whole class advice

Work in pairs, one device between the pair. Take it in turns every question to swap who runs code. You must work at the same pace as your partner and not move on to the next question until you have both written your answer down. If you disagree, write a different answer. You must mark your work before moving on to the next section.

Q1, 2 and 3 are revision questions

Looking for keywords in the question will help.

Q5 Hint variable blocks are orange

How is it giving one point to the score when fish is caught at the moment? If pupils really struggle with this question, tell them we will do more on this in year 6.

Q6

HINT what is underneath pick random 3 to 5.

Q7

The question mentions starting at a % size. Which percent block will be run first in the sequence?

Q8

Firstly, what makes the pollution get larger every second?

Secondly, when you change **size by** you are adding 10. What is the inverse to add?

Q9

Point out the green flag code that creates clones. Then point out the three clone blocks that are triggered when a clone is created.

OCEAN POLLUTION CREATE

Work on your own

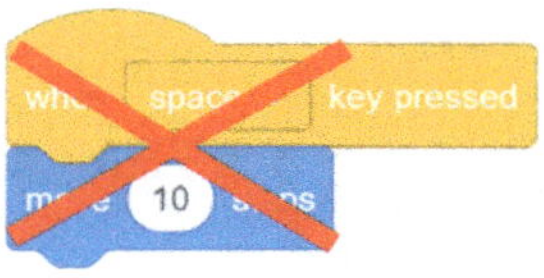
key pressed
10

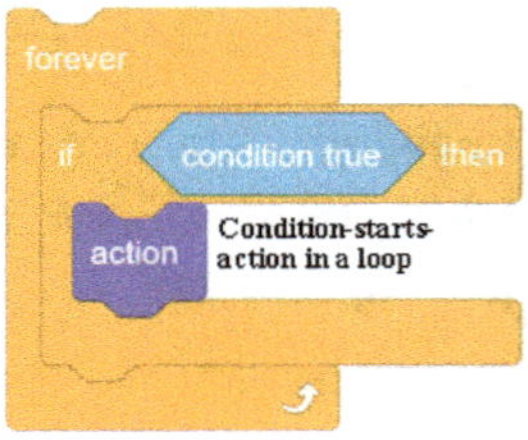
forever
if
condition true
then
action
Condition-starts-action in a loop

You can share design ideas, but must plan and code separately

Examine the plan first to help you plan

PLAN

Design and code your own game that uses **condition-starts-actions**. You can adapt any ideas from the Diving Beetle or other games.

Idea Level *My game will… My characters will be… The aim of the game will be….*

What will your characters do?

Design Level (Draw your game simply and add **condition-starts-action** algorithms)

Teacher & Pupil Assessment Circle the stage that you think you have reached in each row, your teacher will check it.

	Not used a condition checked in a loop	Copied a condition checked in a loop from ocean pollution	Copied and changed condition checked in a loop from ocean pollution	Found own use for a condition checked in a loop
Indefinite (forever) loops	0 marks	1 mark	2 marks	3 marks

	Not used previous programming concepts for real purpose	Used previous programming concepts for real purpose
Used previous programming concept such as count-controlled loops	0 marks	1 mark

	No theme in planning or code	Has a theme in planning or code
Has a project theme in planning or code	0 marks	1 mark

Supporting CREATE

Alternative Method of Delivery

An alternate method to cover this is to work with the whole class on the planning process together using last slides on the introduction to condition starts action in a loop.

Individual Support Ideas Level

There are some example game ideas to copy and adapt on slide 18 on the introduction to condition starts action in a loop.

Whole class advice

Once you have written an idea it is important to break that idea up into objects (sprites, backgrounds, sounds, etc.).

Then take each object and list everything that object will do and how it will do it. For example, turn right using right arrow key. You must break it up into its smallest elements. You can't say steer, because steer is turn right and turn left.

Then, once you have the list of commands, each one must be turned into an algorithm as shown.

You can write a few algorithms and then turn these into code before planning more.

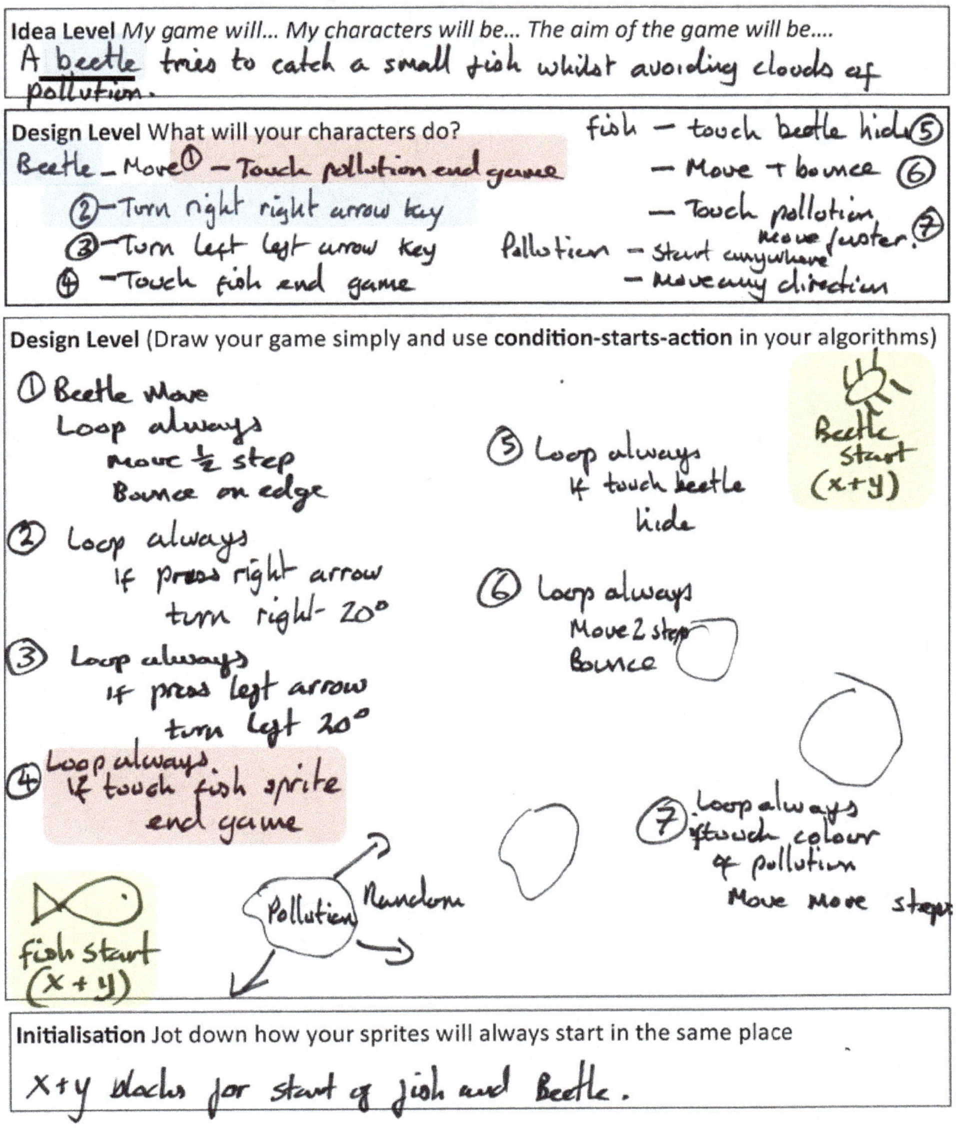

Idea Level *My game will... My characters will be... The aim of the game will be....*

A beetle tries to catch a small fish whilst avoiding clouds of pollution.

Design Level What will your characters do?

Beetle – Move ① – Touch pollution end game
②– Turn right right arrow key
③– Turn left left arrow key
④ – Touch fish end game

fish – touch beetle hide ⑤
– Move + bounce ⑥
– Touch pollution, move faster. ⑦

Pollution – Start anywhere
– Move any direction

Design Level (Draw your game simply and use **condition-starts-action** in your algorithms)

① Beetle Move
Loop always
Move ½ step
Bounce on edge

② Loop always
If press right arrow
turn right 20°

③ Loop always
If press left arrow
turn left 20°

④ Loop always
If touch fish sprite
end game

⑤ Loop always
If touch beetle
hide

⑥ Loop always
Move 2 step
Bounce

⑦ Loop always
If touch colour of pollution
Move more steps

Beetle Start (x+y)

Pollution Random

fish Start (x + y)

Initialisation Jot down how your sprites will always start in the same place

x+y blocks for start of fish and Beetle.

Individual Support Ideas Level

Underline each character and object in your idea and list everything that object will do and how it will do it. For example, turn right using right arrow key. You must break it up into its smallest elements. You can't say steer, because steer is turn right and turn left.

Then point to blue highlighted examples in idea and design level.

Individual Support Design Level list to Design level algorithm

Take one idea such as touch fish end game and turn it into an algorithm.

Then point to pink highlighted examples in design levels to illustrate how that is done.

Remind the pupils how they role-played and wrote everyday conditions in loops.

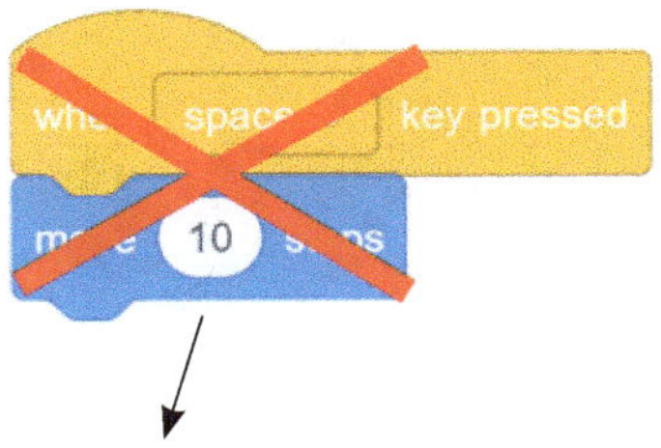

Individual Support Initialisation

Ask pupils where will their sprites start from? Can they use and x and y block to make them start there every time? Which direction will the sprite face when it starts? Can they use a point in direction block to make the sprite start in the same direction each time? What size will their sprite be? Can they use a set size to block to make this the same every time?

Then point to yellow highlighted examples in design levels to illustrate how that could be done.

Banned Scripts

Explain that pupils might have used blocks like these to move or turn, but that these methods of programming do not work in any other programming language. They are there to help very young people make things. In this module they are banned. You can use both blocks but not together or in this way.

PARSONS MARKSHEET ANSWERS

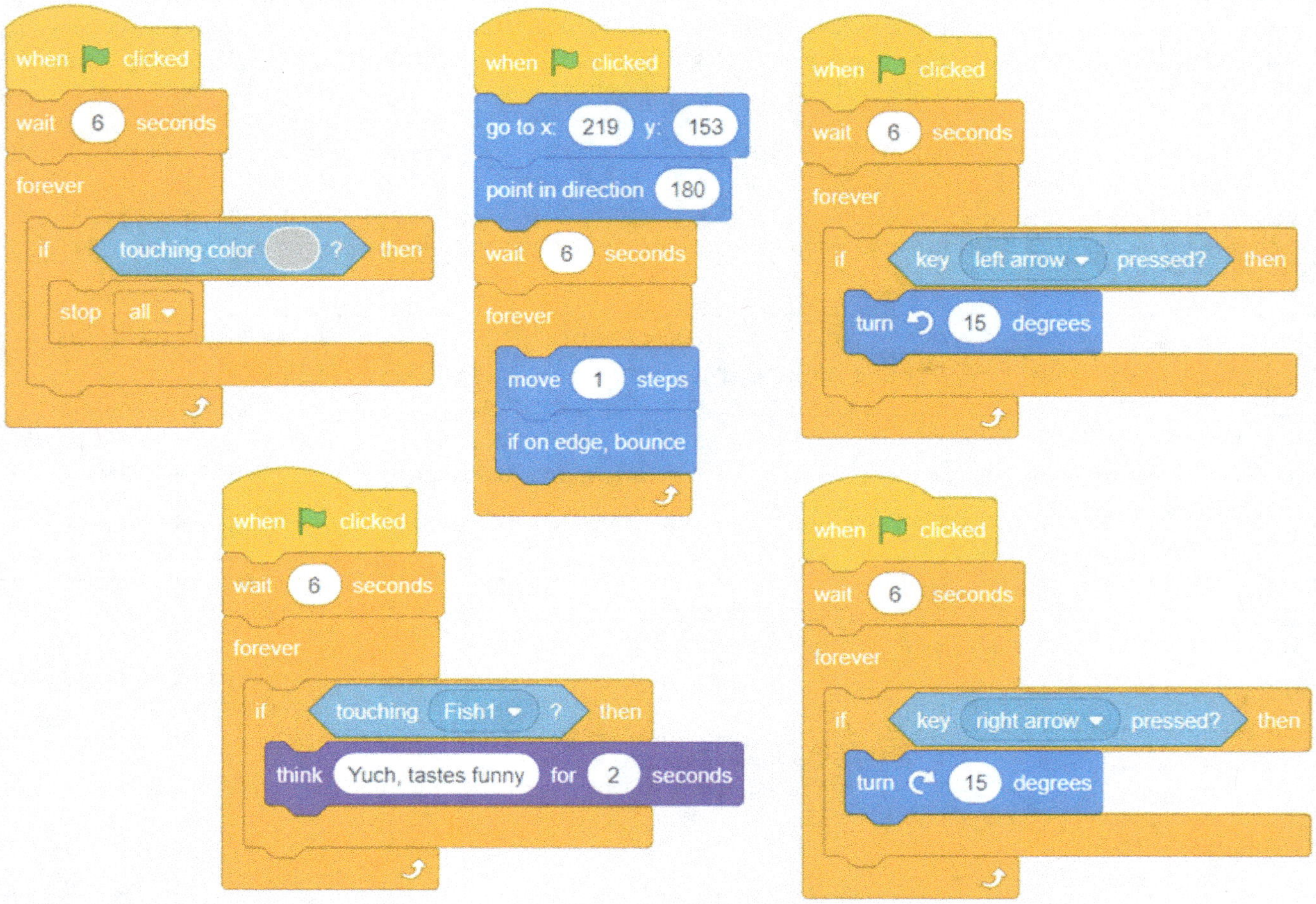

FLOW MARKSHEET

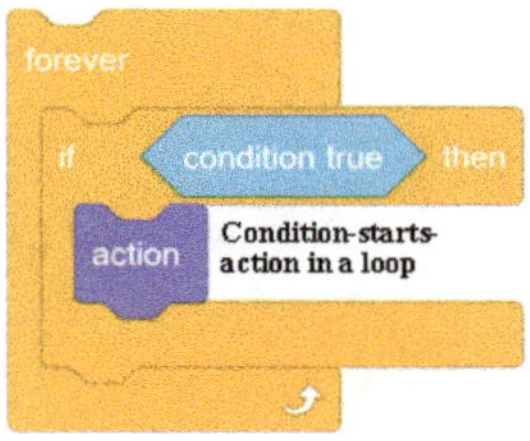

Complete the flow of control pathways for these programming sections. Dots to show actions. Arrows back to show loops. Pathways to show where conditions take two paths. Write in each condition as a question and mark yes and no on the pathways.

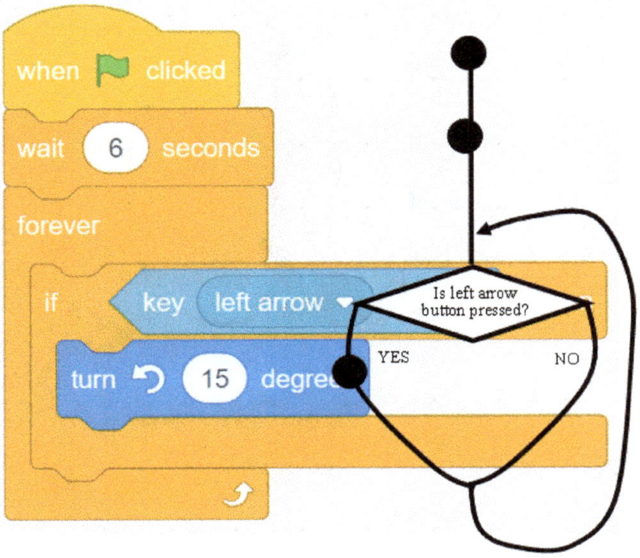

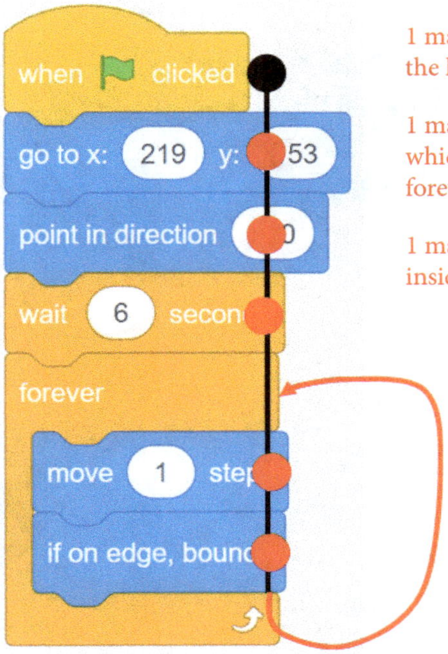

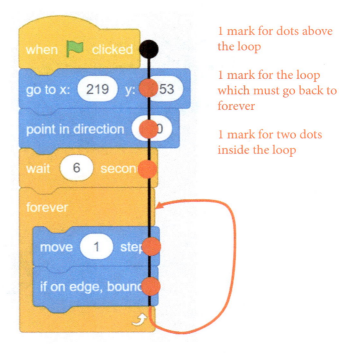

1 mark for dots above the loop

1 mark for the loop which must go back to forever

1 mark for two dots inside the loop

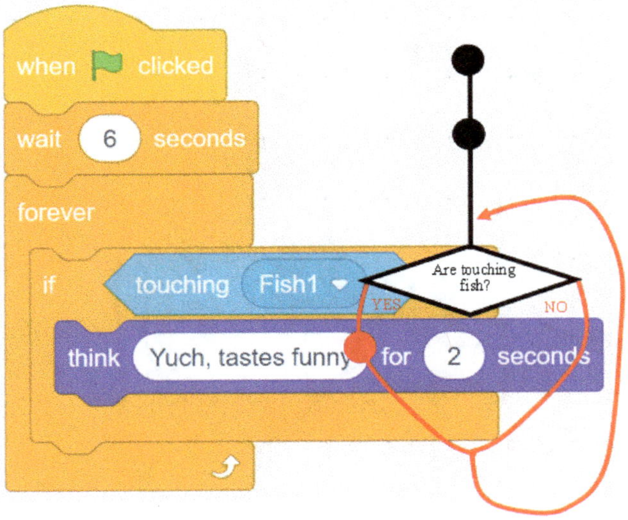

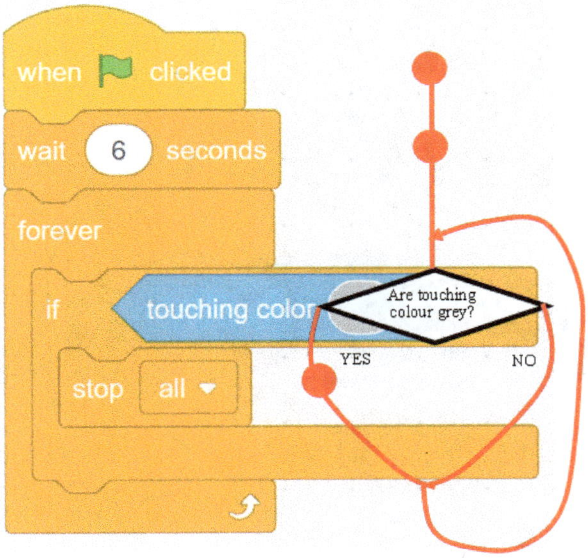

1 mark for the two paths

1 mark for the loop which must go back to forever

1 mark for one dot inside the loop

1 mark for question inside condition

1 mark for yes and no

1 mark for the two paths

1 mark for the loop which must go back to forever

1 mark for one dot inside the loop

1 mark for two dots before the condition

1 mark for question inside condition

1 mark for yes and no

PREDICT MARKSHEET

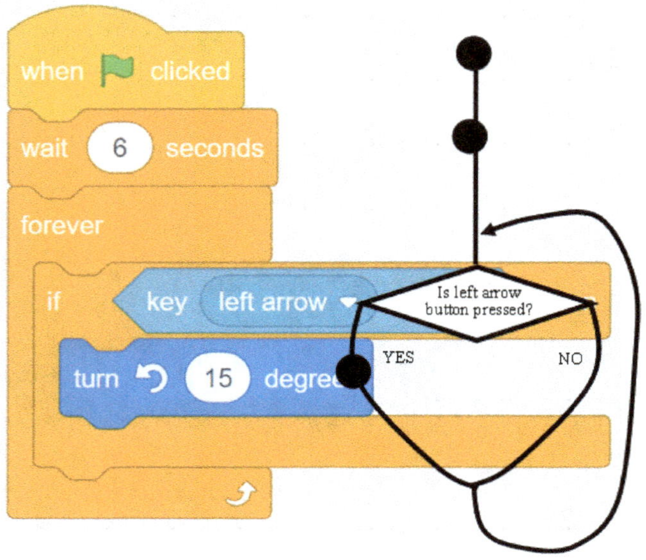

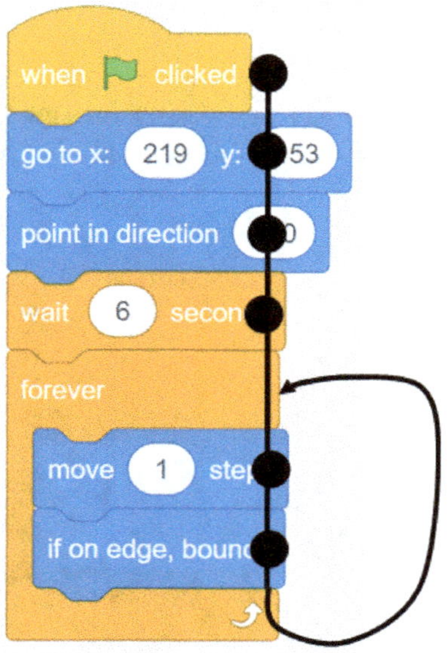

Tick the correct prediction

- ☐ Steer right
- ☐ Explain how to play
- ☐ Steer left (1 mark)
- ☐ Move continuously
- ☐ End game if touching grey pollution
- ☐ Say something if touch a fish
- ☐ Go to next level

Tick the correct prediction

- ☐ Steer right
- ☐ Explain how to play
- ☐ Steer left
- ☐ Move continuously (1 mark)
- ☐ End game if touching grey pollution
- ☐ Say something if touch a fish
- ☐ Go to next level

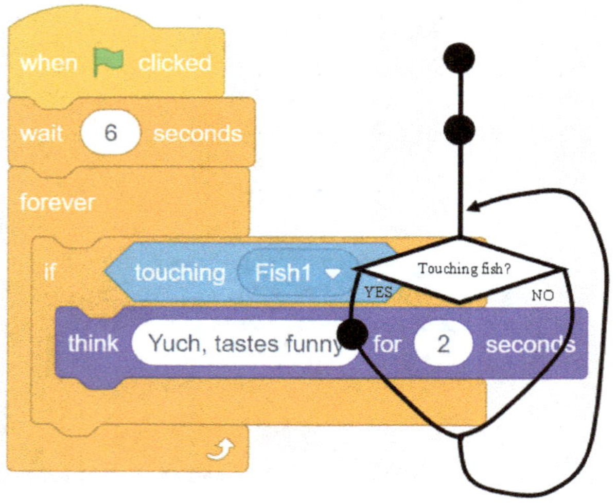

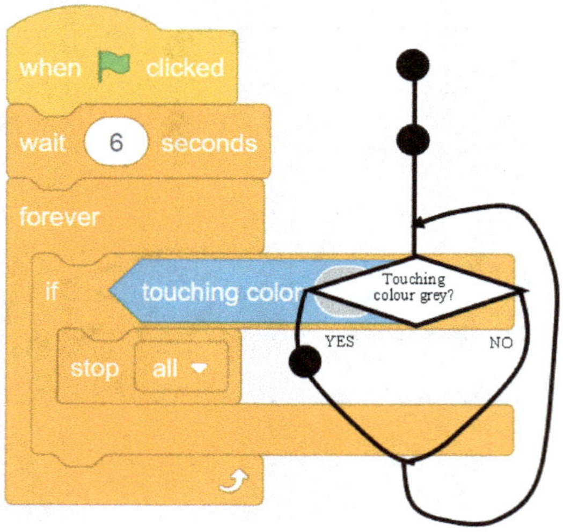

Tick the correct prediction

- ☐ Steer right
- ☐ Explain how to play
- ☐ Steer left
- ☐ Move continuously
- ☐ End game if touching grey pollution
- ☐ Say something if touch a fish (1 mark)
- ☐ Go to next level

Tick the correct prediction

- ☐ Steer right
- ☐ Explain how to play
- ☐ Steer left
- ☐ Move continuously
- ☐ End game if touching grey pollution (1 mark)
- ☐ Say something if touch a fish
- ☐ Go to next level

EXAMINE PLAN MARKSHEET

Work with a partner

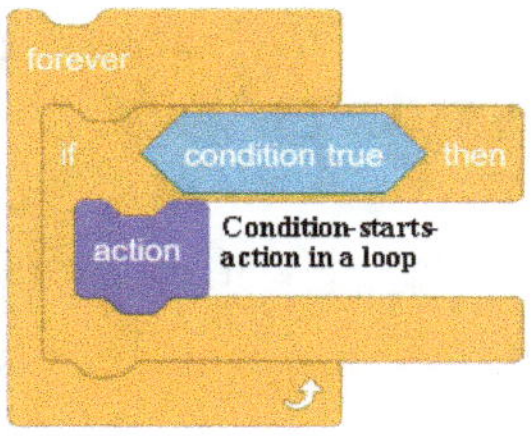
forever
if
condition true
then
action
Condition-starts-action in a loop

EXAMINE PLAN

Have a look at the design of this game. Answer the questions below.

Idea Level *My game will... My characters will be... The aim of the game will be....*

A beetle tries to catch a small fish whilst avoiding clouds of pollution.

Design Level What will your characters do?

Beetle – Move ①
– Touch pollution end game
② – Turn right right arrow key
③ – Turn left left arrow key
④ – Touch fish end game

fish – touch beetle hide ⑤
– Move + bounce ⑥
– Touch pollution move faster ⑦

Pollution – start anywhere
– Move any direction

Design Level (Draw your game simply and use **condition-starts-action** in your algorithms)

① Beetle Move
Loop always
move ½ step
Bounce on edge

② Loop always
If press right arrow
turn right 20°

③ Loop always
If press left arrow
turn left 20°

④ Loop always
If touch fish sprite
end game

⑤ Loop always
If touch beetle
hide

⑥ Loop always
Move 2 step
Bounce

⑦ Loop always
If touch colour of pollution
Move more steps

Beetle start (x+y)

Fish start (x+y)

Pollution
Random

Initialisation Jot down how your sprites will always start in the same place

x+y blocks for start of fish and Beetle.

1. Circle all the conditions inside loops that you can see. (max. 5 marks)
2. Underline all the initialisation (thinking about start positions or clearing old program effects) you can see. (2 marks)

OCEAN POLLUTION
INVESTIGATE MARKSHEET

USE the code (Run the programs lots of times but don't change the code)

Look at the code inside diving beetle sprite

1. What will happen if the diving beetle touches the fish1 sprite *(controlled diving beetle code)?*
   Think Yuch, tastes funny for 2 seconds (1 mark)
2. What loop are all the if then **condition-starts-action** blocks inside?
   Forever loops (1 mark)
3. Which section of code **hasn't** got a condition? *Write down what is inside the loop*
   Move 1 step, If on edge bounce (1 mark for either)
4. What happens if you press the right arrow key?
   Turn right 15 degrees (1 mark)

Look at the code inside fish1 sprite (fish costumes may differ)

Fish1 Sprite Questions

5. What direction is the fish1 sprite pointing at the start of the game (initialisation code)?
   90 degrees or right (1 mark)
6. What code block **creates** a fish1 clone (programmed copy or itself)?
   Create clone of myself (1 mark)
7. How many sections of code start once a clone has been created? *HINT Starting block mentions clone*
   3 (all start with when I start as a clone) (1 mark)
8. If a fish1 clone touches the diving beetle, what two things happen *(controlled by fish1 code)?*
   Change score by 1 or one gets added to score and hide (1 mark for both). It does also say Yuch, but that is not controlled by fish1 code
9. How many seconds before a new fish1 clone is created?
   Between 3 and 5 seconds (1 mark)

Look at the code inside pollution1 sprite

Pollution1 Sprite Questions

10. What size does the pollution1 sprite start at (initialisation code)?
    100% (1 mark)
11. After one second what size will the pollution1 sprite be?
    110% (1 mark)
12. How fast does the pollution1 sprite move?
    0.2 steps (1mark)

CHANGE MARKSHEET

MODIFY (Run the code and make small changes)

Diving Beetle Questions

1. Can you make the diving beetle move faster? What did you change?
   Change move 1 step to a higher number (1 mark)
2. Can you make the diving beetle turn slower? What did you change?
   Change both turn blocks to less than 15 degrees (1 mark)
3. Can you make the diving beetle point to the left when it starts? What did you change?
   Change point in direction 180 to –90 (1 mark)

Fish1 Sprite Questions

4. Can you make the fish1 clone move faster? What did you change?
   Change move 0.5 steps to a higher number (1 mark)
5. Can you make the fish1 clone add two points to the score variable when it is caught?
   Modify change score by 1 to change score by 2 (1 mark)
6. Can you make the fish1 clones appear after 2 seconds rather than randomly?
   Either change pick random to 2 to 2 or remove the random block and adapt wait to 2 seconds (1 mark for either solution)

Pollution1 Questions

7. Modify the code in pollution1. Can you make it start at 200%? What did you change? Is this a good idea? If yes or no why?
   Change set size to 100% to set size to 200% (1 mark). It is not a good idea, as the game is over even faster any similar answer (1 mark)
8. Modify the code in pollution1 so it starts at 300% and gets smaller every second. What did you change to make it get smaller?
   Modify change size by 10 to change size by –10 or similar number (1 mark)

Pollution1 Optional Extension Question

9. Can you modify pollution1 so that it automatically generates 10 pollution sprite clones?

A. You will need to delete all other pollution sprites

B. You will need to add new code to create 10 clones *HINT Repeat 10 create clone of myself*

C. You will need to change the green flag starting blocks for *when I start as a clone*

D. You will need to hide the original pollution1

HINT Examine fish1

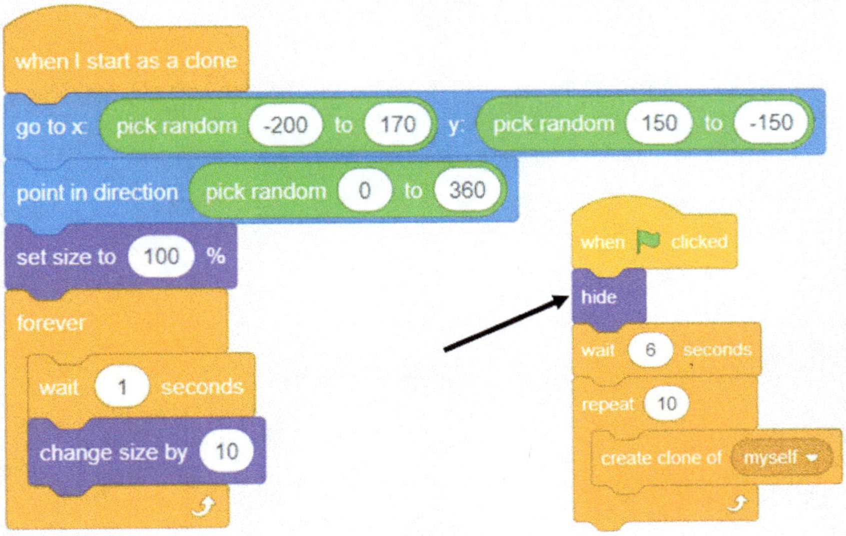

This is not the only way to create pollution1 as a clone. If it works it is correct (5 marks)

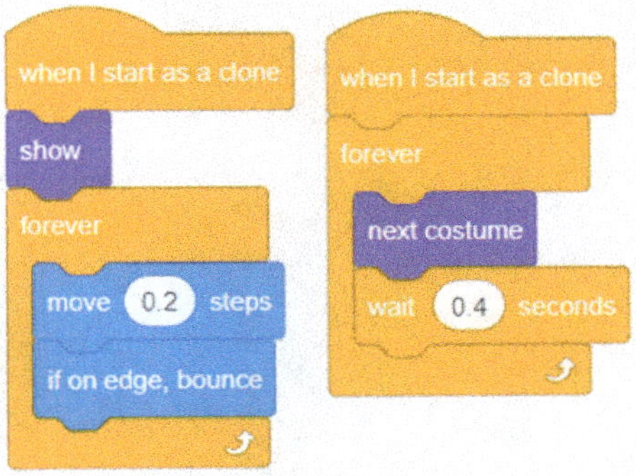

www.ingramcontent.com/pod-product-compliance
Lightning Source LLC
LaVergne TN
LVHW082339070326
832902LV00043B/2710
* 9 7 8 1 9 1 5 0 5 4 2 6 5 *